THE SYNERGY OF MUSIC AND IMAGE IN AUDIOVISUAL CULTURE

The Synergy of Music and Image in Audiovisual Culture: Half-Heard Sounds and Peripheral Visions asks what it means to understand music as part of an audiovisual whole, rather than separate components of music and film. Bringing together revised and updated essays on music in a variety of media – including film, television, and video games – this book explores the importance of partially perceived and registered auditory and visual elements and cultural context in creating unique audiovisual experiences. Critiquing traditional models of the film score, *The Synergy of Music and Image in Audiovisual Culture* enables readers across music, film, and cultural studies to approach and think about audiovisual culture in new ways.

K.J. Donnelly is Professor of Film and Film Music and Director of Doctoral Programmes for Film at the University of Southampton.

THE SYNERGY OF MUSIC AND IMAGE IN AUDIOVISUAL CULTURE

Half-Heard Sounds and Peripheral Visions

K.J. Donnelly

Routledge
Taylor & Francis Group

NEW YORK AND LONDON

Designed cover image: Allstar Picture Library Ltd / Alamy Stock Photo

First published 2024
by Routledge
605 Third Avenue, New York, NY 10158

and by Routledge
4 Park Square, Milton Park, Abingdon, Oxon, OX14 4RN

Routledge is an imprint of the Taylor & Francis Group, an informa business

© 2024 K.J. Donnelly

Library of Congress Cataloging-in-Publication Data
Names: Donnelly, K. J. (Kevin J.) author.
Title: The synergy of music and image in audiovisual culture : half-heard sounds and peripheral visions / K.J. Donnelly.
Description: New York : Routledge, 2023. | Includes bibliographical references and index. | Summary: "The Synergy of Music and Image in Audiovisual Culture: Half-Heard Sounds and Peripheral Visions asks what it means to understand music as part of an audiovisual whole, rather than separate components of music and film. Bringing together revised and updated essays on music in a variety of media-including film, television, and video games-this book explores the importance of partially perceived and registered auditory and visual elements and cultural context in creating unique audiovisual experiences. Critiquing traditional models of the film score, The Synergy of Music and Image in Audiovisual Culture enables readers across music, film, and cultural studies to approach and think about audiovisual culture in new ways"–Provided by publisher.
Identifiers: LCCN 2023018428 (print) | LCCN 2023018429 (ebook) | ISBN 9781032290263 (hardback) | ISBN 9781032290256 (paperback) | ISBN 9781003299653 (ebook)
Subjects: LCSH: Motion picture music--Philosophy and aesthetics. | Motion pictures–Aesthetics. | Motion picture music–Psychological aspects. | Motion pictures–Psychological aspects.
Classification: LCC ML2075 .D6646 2023 (print) | LCC ML2075 (ebook) | DDC 781.5/42–dc23/eng/20230526
LC record available at https://lccn.loc.gov/2023018428
LC ebook record available at https://lccn.loc.gov/2023018429

ISBN: 978-1-032-29026-3 (hbk)
ISBN: 978-1-032-29025-6 (pbk)
ISBN: 978-1-003-29965-3 (ebk)

DOI: 10.4324/9781003299653

Typeset in Sabon
by Deanta Global Publishing Services, Chennai, India

CONTENTS

1

INTRODUCTION

Conceiving Music's Relationship to Image

An episode of *Alfred Hitchcock Presents*[1] begins with one of Hitchcock's on-screen introductions directly addressing the camera. He informs the audience about how the television drama series deals with music: by having the music written and then creating the show and its narrative to fit around the existing music. This may be a joke, reminding the audience that the music is written to fit films and audiovisual drama yet it is simultaneously a double bluff as *Alfred Hitchcock Presents* not only had scored episodes but also instances where recorded cues were edited onto the action and, in fact, were reused many times in some cases. Indeed, this was common with some television shows, such as *Star Trek* (1966, Desilu, Paramount, Norway Corp.), which reused exactly the same recorded cues for similar narrative situations to the point where, through the music, we can understand just how stereotypical such narratives might be. Increasingly, mainstream films have also used pre-existing music, where images are cut to the structure and integrity of the music. So, conversely, Hitchcock's joke is partly true, and perhaps not a joke at all, highlighting uncertainty about incidental music and its often potentially ambiguous position in audiovisual drama and film.

This book endeavours to approach music in audiovisual culture as a complex merged signal rather than as idealized and separate "music" and "the film," which, conceptually and physically, are added together in a simple operation. The relationship of music to the moving image rightly now garners the sort of scholarly scrutiny that it always deserved despite the historical vitriol of detractors in the industry and academia, which impeded the development of a body of theory and analysis on the subject.

DOI: 10.4324/9781003299653-1

It is important to note from the outset that although this book is concerned with music and the moving image, music also has a significant interaction with other elements of the soundtrack, and some might even argue that its interaction with dialogue outweighs its interaction with images. Indeed, music increasingly has been integrated with other film elements. In recent years, the development of converging digital sound technology has allowed sound designers to use musical software to enhance sound effects in films and enabled music composers to produce their own music incorporating elements of sound effects. Such innovation, in line with technological convergence, aesthetic convergence, and harmonizing platforms and industries, has meant that music is no longer simply a "bolt-on" to films and other audiovisual culture but integrated almost genetically on a conceptual level: instigating film titles and narratives, perhaps even inspiring films as spin-offs from existing music, while continuing to inspire and articulate the most emotional and exciting moments of the overwhelming majority of films and other audiovisual media.

The book's title points to the sharp impression but ultimate uncertainty of peripheral vision and the ambiguous potency of half-heard sounds of which we might only be partially aware. It is easy to forget that the impressive and sometimes overwhelming effect of film and television is the product of a mixture of vibrating speakers or headphone drivers and screen projection or dots on an electronic screen. Music regularly works to enhance the effect of the image and vice versa. This mutually reinforcing effect is a form of aesthetic synergy, where the two add up to more than the sum of their parts. Sensuous, rhythmic, and qualitative aspects of each generate a complex interaction, before aspects such as narrative context and cultural associations of the music and images respectively are taken into account. It is therefore not surprising that it is a thanklessly difficult task attempting to account for the effectiveness of music in combination with the moving image. This, I would venture, is one of the main reasons why there are few sustained attempts to provide convincing and authoritative accounts of the power in the "lock" between music and the moving image, or the emotional push and pull that incidental music instigates.

The Synergy of Music and Image

In recent years, music has come to play an increasingly evident and important role in audiovisual culture. As Carol Vernallis rightly notes, there has been a palpable "audiovisual turn" in culture more generally (2013: 33). We have experienced the widening use of "accompanying music" – as ambient mood music or Muzak, on TikToks and short films on the Internet, advertisements, and TV continuity, in waiting rooms and supermarkets, and in video games, let alone on iPods that tether music firmly to the visuals of everyday life.[2] People habitually "soundtrack" their daily lives, aiming to dramatize, sweeten, expand, and direct their experience, in a similar manner to music in cinema, television, video games, and radio (Kassabian 2013). What is sometimes called "media music" has also attained a certain degree of popularity outside its original context in terms of film music and video game music concerts, sales of recordings, and celebrity status for composers such as Hans Zimmer or Ennio Morricone. Furthermore, mediocre music can be transformed through its coupling with impressive and engaging images. This is evident to anyone who has spent time watching a succession of music videos, and the substantial budgets they are assigned confirm the belief in the power of the image as a supplement to the song. Similarly, and reciprocally, there has been an assumption (perhaps more a vain hope) that a poor film can be "saved" by the application of effective music. Music certainly "aestheticizes" the image, making it become something less of a recording of what was in front of the camera and more of an emotional experience. Of course, films and other media do not *need* music. Some manage to do very well without it. For example, the films that conform to the DOGME 95 Manifesto or the earlier films made by the Dardenne brothers, among others, have refused to use incidental music as a matter of policy.[3] Yet the isolated practices of these filmmakers underline just how important music is considered by the overwhelming majority of filmmakers.

It is the case that no matter how "unmusical" we might be, we have obtained a certain "cultural literacy" in music, and more pertinently an audiovisual or "musical-visual" literacy. This enables our immediate understanding of and reaction to music's appearance in films and media. Thus, the music of the cinema has a particular and distinct meaning or effect in the film theatre or on a television set and is perhaps different when listened to on a CD or elsewhere. We can all recognize musical clichés: the jaunty tune that appears for a happy scene, the sombre dirge that accompanies a morose situation. These have become internalized in us to the point that we never really have to ponder them. From the early years of the last century, music considered "appropriate" to the moods of the action was used to accompany silent movies. As such, music for film wrested approaches from a whole tradition of music accompanying other media (theatre, opera, and other live entertainment) and the more recent tradition of music thought to contain and evoke images (what is called "programmatic music"). The breadth of cinema that we have seen and heard has served to condition us to music as an embodiment of certain feelings and ideas, not only emotions but times and places, and much more. A strong tradition exists of the styles, genres, and momentary clichés that adorn almost every piece of music that has ever graced film and other media. Beyond styles as codes of communication, less obvious aspects such as rhythm and texture also have distinctive meaning and effect. The history of music's coupling with the moving image has built up a sense of "synaesthesia," an equivalence of music and image; at least, there is a tradition of using certain forms of music to accompany certain images (and vice versa). Certain sounds appear to invoke certain images. There is certainly a strong sense of what fits what. Figurative images aside, there is a tradition that marries certain visual kinetics with certain types of sound and rhythm. Energetic music tends to complement energetic images, dynamic camera movement, and rapid editing. Busy music gives an impression of movement, although fast repetition can also give the impression of stasis. The "cross-rhythm" of the beat and edits or other punctuations in the image can furnish an abstract sense of aesthetic play or a compelling mesh of movement and the feeling of movement. Either smooth and gliding or sudden and abrupt screen motions often seem to fit the "movement" of music well. The former can be seen in films like *An American in Paris* (1951) as much as in more recent music videos.

There appears to be at the very least a cross-referencing between music and image, and likely more: an intimate level of merged unification. In Powell and Pressburger's *The Red Shoes* (1948), composer Julian Craster declares about a passage in his music, "Anyone who understands anything about music will see a ballroom." Despite some strong representational traditions, sometimes the assumption of direct correlation has been overstated. The metaphor of synaesthesia has displaced the reality of a perceptual condition to stand in for an idea of the intimate and mutually implicating relationship between sound and image (Cf. Cook 2008: 24–56). While sounds can suggest images, perhaps less obviously, images can imply sounds and music. This might be accounted for with recourse to the notion of structural isomorphism, whereby a sense of physical and structural likeness is understood between certain sounds and images. The most obvious would be deep sounds and large objects, or high-pitched sounds and small objects. Perceiving homologies between sound and image has been the foundation for the strong weld between the two, and this is the basis of much 21st-century audiovisual culture.

The Core of Audiovisual Culture

What was originally called "film music," "non-diegetic music," "incidental music," or "score" as an aesthetic and psychological component of film now has pervaded most other areas of audiovisual culture. Indeed, the term "film" has become far less specific in recent years, being increasingly used for short-duration audiovisual objects on the Internet, and for films and television shows of over an hour's length on Blu-Ray or DVD. Indeed, we might understand a "core" of music relations with the moving image that exists across audiovisual media despite their often significant differences.

This book primarily will address film, but also sister media, such as television and video games, where the sound and principles of musical accompaniment from film habitually have been retained and developed. Music in television drama often follows a more direct and simpler approach than film, as many TV programmes owe more to traditions derived from radio. Video games, particularly the expensively developed ones, increasingly have tried to sound like expensive feature films, even though their procedures are by necessity radically different. Indeed, "interactive" or "dynamic" music, which reacts to a range of possible developments in gameplay, still often follows a broad concept of non-diegetic music or accompanying score (Donnelly 2021: 94), even if their procedures are profoundly different.

While the combination of music and the moving image appears to be a distinctive object, it coheres around an aesthetic core and psychological involvement of the user. Indeed, the traditions of sound film have been sustained into other audiovisual media, where they remain as a common core of aesthetic approaches and audience expectations, despite disparities in the respective formats. Of course, all audiovisual culture is far from the same, yet what is formed by the combination of sound and music with moving images follows the same underlying principal processes, both in terms of dominant syntax and construction as well as psychology and perception.

This book embraces incidental music in film, musicals, music videos, and video game music. The fount of audiovisual relations is the model established by the Classical Hollywood studio system (Bordwell, Staiger, and Thompson 1988) in the early 1930s. This might be seen as a form of musical or sonic architecture, particularly in its structural place in the background and enveloping "wall-to-wall"[4] aspect, which attempted to homogenize film music space and thus the very social space of the cinema itself. This model is what Claudia Gorbman called "Classical film scoring" (1987: 70) and Kathryn Kalinak called the "Classical Film Score" (1992: xv–xvi), a blueprint that arguably has fragmented in recent decades yet has not been superseded. This has been a "gold standard" benchmark across the world against which notions of orthodoxy and quality could be measured, as well as aspirations to innovation, experimentation, and subversion. Other broad models of the relationship between music and image are its antecedent, "silent cinema" with its live music, and the more recent development of mainstream cinema (Cutting and Candan 2015; Bordwell 2002; Smith 2013), and what has been called "musical sound design" (Kulezic-Wilson 2020), which mixes music with other sonic elements to create an extended and unified palette. Video game music can sometimes owe a lot to film scoring, despite its wholly different interactive nature.

The film musical, one of the most popular genres of classical Hollywood with its foregrounded songs and dances and alternations of dialogue and number has been resurgent since the Millennium. They regularly involve cutting the images to fit the music in song or dance sequences, with the rhythm and structure of the music defining time and action. Such an approach has moved across into mainstream dramatic film in recent years, particularly in dialogue-free action sequences. Some of the film musicals' assumptions and aesthetics sustained and founded the music video format, while music documentary can sometimes appear close to the musical in format, too, if it focuses on music rather than musicians. Significantly, each of these models embodies a conceptualization of the relationship between sound and image, and one ultimately derived more from film form rather than musical form and logic.

There are three fundamental aspects of audiovisual objects, all of which are able to have a significant impact on the film or other piece of media. These defining characteristics comprise the physical, conceptual, and emotional relationships between sound and image. The physical pertains to whether sound and image are premised as being synchronized or not.[5] Secondly, the conceptual relationship between sound and image often coheres around a sense of whether sound is construed as diegetic or non-diegetic, and sometimes also as on-screen or off-screen.[6] Thirdly, the emotional relationship between sound and image involves whether and to what degree there appears to be an empathetic relationship between the two. This is the psychological relationship between sound and image. Indeed, psychological engagement is central to the medium and music has a significant place in this. A notable characteristic of film (and other media) music is its emotional empathy with events depicted visually, making for an emotionally engaging scenario with characters that the audience identifies with and is emotionally involved with. This is underlined by isolated instances of so-called "anempathetic music," where music appears emotionally indifferent to the events it accompanies (Chion 1994: 8–9).[7] This appears as a distinct effect in itself, which can be remarkably effective.

The Hypnotist

Hugo Münsterberg, arguably the first film theorist, declared that film was tied directly to a mode of human perception and psychology, suggesting something of why film has been able to make such a strong sense of psychological engagement with audiences (Münsterberg 1970: 41). Film inculcates, and perhaps embodies particular psychological states, and

music can be a defining aspect of this, being central to emotional processes as well as helping to clarify understanding.

One highly characteristic aspect of incidental music in films is that it
tends not to occupy the foreground of the film experience. Consequently,
it appears to be apprehended either semi-consciously or unconsciously
by film audiences.[8] Its manipulative aim, most clear in moments of high
emotion, might well be all the more effective for it not being noticed: the
convention of film perception is that we should not become aware of the
music but concentrate on other aspects of the film. George Burt notes, "it
is important to ask to what extent film music is consciously heard generally, or, to put it another way, to what extent should it be heard" (1994:
5). Claudia Gorbman, whose book *Unheard Melodies* has a title that
addressed this point explicitly, notes how far its status leads to its power:

> Film music is ... the hypnotist that lulls us into a hyperreceptive state,
> in order that we receive and identify with the movie's fantasy ... Film
> music is like the medium of a dream, forgotten in the waking state; but
> this medium is itself not neutral. It embodies and disseminates mean-
> ing, all the more powerful in not actively being noticed.
>
> *(Gorbman 2000: 234)*

Moulding mood unconsciously through ambience manipulation is a pervasive technique, evident in all architectural environments and public
spaces, where sound can often also play an imperative psychological role.
Such environmental and tonal aspects form a deep background that is
rarely registered but forms a defining part of the experience. This corresponds to the gestaltist division of figure and ground, where the backdrop
is understood as crucial in that it distinguishes and defines the objects in
the foreground. Indeed, an approach that follows these lines registers that
"background music" is far from insignificant.

So, one of the least registered aspects of sound and music in audiovisual
culture is the significance of their partly perceived facets. For instance,
both quiet, momentary sounds and objects on screen but occupying the
background or edge of the frame, appear as half-noticed, semi-conscious
aspects in peripheral vision and hearing. These can be highly significant
and the phenomenon furnishes the book's title. While many writings
about music in audiovisual culture focus on "what it communicates," its
processes are more complicated and can form a crucial semi-conscious
(or perhaps fully unconscious) background. While music's effect might be
far from simple and unified, part of screen music's startling force comes
from its unity with the image. Inter-modal "crosstalk" between sound
and image forms a whole new signal of its own. As I have noted already,
this is not "music for films" but the forging of a synergetic unity, and

media music composers have a particular skill to know about how images and drama work, while directors on some level know a good deal about music.[9]

While the essential nature of media "incidental" music as a manipulative device, inculcating a sense of mood and perhaps even behaviour in the audience, is registered far less than might be expected by scholars, the technological essence is often almost wholly bypassed in discussions. Understanding audiovisual culture is not the same as understanding its music as "composing," or indeed, seeing film as being simply about writing and acting. Indeed, in some ways, these might be construed as near equivalent constrained approaches. However, we must have at least some idea of how audiovisual culture is constructed to make a viable analysis. One striking issue is that the recorded and technologically mediated component and character have been badly neglected.[10] They provide the hinge, the crucial point of unity between sound and image. As such, they need to be taken far more seriously; technology and mediation often remain forgotten in the rush to discuss "music" or dramatic aspects of film, as if these are fully "present" without technological interference.

Media specificity, technology, and the physical facts of media have in most cases been "written out" of accounts of audiovisual culture more than anyone might reasonably expect.[11] Perhaps this is less than surprising. The "forgetting" of mediation is pervasive in the modern world as a parallel to the increasing penetration of media into all aspects of life.[12] Musical recordings are regularly discussed as if they were unmediated objects, although aficionados often show an awareness of musicians' differences but not of recording techniques. The latter are ignored and often considered "invisible," or perhaps "unheard," with the crucial frame often barely registering for all audiovisual culture.

Audiovisual Music Analysis

Alongside developments in audiovisual culture's prominence, perhaps as might be expected, scholarly writing about the theory and history of "audiovisual" music and culture now has definitely arrived. Indeed, it has developed from the margins to being a notably popular subject for scholars within a quarter century. Claudia Gorbman's aforementioned *Unheard Melodies*, published in 1987, is considered by most to be the progenitor of most of the ensuing research and writing. Although Eisler and Adorno's book *Composing for the Films* (1994 [f.p. 1947]) was 40 years earlier, its influence has been uneven, and its character contrasting and contradictory with practical scoring chapters from the former author and critical theory-oriented chapters from the latter. In the wake of Gorbman's setting out of the scholarly field of endeavour, other important books appeared from Caryl Flinn (1992), Kathryn Kalinak (1992), Royal S. Brown (1994), and Jeff Smith (1998). Recently, there has been a boom in publishing about music and the moving image. A handful of journals, a plethora of monographs, and edited collections and new scholars are appearing constantly with fresh approaches to material. Many of these have "grown up" with the study of music in audiovisual media as a viable academic subject.

The best of this writing always acknowledges that it is far more than a simple "addition" to the images of film. In fact, audiovisual music might be understood as not music at all, or at least as music with profound differences from other music. Indeed, in musical terms, it might be better understood as a context, for any music imported to film transforms into something else through merging with its new surroundings. However, becoming an integral element of a combination with images might also mean the music composed for a film is only a partial object alone without its visual counterpart, while the images without their music can appear lifeless and emotion-free. This often calls for a form of music that is significantly different from other music, setting up a condition of music that has an ability to incorporate images into itself, as much as images can achieve their plenitude through incorporating music. Similarly, pre-existing music, sometimes of well-known origin, must transform to successfully become film music. The process is not the simple addition of music to images, but a complex process of merger and transference between the two media.

Michel Chion's subject-defining book, published in English as *Audio-Vision: Sound on Screen* (1994), establishes a strong sense of film and other media being audiovisual, manifesting what he calls "audiovision," with sound being a significant partner rather than a bit-part player.[13] Such an approach also underlines the sense of music being "film sound" and film sound being "music." Chion discusses the process of "synchresis"; "the forging of an immediate and necessary relationship between something one sees and something one hears" (1994: 5). This is a strong statement about how we should conceive the relationship of sound and image in audiovisual culture. This sense of intimacy and redefining connections is embodied by the "McGurk Effect," which proves the perceptual "crosswiring" of seeing and hearing and which I discuss in my book *The McGurk Universe* (2023). Not only merged into a combined signal but also the addition of music and moving images adds up to significantly more than each separately. If anything needs acknowledgement it is this. Indeed, musicians and filmmakers have been aware of something approaching this ever since the possibility of unifying the two was viable. In the film industry there was a persistent adage that a poor film could be "saved" by good music, while many mediocre songs have been transformed by remarkable images in music videos. Despite this, much analysis persists in retaining a strong sense of audiovisual culture as a "combination" of two distinct things rather than as a "genetic" merging into a complex but unified object.

Our conception of audiovisual culture determines how we analyze it. Analysis of audiovisual culture has been dominated by functional approaches, which look for what sound does for image and what image does for sound. With films and television drama, this has alighted firmly on narrative and "information." The old adage about music in film either being "camera" or "set" is unfortunate in being ocularcentric but nevertheless provides a useful conceptualization. Incidental music can predominantly act as an agent of narration, emphasizing events and dynamics of character and emotional tone, or it can act as a more inert sense of location and atmosphere. Often, it oscillates between the two, yet this divide throws into relief a difference in approach. As narration, film music is a skilled and specialized endeavour, while as atmosphere this might be produced by musicians with no interest in writing to the rest of film and encourages the use of pre-existing music. It is relatively easy to address what musical accompaniment can tell the audience as an addition to other narrative information. It is less easy to address how far music can serve an atmospheric or emotional function, and harder still to look into points where the music might seem to add nothing or contradict our understanding of the drama. So, as I noted, our conception of audiovisual culture defines how we go about analyzing it.

The most sophisticated approaches to music in film and audiovisual culture are beyond merely conceiving the relationship as functional. Music does not simply communicate clear and finite ideas to the audience. Its effect is far more unstable, with its intimations, connotations, and emotional valences that can be less than or excessive to the context of the film. Working in an unstable and uncertain area of human subjectivity, films play with audience emotion and memory, rather than dealing purely with straightforward cognition and a solid "signified." Music is one of the most important agents in engaging this crucial area of activity for audiovisual culture, where uncertainty sits alongside powerful emotions and half-remembered pasts.

Analysis varies between "big closeups" and "long shots." Both are necessary but sometimes I think we have too many case study "closeups" and less sense of wider context. Indeed, conference papers and chapters for edited collections lend themselves to "snapshots" of individual films and their music rather than to synoptic views or more general theorizing. To have meaning, close analyses need to show awareness of wider context or risk autonomous irrelevance. A historical sense is important as is a sense of the determining roles of institutional and aesthetic norms, and industrial and audience expectations.[14] Sometimes, securing a "bigger picture" and seeing the relationship between different scholarship, theories, and approaches can prove difficult.[15] Yet theoretical concerns too often have been shunted to the background by concerns with individual films and the music written for them.

Often, aesthetic imperatives have overwhelmed analysis, with little awareness of institutional, historical, or technological determinants. In recent years, sterling work by some scholars has shone a light on historical and industrial concerns of production that have regularly been ignored by analysis dominated by an idealistic approach to music or audiovisual aesthetics. These clearly are determining and of paramount importance, not least in that they provide clear horizons for what ends up as films and other audiovisual culture.

***

This book brings together for the first time essays written over a long period and published elsewhere. It embraces a wide range of audiovisual culture, including music as the glue that holds together the illusion of film, warding off a psychological collapse (Chapter 2 "The Ghostly Effect Revisited"), the development of incidental music in film, from modern mixtures of music and sound design (Chapter 3 "*Saw* Heard: Musical Sound Design in Post-Millennium Cinema") to the revival of the classical film score (Chapter 4 "The Classical Film Score Forever? *Batman, Batman Returns* and Post-Classical Film Music"). It embraces film music working with and against genre traditions and expectations (Chapter 5 "Europe Cannibalizes the Western: *Ravenous*"), the "resurfacing" of silent and early sound films (Chapter 6 "Music Cultizing Film: KTL and the New Silents," and Chapter 7 "Irish Sea Power: A New *Man of Aran*"), music as a direct psychological effect (Chapter 8 "Hearing Deep Seated Fears: John Carpenter's *The Fog*" and Chapter 13 "Lawn of the Dead: the Indifference of Musical Destiny in *Plants vs Zombies*"), or as atmospheric signature (Chapter 9 "Angel of the Air: Popol Vuh's Music for Werner Herzog's Films"). It has chapters on film musicals (Chapter 10 "Musicals, Commerce, and Race: White Labels and Black Imports"), music documentary and the relationship with the music industry (Chapter 11 "British Cinema and the Visualized Live Album"), and music as imaginative dimension (Chapter 12 "Television's Musical Imagination: *Space 1999*").

As already noted, this volume primarily addresses film, but also deals with audiovisual sister media, such as television and video games, where the sound and principles of accompaniment from film have been retained and developed. Each chapter focuses on specific subject matter as (not fully autonomous) case studies, engaging with the rich history, varied genres, different traditions, and varied audiovisual strategies. This book is not about film/media music, nor is it about film and what music tells us about its stories. It is about the complex interaction of sound and image, as well as the slightly uncertain and at times ambiguous sense that the relationship of sound and image can engender, even when they are firmly merged into a single sensuous and informative signal. Seeing and hearing the medium can be difficult in audiovisual drama, where we are not meant to perceive the frame but merely follow characters and what happens in a successful illusion. Music plays a crucial role in this process and yet, along with the other defining audiovisual stylistic aspects, remains "invisible" and "unheard."

These chapters will include some already published, although amended, material:

2. "The 'Ghostly Effect' Revisited" in Miguel Mera and Ron Sadoff, eds., *The Routledge Companion to Screen Music and Sound* (New York: Routledge, 2017), pp. 17–25.
3. "*Saw* Heard: Musical Sound Design in Contemporary Cinema" in Warren Buckland, ed., *Contemporary Film Theory* (London: Routledge, 2009), pp. 103–123.
4. "Music Cultizing Film: KTL and the New Silents" in *New Review of Film and Television Studies*, vol. 13, np. 1, March 2015, pp. 31–44.
5. "Irish Sea Power: A New *Man of Aran*" in Holly Rogers, ed., *Music and the Documentary Film* (London and New York: Routledge, 2014), pp. 137–150.
6. "The Classical Film Score Forever?: *Batman*, *Batman Returns* and Post-Classical Film Music" in Steve Neale and Murray Smith, eds., *Contemporary Hollywood Cinema* (London: Routledge, 1998), pp. 142–155.
7. "Hearing Deep Seated Fears: John Carpenter's *The Fog*" in Neil Lerner, ed., *Music in the Horror Film: Listening to Fear* (London: Routledge, 2010), pp. 152–167.
8. "Angel of the Air: Popol Vuh's Music for Werner Herzog's Films" in Miguel Mera and David Burnand, eds., *European Film Music* (London: Ashgate, 2006), pp. 116–130.
9. "*Ravenous* and the European Take on American History and the Western" in Kathryn Kalinak, ed., *Music and the Western* (London: Routledge, 2011), pp. 148–164.
10. "Black Imports and White Labels" in *British Film Music and Film Musicals* (Basingstoke: Palgrave, 2014), pp. 166–178. (Thanks to Palgrave for allowing reprinting.)
11. "British Cinema and the Visualized Live Album" in Robert Edgar, Kirsty Fairclough-Isaacs and Benjamin Halligan, eds., *Rock Documentaries* (London: Routledge, 2012), pp. 171–182.
12. "Television's Musical Imagination: *Space 1999*" in K.J. Donnelly and Philip Hayward, eds., *Music in Science Fiction Television: Tuning In to the Future* (London: Routledge, 2012), pp. 111–122.

13. "Lawn of the Dead: the Indifference of Musical Destiny in *Plants vs Zombies*" in K.J. Donnelly, Neil Lerner, and Will Gibbons, eds., *Music in Video Games* (London and New York: Routledge, 2014), pp. 151–165.

Thanks to Genevieve Aoki and Pete Sheehy at Taylor and Francis; and editors of the books where the essays first appeared: Ron Sadoff, Miguel Mera, David Burnand, Ben Winters, Kathryn Kalinak, Neil Lerner, Will Gibbons, Warren Buckland, Phil Hayward, Holly Rogers, Ben Halligan, Robert Edgar, Kirsty Fairclough-Isaacs, Matt Hills, Jamie Sexton, Murray Smith, and Steve Neale. In most cases, their comments allowed for significant improvement of the essays. Indeed, the late and much-missed Steve Neale gave outstanding advice to me on an essay from right at the start of my career as a scholar, and it is included here. Lots of people have helped over the years: thanks to all.

Notes

1 *Alfred Hitchcock Presents* (1955–62, Revue Studios/Shamley), episode "Alibi Me," first tx.11 November 1956.
2 In recent years, football (soccer, if you like) stadia increasingly have used recorded music, sometimes to augment or drown out traditional crowd singing.
3 A lack of music has a value within a system that uses music, too. Moments when we expect music but merely receive diegetic sound are often highly effective. According to David Sonnenschein "the spectators … are drawn into examining the image more carefully and actively, seeking to explain the strangeness of the silence" (2001: 127).
4 What Max Steiner called "100% underscore" (1937: 220).
5 My book *Occult Aesthetics* (2013) describes the regime of sound and image interaction between tight synch and degrees of in and out of synch.
6 See discussion in Heldt (2013), Stilwell (2007), and Smith (2009).
7 This should be related to notions of "congruence" as discussed in Cohen (2015) and Ireland (2018).
8 Annabel J.Cohen extrapolates from her experiments with audience perception of music and slide shows to conclude that film audiences tend to be unaware of music's presence or absence (2000: 366).
9 Indeed, the theory of "neuroaesthetics" understands art as investigations of human perception and cognition, instigated by artists who work on the subject instinctually rather than intellectually or scientifically.
10 An isolated example is Katz (2010).
11 When I was looking into synchronization technology for a section of my book *Occult Aesthetics*, it was remarkable how little interest there was in this technology in scholarly writing. Accounts I came across were specialist technology writing, and those that appeared to be something more than that nevertheless were essentially assemblages of information not far from technical manuals themselves.
12 For instance, it is now not uncommon for English Premier League football to be discussed as if it is a TV show rather than live sporting events, and

indeed from my experience many who talk about it have never visited a football ground and assume it is a set of shots and replays with specialist voiceover commentary.

13 A variation on this is Robert Miklitsch's use of the term "audiovisuality" (2006).

14 There are film music survey history books Cooke (2008) and Wierzbicki (2009).

15 An isolated instance is James Buhler's synoptic *Theories of the Soundtrack* [2018], which touches upon most of the theories that have grown up around audiovisual media.

Bibliography

Bordwell, David, Janet Staiger, and Kristin Thompson, *The Classical Hollywood Cinema: Film Style and Mode of Production to 1960* (London: Routledge, 1988).

Bordwell, David, "Intensified Continuity: Visual Style in Contemporary American Film" in *Film Quarterly*, vol. 55, no. 3, Spring 2002, pp. 16–28.

Brown, Royal S., *Overtones and Undertones: Reading Film Music*(Berkeley, CA: University of California Press, 1994).

Buhler, James, *Theories of the Soundtrack* (New York: Oxford University Press, 2018).

Burt, George, *The Art of Film Music* (Boston, MA: Northeastern University Press, 1994).

Chion, Michel, *Audio-Vision: Sound on Screen*, translated and edited by Claudia Gorbman (New York: Columbia University Press, 1994).

Cohen, Annabel J., "Congruence-Association Model and Experiments in Film Music: Toward Interdisciplinary Collaboration" in *Music and the Moving Image*, vol. 8, no. 2, Summer 2015, pp. 5–24.

Cohen, Annabel J., "Film Music: Perspectives from Cognitive Psychology" in James Buhler, Caryl Flinn, and David Neumeyer, eds., *Music and Cinema* (Hanover: Wesleyan University Press, 2000).

Cook, Nicholas, *Analysing Musical Multimedia* (Oxford: Oxford University Press, 1998).

Cooke, Mervyn, *A History of Film Music* (Cambridge: Cambridge University Press, 2008).

Cutting, James E., and Ayse Candan, "Shot Durations, Shot Classes, and the Increased Pace of Popular Movies" in *Projections*, vol. 9, no. 2, Winter 2015, pp. 40–62.

Donnelly, K.J., *The McGurk Universe* (New York: Palgrave, 2023).

Donnelly, K.J., *Occult Aesthetics: Synchronization in Sound Cinema* (New York: Oxford University Press, 2013).

Donnelly, K.J., "The Triple Lock of Synchronization" in Melanie Fritsch, and Tim Summers, eds., *The Cambridge Companion to Video Game Music* (Cambridge: Cambridge University Press, 2021).

Eisler, Hanns, and Theodor Adorno, *Composing for the Films* (London: Athlone, 1994 [orig.1947]).

Flinn, Caryl, *Strains of Utopia: Gender, Nostalgia and Hollywood Film Music* (Princeton, NJ: Princeton University Press, 1992).

Gorbman, Claudia, "Scoring the Indian: Music in the Liberal Western" in Georgina Born, and David Hesmondhalgh, eds., *Western Music and Its Others: Difference, Representation and Appropriation in Music* (Berkeley, CA: University of California Press, 2000).

Gorbman, Claudia, *Unheard Melodies: Narrative Film Music*(London: BFI, 1987).

Heldt, Guido, *Music and Levels of Narration in Film: Steps Across the Border* (Chicago, IL: University of Chicago Press, 2013).

Ireland, David, *Identifying and Interpreting Incongruent Film Music* (New York: Palgrave Macmillan, 2018).

Kalinak, Kathryn, *Settling the Score: Music and the Classical Hollywood Film* (Madison, WI: University of Wisconsin Press, 1992).

Kassabian, Anahid, *Ubiquitous Listening: Affect, Attention, and Distributed Subjectivity* (Los Angeles, CA: University of California Press, 2013).

Katz, Mark, *Capturing Sound: How Technology Has Changed Music* (Los Angeles, CA: University of California Press, 2010).

Kulezic-Wilson, Danijela, *Sound Design Is the New Score: Theory, Aesthetics, and Erotics of the Integrated Soundtrack* (New York: Oxford University Press, 2020).

Miklitsch, Robert, *Roll Over Adorno: Critical Theory, Popular Culture, Audiovisual Media* (Albany, NY: SUNY Press, 2006).

Münsterberg, Hugo, *The Film: A Psychological Study* (Minneola, NY: Dover, 1970).

Smith, Jeff, "Bridging the Gap: Reconsidering the Border Between Diegetic and Nondiegetic Music" in *Music and the Moving Image*, vol. 2, no. 1, Spring 2009, pp. 1–25.

Smith, Jeff, "The Sound of Intensified Continuity" in John Richardson, Claudia Gorbman, and Carol Vernallis, eds., *The Oxford Handbook of New Audiovisual Aesthetics*(New York: Oxford University Press, 2013).

Smith, Jeff, *The Sounds of Commerce: Marketing Popular Film Music* (New York: Columbia University Press, 1998).

Sonnenschein, David, *Sound Design – The Expressive Power of Music, Voice, Sound* (Studio City, CA: Michael Wiese Productions, 2001).

Steiner, Max, "Scoring the Film" in Nancy Naumburg, ed., *We Make the Movies* (New York: Norton, 1937).

Stilwell, Robynn, "The Fantastical Gap Between Diegetic and Nondiegetic" in Daniel Goldmark, Lawrence Kramer, and Richard D. Leppert, eds., *Beyond the Soundtrack: Representing Music in Cinema* (Berkeley, CA: University of California Press, 2007).

Vernallis, Carol, *Unruly Media: YouTube, Music Video, and the New Digital Cinema* (Oxford: Oxford University Press, 2013).

Wierzbicki, James, *Film Music: A History* (London: Routledge, 2009).

2

THE GHOSTLY EFFECT REVISITED

In his chapter in *The Sounds of Early Cinema*, Tom Gunning suggested that the widespread advent and acceptance of recorded and synchronized sound cinema in the late 1920s was likely a product of the desire to reunite hearing and vision, which had been divided by technology (photography, phonograph, and film) a few decades earlier. This is an intriguing idea. There was "a desire to heal the breach," as he puts it (Gunning 2001: 16). This seems like an unfashionable, sentimental, and untestable hypothesis, yet one that attempts to account for the emotional character at the heart of cinema that is more easily avoided by most historians and aestheticians.

To address the question as to why films used music right from their inception as a public event, various answers have been put forward. In *Composing for the Films* (1947) Hanns Eisler and Theodor Adorno suggest that music dissipated the "Ghostly Effect" of the moving image that is particularly evident during silence.[1] They state that it is not only a silent cinema phenomenon but also sustains in the cinema of recorded sound.[2] Indeed, we should be careful, as the Ghostly Effect is not simply a lack of sound leaving the silent moving image disturbing, but the naked moving image itself, allowing its true nature to become apparent. This is the mechanical nature of cinema, as well as its inherent reminder of our own mortality, where the flimsy illusion of life acts as a reminder of the ephemeral and impermanent nature of life itself.

Tantalizingly, they failed to go into much explanatory detail. This not easily verifiable hypothesis attempts to account for the emotional character at the heart of cinema that is more easily avoided by most historians, musicologists, and aestheticians. However, as a theory the Ghostly Effect

DOI: 10.4324/9781003299653-2

has been engaged by a large number of writers about sound and music in the cinema, although in many cases only briefly (Rosen 1980; Gorbman 1987); Carroll 1988: 215; Larsen 2007). This appears to be not a very usable theory for the purposes of analysis and I remain convinced that as a theoretical concept, more mileage could be made from the notion of the Ghostly Effect.

Within a short space in their book, Adorno and Eisler promulgate a number of concepts tied to the notion of the Ghostly Effect. These include the antithetical character of film and music, film's relation to the "ghostly shadow play," the magic function of music, the depiction of the living dead on screen, and shock and "exorcism." These are all related ideas, used to give dimension to the notion of an inherent Ghostly Effect in film and the medium's mechanisms for dealing with this problem. As a general backdrop, they state that the film medium and music have "an antithetic character" (Eisler and Adorno 1994: 75). This appears to be a fundamental point. Some analysis of music and film assumes that it merges into a whole, while some assume that the two arts remain distinct. Adorno and Eisler are explicit in their analysis, declaring that film and music are not organic partners; music and image have different functions. So, they constitute not an unproblematic unity but an alliance, although they see music as retaining a sense of separation.[3] This corresponds with some of the more recent theorizations of "intermediality," which approaches arts as composites where aspects of each individual medium might remain conceptually distinct.[4] This is an important question for analysis which is rarely directly addressed. How far do (or can) film and music merge or do the components always remain distinct? The gluing together of different parts is a key to upholding film's beguiling illusion and avoiding the detrimental Ghostly Effect. Films are always under the threat of spectral collapse.

Memento mori

Eisler and Adorno emphasize the verity that cinema was always connected with ideas about death and reanimation, particularly spectres and the undead: "The pure cinema must have had a ghostly effect like that of the shadow play – shadows and ghosts have always been associated" (Eisler and Adorno 1994: 75). Indeed, there was a consistent early association of moving images with death and the supernatural.[5] For instance, Tom Ruffles in *Ghost Images: Cinema of the Afterlife* (2004) points to a continuity with popular phantasmagoria shows and spiritualist séances rather than film having a direct lineage from the theatre and literature. Indeed, the living dead appearing on screen is at the heart of cinema, where film was able to reanimate those who were absent or dead, through a process of conjuring a convincing illusion. Eisler and Adorno continue: "The need was felt to spare the spectator the unpleasantness involved in seeing effigies of living, acting and even speaking persons, who were at the same time silent. The fact that they are living and nonliving at the same time is what constitutes their ghostly character" (1994: 75) The simultaneous state of alive and dead which the screen enabled was disturbing not only because it depicts an in-between state, but also because it stands as a reminder of death for the audience. As in effect a memento mori, film contains at its heart a potentially negative thing – a reminder of our own mortality. In narrative terms, films allow us to experience immortality (in vampire films such as *Dracula* and the *Twilight* films, for example) but they also inevitably remind us that we have a limit. Indeed, dying is a commonplace element in films and on occasion films can collapse a person's whole lifetime into just a few minutes. But beyond this, on a material level, Adorno and Eisler propose that film reminds us of death by showing "dead" images through its mechanical illusion of life. This plays out as an unconscious process, pushed to the back of our minds to allow film to remain a compulsive and enjoyable medium.

So then, a defining aspect of film is that it is comprised of the shadows of the dead, an uncanny yet compelling illusion of life This is the heart of film, and a property exploited wholeheartedly by horror films, although also evident in some other types of film. In essence, the Ghostly Effect is the threat of physical "disintegration" of the film and likewise by implication of the human body and psyche. Film is always teetering on the brink of the collapse of its own powerful illusion. Sometimes, all it takes is for an audience member to refuse to accept the illusion to render it perceived as disparate constituent elements. It can seem that these elements offer a thin and flimsy approximation of life, mechanically held together into a simplistic whole. Yet the one- (perhaps two-) dimensional "life" depicted might resonate strongly with that of the audience. The collapse of this illusion alienates the audience and reminds them of their own social alienation. In this way, potentially, film might be understood as an unstable medium that despite its alluring illusion constantly threatens to remind the audience of their alienated relationship with society, as well as their mortality. Eisler and Adorno state that this phenomenon of illusory life "requires" music to dissipate the effect and ritualistically ward off its associated evil. Although their theory sounds most pertinent to silent cinema, they contend that this phenomenon sustains in the cinema of recorded sound. The Ghostly Effect persists and thus music is still required for the same purposes. They state of sound cinema: "Their bodiless mouths utter words in a way that must seem disquieting to anyone uninformed" (Eisler and Adorno 1994: 76). This situation can be apparent for audiences not used to slack dubbing or failures of synchronization. Even an awareness of the mechanical merging of sound and vision can lead to a bemused rather than absorbed reaction to sound film.

Aspects of the Ghostly Effect might be exploited directly as an infrequent but disquieting effect by films. For instance, the manipulation of mechanical rather than organic movement allied with disturbing silence is highly evident in the horror film *Dead Silence* (2007). This film is premised upon uncanny seemingly alive mechanical ventriloquist dolls and exploits the threat of "seeing behind the curtain" of film as a medium, with startling moments of "mechanical cutouts" of sound. At one point, the film's protagonist Jamie drives in a car with the ventriloquist's dummy Billy sitting in the back seat. Suddenly, the car and all other diegetic sounds disappear leaving an unearthly total silence, underlined by a shot of Jamie looking around concerned. In the midst of the eerie lack of sound, an acousmatic – unsynched, offscreen, possibly even non-diegetic – metallic scraping sound occurs, and in a dramatic shot the dummy Billy subsequently turns his head to look at Jamie. This is an effective and unsettling moment, enhanced by the film's intimation that sound might have broken down, allied with the implications of mechanical life (the dummy) and meditation upon the status of life and death. Later in the film, Jamie digs up Billy's grave. Again, and equally suddenly, diegetic sound and non-diegetic music halt abruptly; Jamie then looks around concerned, after which we hear a gradual and quiet return of diegetic sound. Here, as in the previous example, the withdrawal of sound threatens the continued illusion of film but is then pulled back into the narrative frame through the on-screen character's response, which signals unambiguously that he is experiencing the same loss of sound as the audience. The threat is invoked and then dissipated. This is an example of film playing around with its own mechanical and illusory nature, and thus exploiting as well as denying the efficacy of the Ghostly Effect of cinema. *Dead Silence*'s representational regime moves from its conventional "normality" to a moment of the abnormal supernatural, which is expressed in stylistic terms as unconventional. Equally, aesthetic aspects can (and usually do) function as a constant reassurance for the audience. Music is able to *reassure*, or make conventional, such moments in films. Through engaging aesthetic convention, music is able to render such disturbing moments less threatening by making them conform to convention and remain consistent with expectations. It also indicates to the audience members how they are expected to react. This facet of film music often receives less attention than it deserves. Indeed, what might almost be thought of as a "making banal" function for music is not as engaging as discussing music's more esoteric and powerful functions.

As part of dealing with the Ghostly Effect, Eisler and Adorno discuss the magic function of music, where its charming and reassuring nature works against the dark nature of film (the mechanical moving image's nature). As a premise, music and film are approached as two fundamentally different discourses and arts, which can never lose their separate natures. They note: "The magic function of music … probably consisted in appeasing the evil spirits unconsciously dreaded. Music was introduced as a kind of antidote against the picture" (Eisler and Adorno 1994: 75). Their approach and language confirm that theirs is no orthodox "cultural history" but rather a "psychic history," which points to film music as a "protection." Thus, film music is not simply a mask of cultural manipulation, which Adorno's "culture industry" writing might suggest, but an absolute necessity for "safe" consumable film.

Eisler and Adorno go on to state that "music was introduced … to exorcise fear or help the spectator absorb the shock" (1994: 75). While again it sounds as if they are using some stark but rich metaphors to describe the process, they retain a sense that there is something inherently supernatural about film, and while it may contain something of the shock of technological modernity, it requires a ritualistic practice to render it safely consumable. This "shock" aspect is reminiscent of Robert Spadoni's discussion of the uncanny effect of sound added to image at the turn of the 1930s. In *Uncanny Bodies: The Coming of Sound Film and the Origins of the Horror Genre*, he argues that early sound cinema had an uncanny effect, where its disturbing body mode comprising images and sounds was perceived as disturbing by "heightened" audience members, who took in more than the simple illusion of unified sound and image but instead were aware of the technological basis of the disquieting effect of pseudo-life (Spadoni 2007).

We can always make ourselves aware of film as a manipulative illusion. Film works hard to retain its illusory effect and suspend our disbelief. Music's place in the process might be conceived as one facet of a *misdirection* process: hiding film's nature through compensation and directing attention elsewhere. Explicit examples of musical misdirection include the use of the comic piece of library music *The Gonk* in George Romero''s *Dawn of the Dead* (1978) to accompany images of zombies wandering aimlessly around a shopping mall. Without the music, the images are far more disturbing, not least because the film's satire of the emptiness of modern consumerism becomes more naked: we are the "dead" people wandering aimlessly around the shopping mall! From a different point of view, the use of some of Krzysztof Penderecki's music in *The Shining* (1980) reminds the audience that they are watching something serious and deeply upsetting. During the sequence where Jack turns on Wendy and ultimately is knocked unconscious by her baseball bat, the dialogue is on the brink of comedy (bolstered by Jack Nicholson's burlesque and pyrotechnic acting performance). The use of Penderecki's music (*Polymorphia* edited together with his *Utrenja: Ewangelia*) at this point, behind the almost comic scene not only holds it within the frame of horror, warding off its humorous aspects but also redoubles the effect of the scene through the slight uncertainty of the mixture of comedic and disturbing elements sitting side by side. Such misdirection might be a risky process, where the audience might lose the illusion and be confronted with the reality of cinema as a manipulative mechanical operation, and its approximation of life being a reminder of the transience of our own lives. The Ghostly Effect is *not* simply silence in films but manifests the naked image: allowing its true and disturbing nature to become apparent. While films like *Dead Silence* are a rarity in that their misdirection is *lost* momentarily as a perceptual and emotional effect, some horror films retain diegetic sound but disorder and perhaps problematize the illusory whole of the film images and sounds.

The Ghostly Effect of the *Blind Dead*

The Ghostly Effect likely has contributed to and retained a notable place in the horror film genre. In the 1970s, there was a series of Spanish horror films directed by Amando De Ossorio and focusing on the evil characters of the *Blind Dead*. These ghosts of the medieval Knights Templars are both faceless in that they have decaying skulls and are wordless: both blind and mute. These films began with *Tombs of the Blind Dead* (1971), which was succeeded by sequels *Return of the Blind Dead* (1973), *The Ghost Galleon* (1974) and *Night of the Seagulls* (1975). Befitting films with noiseless central characters, dialogue is often marginalized in these films. Indeed, sounds and action are almost always more atmospheric than dialogue, and thus the horror film is often a repository of the traditions of the "sound film."[6] In the *Blind Dead* films, the receding of dialogue opens up a space for the use of different sounds and music. The Blind Dead themselves encompass a conspicuous audiovisual rendering, comprising extreme slowness of movement, slow-motion imagery, silence, wind sounds, and music particular to them, amongst other things. While such a scheme generates a highly distinctive aesthetic effect, it emanates at least partly from the films' mode of production, which involved shooting without location sound and adding all sound in post-production. In other words, all the sounds were added later and constructed into a whole, in a process remarkably similar to the addition of incidental music. In certain ways, such a practice encourages both art and artifice in film sound, as well as arguably propagating an aesthetic sense of sound that is similar to a musical understanding. This procedure of shooting without location sound was not uncommon in popular European cinema and is perhaps most evident in Italian popular cinema like spaghetti westerns.[7] In the

Blind Dead films, little dialogue means more space for silence, music, and strange sounds. This separation of image and sound in production is most evident where films are not trying to furnish a sense of regularity, and these films in particular during the sequences of Blind Dead attacks.

In the fourth film in the series, *The Night of the Seagulls*, Dr. Henry Stein and his wife Joan arrive at their new home in a rural seaside village in an undefined country. They get a cold reception. At night, they hear bells tolling, strange singing, and seagulls crying. The castle has Templar tombs which open as the villagers lead a young woman to be sacrificed. To ensure continued good fishing, every seven years the villagers sacrifice seven young women on successive nights to the Templars by tying them to a rock on the beach and allowing them to be taken and killed. With help from Teddy (the "village idiot"), Henry and Joan save their friend Lucy from being sacrificed, leading to a siege of their house.

The audience learns that apparently the souls of the sacrificed women come back as seagulls. These seagulls are almost always off-screen, signified by their sound only, in a manner not unlike non-diegetic music. *Night of the Seagulls* uses bizarre "day for night" shooting, which contributes significantly to the film's thick atmosphere. While the film structurally consists of fairly standard horror film set-piece killings, these are a succession of rituals which are accompanied often to a great extent by music specific to the Blind Dead.[8] The silence of the figures seems to demand sounds. Their music might be approached as *compensatory*, underlined by the further addition of "overcooked" diegetic sounds, which simultaneously detract from the silence of the Blind Dead figures and also emphasize their mute and quiet status. For instance, the sequence where Lucy is tied to the rocks and awaits the arrival of the Blind Dead is startling in its audiovisual terms.

This sequence is overrun by plesiosynchronous sounds, which accompany a rich variety of images. There are shots of Lucy tied to the rocks, the Blind Dead riding on horseback, images of the sea, and a startling insert of seagulls flying against the sky. The Blind Dead appear often in slow motion, conventionally matched to normal-speed sounds of the sea and their horses' hoof falls, but also, strangely, the same sounds are rendered also in slow motion. The fact that the sounds are not matched precisely anyway means that the slow rendering of the soundtrack is not a representational necessity but an aesthetic choice. Indeed, this is a crucial component of the film's strategy in this sequence of using an "overdone" foley allied with a hard metallic reverberation treatment. This further removes direct synchronization and a sense of sound and image being part of the same thing.

In terms of visuals, there are some remarkable aspects, which the extraordinary sounds de-emphasize, making the audience less consciously aware of aesthetic disturbances, while retaining the bizarre effect. For instance, there is a shocking change in screen direction. This is illogical in that it shows the Blind Dead on horseback, proceeding from their lair to the sacrificial rock. One shot shows them moving left to right along the beach while a later one shows them moving from right to left – crossing the conventional "axis of action" that has persisted since film's early years. Indeed, such a lack of convention appears to be an essential ingredient of the disorientating, supernatural world on screen. Another aspect to note is point of view in the sequence. Near the start we have a bystander's view of Lucy being taken to the sacrificial rock, which establishes audience point of view with a naive and distant understanding of the events unfolding. The successive point of view from a matched eyeline is from Lucy herself, supplying a terrifying shot of the Blind Dead closing in on her. Yet this is not the concluding point of view, as the eyeline match and then the camera position situates the audience with the Blind Dead's viewpoint of Lucy. This is something of a horror film convention, where the victim is shown from the attacker's point of view. However, this has unnerving implications in that it aligns our view and identification with the perpetrator of violence,[9] although few are as direct as this case, where the audience receives a technical point of view shot rather than merely a shot "with" the Blind Dead. Perhaps the implications go further here: we are forced to adopt the position of the Blind Dead (even though they cannot see), which suggests we share something of the half-life, half-death of the evil protagonists. Films such as the Blind Dead series cannot help but provide reminders of our own mortality by not only showing death but also connecting us with the uncanny walking dead on screen. Although not a hollow illusion, this appears to be exploiting the Ghostly Effect in that we are disconcerted as the mechanism of illusion is taken apart. Although it threatens to fall into its constituent parts, something of the continuity remains and the audience is not alienated but disturbed.

As the Blind Dead are silent, they receive a form of "compensatory sound," which consists of loud diegetic sound and non-diegetic music, as well as plesiosynchronous sounds (most obviously here the sound of the sea waves). This extraordinary amalgam of sounds that are not quite matching the activity of the images makes for distinctive passages of bizarre, vaguely disturbing dislocation. The fact that in the *Blind Dead* films the ghostly characters are highly sensitive to sound (indeed, they can hear their victims' heartbeats) matches the post-production's building up of sound into a varied and dramatic object which has a certain effect in such a "sound-sensitive" film environment. This is not simply relevant to *The Night of the Seagulls*. There is a wider phenomenon of "compensatory sound" in film and television. For instance, in television documentaries it is now common to have old footage shown with general plesiosynchronous sound added, or even on some occasions having the sound of a projector rattle added. Is this due to an increasing embarrassment about silence, particularly in light of television being so rarely a quiet medium? Or is this a fear of the anticipation set up by silence in audiovisual convention? Or does this mark attempt to "normalize" visual footage and ward off the Ghostly Effect? Traditionally mainstream films have tended to wash dialogue-free and even simply quiet scenes with incidental music and even allow film composers to let loose a little.[10] Even the *Blind Dead* series' quietest moments include added wind sounds to avoid any sustained silence,[11] which appears to add up to something of a "normalization" strategy to calm the audience and reassure the illusion of film.

Most clearly in sound films, through withholding perceptual and communicative senses the Ghostly Effect appears almost to threaten the audience with muteness, or at least to suggest something of a mute existence. Adorno and Eisler note that

> Motion-picture music corresponds to the whistling or singing child in the dark. The real reason for the fear is not even that these people whose silent effigies are moving in front of one seem to be ghosts ... But confronted with gesticulating masks, people experience themselves as creatures of the very same kind, as being threatened by muteness.
>
> *(Eisler and Adorno 1994: 75)*

There is an undoubted threat of deafness engaged by speaker and headphone cut-out, while voiceless characters on screen might problematize the audience's notion of human form and physicality (Cf. Mamula 2015). According to probably the earliest film theorist, Hugo Münsterberg in *The Photoplay* (1916), the medium of film is an objectification of (perceptual-cognitive) mental processes. However, he was addressing silent cinema, which at the time had unpredictable musical accompaniment and he was more interested in the rendering of the world as condensed and time-compressed imagery. This corresponded with Freud and his more recent disciples, yet Münsterberg's focus on film as an analogue to human perception suggests how direct and startling aspects can be for the audience. Film manifests something approaching a *physical threat*. On rare occasions we may jump in the cinema. Added to a sense of identification, empathy or at the very least an understanding with the characters on screen, we can also feel their limitations, whether it be on a level of hearing, seeing, or speaking. Hearing without seeing is more prominent in the cinema than seeing without hearing. While this strategy has been used to express the world as perceived by a deaf character, it can also be used as a disquieting strategy in thrillers or horror films. Of course, infants are able to hear before they can see, and the removal of this primary stimulus can have a substantial effect. Anthony Storr notes in *Music and the Mind*:

A dark world is frightening. Nightmares and infantile fears coalesce with rational Anxieties when we come home at night through unlit streets. But a silent world is even more terrifying. Is no one there…? … we are dependent on background sound of which we are hardly conscious for our sense of life continuing. A silent world is a dead world.

(Storr 1997: 27)

The withholding of sound is certainly able to have a horrifying effect.[12] Going further, death might be understood in neurological terms as the removal of all sensory stimulation. The Blind Dead are both blind and mute, going some way toward this, although they are clearly dead, too. The Ghostly Effect is not simply "silence" but the muted image, and these are not the same. The latter is a disconnected illusion that lacks dimension and is unconvincing and, crucially, alienating for the audience. It is not an absence so much as the actuality of film's electro-mechanical illusion.

Conclusion

The Ghostly Effect is the failure of illusion, perhaps most commonly occurring when too little care is taken to hold the illusion together, serving to remind us of our own alienation and fragile, limited life, while its "reanimatory" aspects (and approximation of "life") reference death and remind us of our own mortality. These are not "signifieds" but vague impressions, and likely an unconscious permeation which most clearly breaks the surface in horror films. While these are qualities of the physical parameters of film (as a medium of the flat, partly-dimensional moving image accompanied by sounds that may or may not be closely synchronized), I would suggest that this essential quality has also been exploited by some films.

Of the theories as to why cinema included musical accompaniment from its beginning, none is definitive or fully convincing but Eisler and Adorno's theory is the most intellectually challenging. I am interested less in its accounting for music's role in cinema and more in the theory's foundational ideas and their implications. What are the implications of this theory? The Ghostly Effect describes film's essence: the electrical- mechanical reality of cinema as a creator of illusion and machine of manipulation. Film contains at heart a potentially negative thing – reminding us of our mortality, but it precisely works to contain this and dissipate this negativity. A functional misdirection is likely one of film music's principal functions, although this is not approached in any decisive manner of construction but more through an underlying general function. Furthermore, it has for a long time been my suspicion that horror films (and other disturbing fare) engage most directly with some of the essences of cinema as a medium.

What can the notion of the Ghostly Effect do for us in terms of analysis? Addressing the Ghostly Effect reminds us that film is an illusion. Indeed, such a powerful illusion that poor film analysis simply tells us what happens as if we are dealing with actual events rather than projections on a screen or lit electronic screens, allied with speakers or headphones. Analysis thus should be aware of the fragility of the illusion, but also be aware of the potency of its convincing power. Similarly, analysis should also be aware that film music is not like any old music, but is something far more: ritualistic, magic music. Its efficacy derives from its position rather than necessarily simply its musical qualities.

Notes

1 Adorno wrote "most of" this chapter of their book (Schweinhardt and Gall 2014: 143).
2 One criticism (of many) might be that this theory lacks an historical dimension. Audience attitude to film and music has doubtless changed between the time of their writing and now. They suggest, however, that the Ghostly Effect is an essential element of the medium (the union of audio and visual) that remained from the 1890s until their book in the 1940s and beyond.
3 But we should not forget that Adorno and Eisler are "music people," who have a vested interest in dealing with film music as "music." Indeed, they are light on film analysis and stick more with what they know.
4 "Multimediality," on the other hand, simply superimposes one medium upon another, while "transmediality" incorporates material from one into another medium (Wolf 1999: 39–40).
5 For instance, its continued validity is indicated by writings such as Perez (2000).
6 In 1929, film director René Clair championed the sound film in opposition to the more conventional talkie. The former used the possibilities of sound in film rather than being a slave to reproducing dialogue for talking actors on screen (Clair 1985: 92).
7 This remains in some quarters, and directors such as Hitchcock marked a continuation of silent cinema through sequences lacking directly recorded sound. Indeed, shooting without sound is in effect shooting silent film. For more on the persistence of a a silent film aesthetic, see Donnelly (2013), chapter 8.
8 The highly distinctive music was written by Antón García Abril.
9 Although a point of view shot does not necessarily force us to identify with that character position. It is not a straightforward equation (Clover 2000: 152).

10 Altman, Jones and Tatroe note that there was a convention in the 1930s where films tended toward a continuous sound level despite a dynamic interaction of soundtrack elements (2000).
11 Silence has been discussed effectively by Claudia Gorbman (2007) and Danijela Kulezic-Wilson (2009: 1–10).
12 For instance, in "traumatized' television," which involves a mute end to a television show after a particularly shocking or sad incident. For example, *Game of Thrones* after the "Red Wedding" or *Doctor Who* after Adric's death. Is this for the purposes of reverence or an analogue physical shock? This conduit moves us rapidly to "outside" the programme while retaining our emotional reaction but violently reinserting us to the "real world" outside the show.

Bibliography

Altman, Rick, McGraw Jones, and Sonia Tatroe, "Inventing the Cinema Soundtrack : Hollywood's Multiplane Sound System" in James Buhler, Caryl Flinn, and David Neumeyer, eds., *Music and Cinema* (Hanover, NH: Wesleyan University Press, 2000).

Carroll, Noel, *Mystifying Movies: Fads and Fallacies in Contemporary Film Theory* (New York: Columbia University Press, 1988).

Clair, René, "The Art of Sound" in Elisabeth Weis, and John Belton, eds., *Film Sound: Theory and Practice* (New York: Columbia University Press, 1985).

Clover, Carol, "Her Body, Himself: Gender in the Slasher Film" in Stephen Prince, ed., *Screening Violence 1* (New York: Continuum, 2000).

Donnelly, K.J., *Occult Aesthetics: Synchronization in Sound Film* (New York: Oxford University Press, 2013).

Eisler, Hanns, and Theodor Adorno, *Composing for the Films* (London: Athlone, 1994).

Gorbman, Claudia, "The Return of Silence" in *Offscreen*, vol.11, nos.8–9, August–September 2007. https://offscreen.com/pdf/gorbman_forum1.pdf.

Gorbman, Claudia, *Unheard Melodies: Narrative Film Music* (London: BFI, 1987).

Gunning, Tom, "Doing for the Eye What the Phonograph Does for the Ear" in Richard Abel, and Rick Altman, eds., *The Sounds of Early Cinema* (Bloomington, IN: Indiana University Press, 2001).

Kulezic-Wilson, Danijela, "The Music of Silence" in *Music and the Moving Image*, vol. 2, no. 3, Fall 2009, pp. 1–10.

Larsen, Peter, *Film Music* (London: Reaktion, 2007).

Mamula, Tijana, *Cinema and Language Loss: Displacement, Visuality and the Filmic Image* (London: Routledge, 2015).

Münsterberg, Hugo, *The Photoplay: A Psychological Study* (London: Appleton, 1916).

Perez, Gilbert, *The Material Ghost: Films and their Medium* (Baltimore: Johns Hopkins University Press, 2000).

Rosen, Philip, "Adorno and Film Music: Theoretical Notes on *Composing for the Films*" in *Yale French Studies*, no. 60, "Cinema/Sound," 1980, pp. 157–182.

Ruffles, Tom, *Ghost Images: Cinema of the Afterlife* (Jefferson, NC: McFarland, 2004).

Schweinhardt, Peter, and Johannes C. Gall (translated by Oliver Dahin), "Composing for Films: Hanns Eisler's Lifelong Project" in David Neumeyer, ed., *The Oxford Handbook of Film Music Studies* (New York: Oxford University Press, 2014).

Spadoni, Robert, *Uncanny Bodies: The Coming of Sound Film and the Origins of the Horror Genre* (Berkeley, CA: University of California Press, 2007).

Storr, Anthony, *Music and the Mind* (London: Harper Collins, 1997).

Wolf, Werner, *The Musicalization of Fiction: A Study in the Theory and History of Intermediality* (Amsterdam: Rodopi, 1999).

3

SAW HEARD

Musical Sound Design in Post-Millennium Cinema

Film sound has experienced some radical developments in both technological and aesthetic terms over the last 30 years or so. The traditional basic speaker system in cinemas in many cases has been replaced by a multi-speaker system which involves a significant spatialization of film sound allied to a remarkable improvement in sound definition. These changes augur an altered psychology at the heart of much new cinema, instilled by sound's increased importance for films.

> The sound of noises, for a long time relegated to the background like a troublesome relative in the attic, has therefore benefited from the recent improvements in definition brought by Dolby. Noises are reintroducing an acute feeling of the materiality of things and beings, and they herald a sensory cinema that rejoins a basic tendency of ... the silent cinema. The paradox is only apparent. With the new place that noises occupy, speech is no longer central to films.
>
> *(Chion 1994: 155)*

Michel Chion points to technological developments in cinema that have had a notable impact on film aesthetics. Any movement from a speech-centred cinema to one that allows more prominence to "noise" is potentially a move from a cinema dominated by synchronized dialogue to one with significant amounts of asynchrony and sound as an effect in itself, be that through loud music or featured sounds.

The series of *Saw* (2004), *Saw II* (2005), and *Saw III* (2006) demonstrate a situation where film music has an intimately close relationship

DOI: 10.4324/9781003299653-3

with the film's overall sound design: where there is a convergence of sound effects, ambient sound, and music. On the one hand, this might be attributed to the development of digital surround film sound and the corresponding importance of sound design in mainstream films. On the other, though, it might be accounted for by social and cultural aspects: there has been a gradual but exponential increase in the degree of ambient sound and ambient music over the past few decades. Sound effects are often less used to bolster a sense of verisimilitude than they are as an aesthetic effect, as, to all intents and purposes, music. Sound design in these films might be understood as essentially musical in nature, following a musical logic rather than any other.

The first film in the series, *Saw*, has a highly distinctive soundscape, which I will be discussing in this chapter. There is no solid demarcation between incidental music and sound design: consequently, sound effects can sound synthetic and music can sound like sound effects. The film has a very intimate relationship of sonic elements that made it unconventional at the time, whereas films not following the dominant conventions of music-sound effects-dialogue atomization are far more common in recent years. The film's music was written and performed by first-time film music composer Charlie Clouser. Up to this point, he was known for his remixes of existing songs, adapting and rebuilding sonic material rather than "creating" as such. Hence, it might be possible to approach Clouser's work in the *Saw* films as an adaptation, a partial remix, of the sound world as a whole rather than the music alone. Clouser's music in the films is often unmelodic, unmemorable, and anempathetic but focuses

instead on texture and timbre and plays upon a confusion between what might be termed "film music" and "sound effects." The films wield sound often either explosively or in a disconcerting and semi-dislocated manner. Furthermore, *Saw* illustrates the assimilation of new technologies and new techniques and concomitantly different assumptions about cinema's diegetic world and the place of sound in this.

Transformation

In certain recent films there has been a notable fusing of elements of the soundtrack, much as classical musicals fused music with dialogue (or more accurately we should use the term "voices"), some recent films have fused music with sound effects, creating a sonic continuum. Music in film has a significant interaction with other elements of the soundtrack as well as with the images, and one might even argue that its interaction with dialogue outweighs its interaction with images. In recent years, the development of converging digital sound technology has allowed sound designers to use musical software to enhance sound effects in films and allowed music composers to produce their own music incorporating elements of sound effects. Such developments, in line with technological convergence, aesthetic convergence, and harmonizing platforms and industries have meant that music is no longer simply a "bolt-on" to films but integrated almost genetically on a conceptual level: instigating film titles and narratives, perhaps even having films as spin-offs from existing music, while continuing to inspire and articulate the most emotional and exciting moments of the overwhelming majority of films and other audiovisual media.

Technology has played an important part in recent developments in film sound and music, and technological determinism is always an attractive if too easy answer. The availability of relatively cheap and easily programmed keyboard synthesizers at the turn of the 1980s led to an explosion of popular music and musicians premised upon the use of these instruments. This had a notable impact on films. In the 1970s, John Carpenter's scores for his own films sounded unique in their use of simple textures with monophonic synthesizers, but by the next decade they were sounding more like some of the contemporary pop music they had partly inspired. Greek keyboard player Vangelis came to some prominence for his scores for *Chariots of Fire* (1981) and *Blade Runner* (1982), and while rock keyboard players like Rick Wakeman and Keith Emerson had dipped their toes into film scoring, by the mid-1980s pop groups using drum machines and synthesizers were producing scores, such as Wang Chung's for *To Live and Die in LA* (1985). The revolutionary development from analogue to digital sound has had a notable impact on many aspects of cinema (Sergi 2004: 30), and on music and sound perhaps more than most other areas, allowing minute alteration and precise manipulation of all aural aspects. By the turn of the Millennium, it was possible for musical scores to be constructed and fitted to a film on a computer screen at home using AVID (or similar) and digital audio workstation (DAW) technology. Consequently, filmmakers like Robert Rodriguez are easily able to construct the scores for their films themselves, making film less of a collaborative medium, and making music less collaborative perhaps than ever. The elevation of the DAW has revolutionized music production, allowing easy construction of relatively high-quality music on a home computer, although most of the top Hollywood film composers only use them for "mock-ups" until the final recording with an expensive orchestra. However, the development of sequencing software has had a direct influence on the styles of music being produced in the popular music arena. Examples of the dominant types of software sequencer include Steinberg Cubase, Sony Logic, Ableton Live, and Propellerheads Reason. One of the central tenets of such computer technology is that music can be reduced to recorded components that are then processed, through audio enhancement/distortion and through the process of looping, where a passage of music is repeated verbatim. This latter aspect was responsible for the proliferation of dance music in the 1990s that was developed in home studios, with an emphasis on the manipulation of sound samples, pre-recorded passages of music, which could be adapted, treated, and woven together into a new musical composition. Such music technology instils an awareness of sound and the ability to manipulate electronically. This encourages a "sound for sound's sake" approach focusing on the manipulation of sound on a basic level (e.g. reverb, filters, placing in stereo mix, etc.) more than the traditional virtues of composition enshrined in so-called "classical training" (harmony, counterpoint, orchestration, etc). This can lead to confusion about what might constitute "music" and what might constitute "non-musical sound," and at the very least has challenged the limited concepts of music that were in wide circulation. Such technology is not only used by "musical" people but also by sound designers and editors, who use digital technology and techniques to "manipulate" sound effects the same way that composers use the same procedures to "compose" music. While on the one hand, composers are more aware of sound as an absolute than perhaps ever before, film sound people are approaching soundtracks in a manner that might be termed "musical," or at the very least betrays a musical awareness of the interaction of elements and their particular individual sonic qualities.

Saw evinces a unified and complex field of music and sound effects. This inspires a certain sonic (and audiovisual) complexity, while the more self-contained nature of the soundtrack inspires less in the way of extended passages of synchronization. One context for this is the use of digital electronics for both music and sound effects, which means that music increasingly is conceptualized in sonic terms (or at least in electronic terms of basic sound manipulation, dealing with concepts such as envelope, filtering, etc.). On the other side of the coin, there is an increasingly "musical" conceptualization of sound design in such films, where sound elements are wielded in an "artistic" manner, manipulated for precise effect rather than merely aiming to duplicate on-screen activity. Consequently, the distinct psychologies of music and sound effects mix. There is a notable collapse of the *space* between diegetic sound and non-diegetic music. This manifests a collapse of mental space, between the film's "conscious" and its "unconscious." Rick Altman wrote about the differences between diegetic and non-diegetic music: "By convention, these two tracks have taken on a quite specific sense: the diegetic reflects reality (or at least supports cinema's referential nature), while the [non-diegetic] music track lifts the image into a romantic realm far above the world of flesh and blood"(Altman 1987: 11). In a similar manner, the unified field of sound merges these distinct channels, potentially mixing (by the film's terms) the objective and subjective, fantasy and reality, fixed perception and unstable reverie, conscious and unconscious, and not least, musical and communicational.

The convergence of music with ambient sound and sound effects contravenes the film tradition of solid demarcation between such elements. As I have suggested, sound design in films might be understood as essentially musical in nature. After all, sound designers use "musical software" and digital products designed primarily for the production of music (such as the industry standard ProTools). This has led to a more *aesthetic* rather than *representational* conception of sound in the cinema. For long, cinema sound was thought of in terms of clarity of dialogue and uncluttered but functional composition of diegetic sound elements. This is particularly evident in films which have recourse to technical as well as representational extremity, most notably in the horror film. The concomitant lack of synchronization in this equation adds up to a degree of mental uncertainty, emphasized by the film for the purposes of horror. At times, the *Saw* films seem to have soundtracks that have a dislocated nature, having become at least partially uncoupled from the image track of the film.

Traditions

Film incidental music's effects include eliciting and affirming emotion, clarification or provision of information (such as mood and setting), providing a sound bath that immerses the audience in the film world, as well as the more traditional functional aspects that include attempting to provide continuity across edits and joins between shots and time-spaces. As such, the score can also furnish a sense of, or emphasize filmic movement while also functioning to clarify and articulate a formal structure for the film (through punctuation, cadence, and closure). Related structural functions might also include anticipating subsequent action in the film, and commenting on screen activities or providing a further symbolic dimension not evident in other aspects of the film. In separate writings, Noel Carroll (1996: 139), Jeff Smith (1998: 6), and Roy Prendergast (1992: 213–222) all quote a newspaper article where in the 1940s respected concert hall composer Aaron Copland posited five categories of film incidental music function. These functions are: "creating atmosphere, highlighting the psychological states of characters; providing neutral background filler, building a sense of continuity; sustaining tension and then rounding it off with a sense of closure" (Copland 1949: 28). Music has many material functions. It regularly has an enormous influence on the pacing of events and "emphasizing the dramatic line" (Burt 1994: 79). David Raksin notes that it was common to enter before the required emphasis, with what was called "neutral" music in the trade (quoted in Burt 1994), before being more emphatic with the music or making a specific musical effect. Such neutral music has given rise to pejorative descriptions of film music as "wallpaper" or "window dressing" which, perhaps in some cases, is justified. Music regularly performs an instructive role, creating meaning through representing ideas, objects, and emotions. Indeed, it performs a primary role in eliciting emotional responses in the audience, and in providing consent for the audience's emotional responses.

Without assuming an unassailable cinematic ideal of sound and image in harmony, it should be admitted that in mainstream films sound overwhelmingly is functional. It works to elide itself as contract more than perhaps any other element of film. Some theorize that we perceive the diegetic world on screen as an unproblematic reality (on some level) (Kracauer 1960: 33–34), and sound is one of the principal elements that convince us that the space on screen is "real." After all, one might argue that most sounds in films exist essentially to bolster or "make real" the images we see on screen and the surrounding world we imagine. Consequently, when we see faces on screen talking we expect to hear what they are saying, when a car drives past we expect to hear those sounds corresponding. The fact that we hear a representation of those sounds, a convention allowing crisply heard voices and unobtrusive car engine sounds rising then falling in pitch and volume, but not intruding on the important conversation, underlines just how conventional film sound is. Certainly, this is apparent if it is compared to the sounds recorded from an integrated microphone mounted on a home video camera.

However, having stated this, film sound still retains a principal function that is to guarantee the illusionistic world on screen. Random sound effects used in avant garde films might serve as an obtrusive reminder of the fabricated nature of film sound (and indeed synchronized cinema more generally), and point to our expectation of film sound to be merely a vehicle for the illusions on screen. Now this is a very different traditional function from that of music in films. Perhaps such a unity of sound effects and music might be approached as just moments of aesthetic effect, where sound effects are precisely sonic *effects*, such as the disconcerting noise from the attic early in *The Exorcist* (1973). This instance is not simply a sound – it is an emotional effect, more like an emanation from the id, a manifestation of primary psychology. Such opportunities are opened by the recession of sound's representational function, which frees it to fulfil more in the way of direct emotional and aesthetic roles, in short, making film sound more like, or perhaps even a part of, the musical dimension of films. Consequently, great care can be taken with qualitative aspects of certain sounds, as the sounds have value in themselves rather than being conventionally representative of sounds from a small repertoire of stereo-typical sounds (as remains the case in much television production).

Michel Chion discusses the new sonic space offered by directional multi-speaker surround sound as a "superfield," which changes the perception of space and thereby the rules of [audio-visual] scene construction" (1992: 149–150). Although it retains much of the tradition of monaural film, he insists that it is an extension of off-screen space and qualitatively different from previous sonic space, while similarly, Phillip Brophy uses the term "acousmonium" to articulate the new tactile and multidirectional space (2004: 28). Chion goes continues with his description:

> I call superfield the space created, in multitrack films, by ambient natural sounds, city noises, music, and all sorts of rustlings that surround the visual space and can issue from loudspeakers outside the physical boundaries of the screen. By virtue of its acoustical precision and relative stability this ensemble of sounds has taken on a kind of quasi-autonomous existence with relation to the visual field, in that it does not depend moment by moment on what we see onscreen.
>
> *(Chion 1992: 150)*

This new field is not simply one of dialogue and sound effects, but one where their interaction with music can be the key to its organization. This development has inspired new aesthetics. According to Chion, Dolby multitrack favours passive offscreen sound, which works to establish a general space and permits more free movement for shots (and more of which are close-ups) within that space, without any spatial disorientation of the viewer-auditor (Chion 1992: 85), although there is a corresponding tendency to keep speaking characters on screen as spatial anchors.

A further part of this process, evident in some films, is the convergence of music and sound effects, with a concomitant collapse of the strict demarcation between the two that reigned earlier. Of course, to a degree, it has always been impossible to fully and clinically separate musical score from sound effects. Music regularly has mimicked, emphasized, or suggested certain sounds in the diegesis. Similarly, sound effects in films are regularly more than simply an emanation from the illusory diegetic world constructed by the film. They often have symbolic or emotional effects that outweigh their representational status. Indeed, it might be argued that much music in general has spent a lot of time and energy in attempting to approximate, or at least take inspiration from, the natural world, from birdsong to the rhythmic sounds of machinery. So, talking in terms of a solid distinction between the diegetic sound effect and musical accompaniment becomes difficult upon closer scrutiny and deeper thought. However, in terms of film production, there has been a relatively solid divide: musicians and composers produce music for film, and foley artists and sound editors are responsible for constructing a conventional series of sound effects to accompany on-screen action. The advent of digital sound technology and the relative accessibility of complex sound-treating equipment have had a notable impact on the production process. An early example of this was the development of special sound for *Evil Dead 2* (1987), where the sound of a rocking chair creaking was merged with sound recordings of a scream, using digital synthesizers to fuse the sounds on a genetic level. A more recent example of the process is *Resident Evil* (2002). The film begins with a voice-over narration accompanied by metallic and booming "non-musical" sounds, leading into a loop of one of the electronic themes Marilyn Manson wrote for the film as the action follows the events of a laboratory accident. Shortly afterwards, when protagonist Alice studies what appears to be her wedding photograph, we hear music that sounds like it was composed from various "non-musical" sound samples, in other words, reorganized and repeated shards of sound effects. Her contemplation is halted abruptly by a nearby door opening. Sonically, this involves a very loud and percussive sound matched to the image of an automatic door. Yet the consistency of the sound is certainly not at odds with the preceding music, firmly supplying the impression of a continuum of organized sound that is able to be more rhythmic and more melodic while retaining a foot in diegetic sound effects and ambiences.

Such a unified field of music and sound effects is evident in a good number of recent films, although this marginal tradition might be traced back to an origin in silent cinema, where the live music performed to accompany the film in many cases "did" the sound effects. This tradition is probably more evident in the film scoring tradition where music will mimic or suggest certain diegetic sound effects, even though they may well be present on the soundtrack anyway. There was a minor tradition of certain sound films having a sonic continuum that fully merged music and sound effects. Probably the best example is *Forbidden Planet* (1956), which had a soundtrack of "electronic tonalities" by Louis and Bebe Barron. For the purposes of film production this could not be credited as "music," and indeed its origins in recordings of "cybernetic sound organisms" that were then collaged to fit the film evince a process far removed from the dominant traditions of Hollywood film scoring. There is a direct confusion of the origins of sounds. Some of the electronic sounds appear to be functioning like incidental music, some clearly are synchronized with images on the screen (such as the monster, for example). Others appear to be environmental, marking the ambience of the unfamiliar alien planet, and adding to the sense of the exotic and uncharted that the film represents. In his study of the sound and music for *Forbidden Planet*, James Wierzbicki notes that this was not an isolated case, and through traversing the membrane of conventional sound functions pointed to a new psychology:

> In contrast [with traditional orchestral scores of the time], electronic sounds in scores for many 1950s science-fiction films were strikingly non-traditional, and thus they tended to blur the long-standing boundary between non-diegetic underscore and diegetic sound effect. Electronic sounds did not simply accompany "foreign" narrative objectives; in many cases, they seemed to emanate directly *from* them.
>
> *(Wierzbicki 2005, 26–27)*

Similarly, Alfred Hitchcock's *The Birds* (1963) has a soundtrack that mixes sound effects and music. It contained no underscore in the traditional sense. Instead, it used electronic "sound design" (apparently Herrmann's idea), which was recorded in Munich with experimentalists Remi Gassmann and Oskar Sala. Hitchcock's regular composer at the time, Bernard Herrmann was "advisor" and the final product, while using synthetic bird noises, remains related to the *musique concrète* produced by experimenters such as Pierre Schaeffer and Pierre Henry in the 1940s and 1950s. *The Birds'* sound design approached music as merely another element of the soundtrack and replaced a musical underscore with "sound effects" that nevertheless are fairly musical in their inspiration. While the soundtrack appears to represent bird sounds that match the action on screen, they are in fact produced electronically and only vaguely synchronized with the birds on screen. It might be more apt to characterize the soundtrack to *The Birds* as a continuum of ambient bird sounds most clearly in the sequences of bird attacks.

Another film that has a soundtrack that goes beyond simple sound effects and music is David Lynch's *Eraserhead* (1977), which makes particularly harrowing use of ambient sound in the background throughout the film. The sound design for the film, by Alan Splet, collaged industrial sounds, metallic noises, rumbles, and wind into a disturbing and continuous sonic backdrop for the film's action. It is not unchanging and moves to the foreground at times. Arguably, it takes something from the general function of film scores, which provide a sonic backdrop and a vague mood for the action. The fact that these sounds were not easily classified as non-diegetic music meant that they were more satisfactorily accounted for as acousmatic sound effects: seemingly the sounds emanating from some dreadful but indistinct industrial machines somewhere in the distance. Indeed, Alan Splet's sound work was far more than merely recording and compiling sounds for use in films. An available three-disc set, *Sounds From a Different Realm*, showcases Splet's work along with his collaborator Ann Kroeber. Some of the pieces are called "Unusual Presences" and illustrate the construction of nearly autonomous sound environments, some of which were used in David Lynch's films. Despite the collection nominally being a sound effects set, they manifest a sustained "canned atmosphere" rather than being simply "recorded sound effects" ready for general use.

Film Sound as Music (and Film Music as Sound)

The effect of a unified field of sound and music is the destruction of the conventional use of sound in films, with a concomitant questioning of the relationship of sound to image. Certain contemporary films evince a unified sound design that conceives of the film's sound in holistic terms rather than as the traditionally separate music, dialogue, and sound effects. Miguel Mera and David Burnand note:

> Modernism is inherent in the technologically enabled means of audio production in filmmaking that encourages the alliance of music and sound design as a recorded and edited form, and thus is at odds with the rehashed nineteenth-century orchestral scores typical of classic cinema, flown into the virtual orchestra pit of the movie theatre.
>
> *(Mera and Burnand 2006: 5)*

Such films with a unified sound field deal with it in highly sophisticated terms. Sound effects are not simply about matching what the screen requires to verify its activities. Instead, sound effects can take on more of the functions traditionally associated with music, such emotional ambiences, provision of tone to a sequence, or suggestions of vague connections.

In short, film sound as a unified field has taken a high degree of its logic from music, and more specifically from music in films in the form of non-diegetic or incidental music. Films such as *7even* (1997) or *Ju-On: The Grudge* (2003) have notable sequences where sound could be construed as music or as sound effects. In both cases, the ambiguity is doubtless part of the general effect of the film. In *Donnie Darko* (2001), a voice (belonging to "Frank") appears in the night, telling Donnie to wake up. This is accompanied by deep ambiguous rumbles and what might be construed as supernatural sounds. It certainly is not easily recognizable as a film score, but equally fails to identify itself as sound effects for anything in the diegetic world. There is a seemingly organic mixture of diegetic sound and music evident in the London Underground-set *Creep* (2004). At the start of the film one of a pair of sewage workers disappears down a tunnel and as the other searches for him, the soundtrack embraces deep sub-bass rumbles that are ambiguous as to whether they are diegetic or not. As his desperation grows, the music grows in volume, featuring metallic sounds and developing from the deep rumbles into a more clearly organized pattern, and thus more clearly becomes "music."[1] Like much of the film, this sequence exploits the dramatic and psychological possibilities of an extended range of bass tones available to 5.1 Dolby sound.

Indeed, since the advent of multitrack recording technologies in the 1960s, Dolby stereo and surround sound in the 1970s and digital sound technology in the 1980s, soundtracks have become increasingly complex and sophisticated. Indeed, Elisabeth Weis points to the exponential expansion of sound resources indicated by the number of sound technicians working on recent films in comparison with the number on a film during the heyday of the Hollywood studio system (Weis 1995: 42–48). The division of labour is often quite precise, although the supervising sound editor or sound designer will tend to have dominion over all sonic resources. Many directors have a significant input to the final sonic character of their films, while ones like David Lynch also design the sound for their films. Film soundtracks are constructed with great care and creativity. Any attempt to approach the unified soundtrack as simply "sound effects" is doomed – doomed to banal answers. The only viable approach is from a musical point of view. After all, music has been the "science" of sound for a very long time, and it is clear that aesthetic impulses are highly significant in determining film soundtracks, rather than representational concerns (to make sounds match screen action).

Sometimes it seems easy to forget that for centuries we have had a theory of organized sound relevant to the cinema: music. Music is at heart about organizing sound events in time and some of its dominant concepts are highly evident in sonic organization in films. For example, the general ambience assigned to a space is conceived as "backing" to the "aria" or singing voice of dialogue. A more recent tradition has been concerned with making sound recordings into music: *musique concrète*, which developed in France after World War Two and was based on the manipulation and distortion of sound recordings on magnetic tape. While it would be a massive reduction to suggest that it is similar to film sound, there nevertheless are shared points of interest and assumptions. It is hardly fortuitous that the primary theorization of film sound comes from an individual with a background in electroacoustic music and a training in *musique concrète*. Michel Chion has introduced a large number of terms and theories from this body of thought and praxis into the study of film. As one of the few areas to deal with sound, often in musical terms, *musique concrète* should be a stopping-off point (however brief) for any analysis of film soundtracks.

Saw's Musical Sound

The *Saw* films centre upon the activities of the "Jigsaw Killer," a serial killer who is at pains to threaten or kill people in creative and imaginative ways apt to each individual. This involves a high level of invention, as well as meticulous planning leading to a tortuous route of potential escape for the protagonists of the films. The first film starts with two men coming to in a basement of a deserted building, both handcuffed securely but with clues about possible escape (and redemption for their sins). It is notably based on an aesthetic of matching a sumptuous soundscape to what are often overwhelmingly static visuals. Apart from flashback sequences, the whole film takes place in one room. The soundtrack thus serves to provide some variation for the audience and remove the potential for boredom. While the narrative is gripping, the visuals are often quite pedestrian and the soundtrack's use of unusual timbres and unfamiliar activities compensates for this to a degree. Thus, the limited diegetic space inspires a sonic drama of space, where the drama of aural elements encourages a feeling of space that is denied by the film's visual construction. The claustrophobia of the film is highly effective but is enhanced or thrown into relief by a feeling of expanded space in the soundtrack. There is copious use of reverb and echo, which makes the film feel like it is taking place in a large arena of emptiness rather than an overlit basement room. This provides a striking mismatch of claustrophobic visual space with expansive and echo-laden sonic space: this mismatch is dramatic in itself. Furthermore, it makes for a psychological mismatch between the image track and the soundtrack which is further enhanced by the uncertain status of much of the sound (as being diegetic sound effects being non-diegetic music). The limited diegetic space forces sonic space's elevation in importance to the point where the film's sonic space manifests an expansion of experience, but simultaneously a fragmentation of the vaguely coherent subject position of the spectator (as theorized long ago and far away). In *Saw*, the Jigsaw Killer hears (rather than sees) the proceedings throughout, unperceived by the two protagonists. The film could be characterized as a "point of audition sound" acousmonium for him (offering a sonic experience close to ours as the audience: could this be seen as an aural *Rear Window* [1954]). Thus, the spectator-auditor position in the film might be construed in this way to furnish the auditory equivalent of the person sitting in the film theatre.[2]

The film's music composer, Charlie Clouser, started off as an electronic music programmer, being involved in television incidental music before becoming known as a member of industrial rock group Nine Inch Nails and subsequently as a remixer for many rock groups, producing new versions of recordings that have a highly individual stamp on them.[3] Clouser joined the *Saw* project after director James Wan had used a number of Nine Inch Nails pieces in the film's temp track (Sacks 2004). Clouser had been a member of that group in the mid and late 1990s. A background in electronic sound manipulation is advantageous for a film that requires something radically different from a conventional orchestral film score, and indeed, Clouser approached the score in a far from traditional manner. He was interested in using non-musical sounds, such as metallic clashing and banging, in

[s]ounds that might have originated in the sound effects. Subconsciously, I think almost sound as though these might be unseen characters to attack, on the other side of the wall. ... [There was also a concern with] [b]lurring the line, and having industrial sounds that spring from the background of the movie [which] might make the viewer less aware of the music as music and that more aware of the general sense of tension and anxiety we were trying to create.

(Sacks 2004)

Director James Wan wanted to use the score precisely as an effect, for psychological impact rather than merely for emotional impact. Clouser noted:

Usually, I don't try to use sounds that will clash against the sound design – doors slamming, gunshots, things like that. But because of the character of the music that James [Wan] wanted it would involve a lot of metal screeching and banging types of sounds, which were going to get in the way of the sound effects, so it was the skillful [*sic*] mix that kept everything together.

(Clouser 2004).

While the final mix may accommodate Clouser's sounds as well as sound effects, it works with similar sonic material in what appears to be a unified field of sound and music. It is little surprise that when asked to list influences on his work Clouser mentioned Louis and Bebe Barron, who provided the electronic sounds/music for *Forbidden Planet* (Clouser 2004).

The likely main source of *Saw*'s temp track was Nine Inch Nails's 1999 double album *The Fragile*, which included slow atmospheric music as well as more up-tempo and noisy songs. While Trent Reznor was (and remains) the principal player in the group, Clouser was a mainstay at this point. An indication of Clouser's importance for the textural and ethereal tracks is his sleevenote credit on the track *The Great Below*, for "atmospheres." The *Saw* scores are premised upon music as provision of atmosphere, although they might be characterized as a distinct alternation of non-musical sounds and spare synthesizer tones, with kinetic mechanical drum patterns, characteristic of certain industrial rock groups, particularly Nine Inch Nails. Clouser noted that he used the sections with energetic percussion patterns "to build adrenaline" (Sacks 2004). These sections include the speeded-up images of a man caught in razor wire and for some of the "reverse bear trap" sequence, where a character must beat a time limit to remove a piece of potentially fatal headware.

While the drum-based passages provide energy, much of the rest of the music is sparsely textured. The type of music Clouser concentrated on focuses on the vertical aspect. Tracks:

> usually have a level of density, which is greater than most scoring cues, in terms of the number of things happening and how much attention you have to pay to them to decode it all. That kind of works against a lot of people coming from a record background when they're scoring because they wind up making it sound like a record and it might be too busy or too dense to serve as "background."
>
> *(Clouser 2004)*

While many forms of music that work outside the cinema can be reined into films effectively, Clouser points to a concern with momentary texture and the vertical (momentary) aspects rather than the melodic or developmental. In fact, throughout *Saw* tends to use emotionally "cold" sound/music, lacking any emotional warmth to the characters and being partially disconnected from proceedings. This lack of empathy can be related to Michel Chion's notion of "anempathetic music," where mechanical music or music that follows its own logic continues across emotional action without any care for matching its mood with that of the images (Chion 1994: 8). In *Saw*, the connection of sound to images can be vague and the music provides atmosphere and energy that match screen mood and action, but the music refuses to provide music that "connects" with the characters on an emotional level, refusing to take advantage of one of the principal functions of film music, which is to allow the audience to empathize with the characters on screen.

One aspect of Clouser's score that is instantly striking is the sheer variation of sounds in circulation. It utilizes a wealth of electronic tones as well as sounds derived from sound samples. However, it is nevertheless "scored" in the traditional sense. For example, it uses deep drones conventional to horror films and dramatizes and punctuates the voice of the Jigsaw Killer as it appears played on a tape. That Charlie Clouser conceived his music in terms of sound elements that would form a sonic foundation for each scene (Sacks 2004), denotes a process closer to soundscape creation than to traditional film scoring. A sound art infusion to film is further evident in *Saw* in that Clouser's electronic score makes copious use of sounds originating with metal sound sculptures. These were Chas Smith's metal sculptures that were designed to be bowed and scraped to create sounds.[4] Clouser used recordings of these as raw material, manipulated in digital samplers but often retaining their original metallic sonic character.

Upon the two protagonists noticing a dead body lying on the floor between them, there is a series of shots of the body that include a revolving shot and close-ups of the body's bloodied head and the gun clasped in its hand. Each shot appears regularly and is accompanied by a sonic "hit," making for a regular rhythmic pulse of sound and image. Matching the dramatic and unusual visual, the sound also acts unconventionally, including some reversed sounds and the music alternating between the front two speakers, a rarity in films and highly obtrusive sonic activity.

When Adam tries to get the tape player from the dead body's hand, as there is a shot showcasing the tape player in the hand simultaneously there is an echoed drum "hit," marking and synchronizing the action. In the wake of this, as Adam uses his shirt and some cloth to try to obtain the tape player, the music moves through a number of fairly distinct sonic passages: starting with a high, falling ethereal monody interrupted by a sound reminiscent of a distant train passing, then a short, high-pitched squeaky sound, then a deep drone (that sounds like an electronically treated male voice choir), a brief burst of repeated guitar feedback. Then, as Adam picks up the cloth to use, we have a synchronized metal sound, similar to that of a bowed cymbal, followed by echoed deep sounds (like a large water tank being hit). Sonically, this sequence seems a clear succession, which likely emanates from the ease with which contemporary digital technology encourages the use of sonic loops (particularly of the digital audio workstations [DAWs] and their ease of manipulating samples and musical "blocks"). This is further underlined by the moment when

Adam finds a saw in a bag in the toilet cistern, which is accompanied by what sounds like heavily echoed guitar feedback looped and repeated into a single musical figure.

Overall, *Saw* has sections with sparse dialogue, which therefore lack the most regular and clear lynchpin of synchronized sound and image. Furthermore, the fact that *Saw* is premised upon two characters (Lawrence and Adam) chained up in one room allows for dialogue without showing the speaking characters. The audience is aware of the spatial set-up and thus the camera has more freedom of movement. Chion notes that the development of the sonic "superfield" has erased the tradition of spatial scene construction in films by losing the requirement for establishing (and re-establishing) long shots

> because in a more concrete and tangible manner than in traditional monoaural films the superfield provides a continuous and constant consciousness of all the space surrounding the dramatic action ... such that the image now plays a sort of solo part, seemingly in dialogue with the sonic orchestra in the audiovisual concerto.
>
> *(Chion 1994: 150–151)*

The sonic aspect of *Saw* certainly evinces much variation, but also consistently uses sounds of obscure origin, such as drones, scrapes, and loud bumps, all of which could be construed as diegetic sounds but more likely are non-diegetic, lacking any origin in the film world on screen.

To describe such sounds, with unapparent origins, Chion invokes the concept of the "acousmatic," a term initiated by Jérôme Peignot but developed by Pierre Schaeffer, and defined as "sound that one hears without seeing the cause" (Chion 1994: 71). The antonym of this is what Chion calls "visualized sound," as a correspondent with Schaeffer's notion of "direct sound" (with a clear origin). There is an essential ambiguity to such sounds. Their origins are immediately obscure, although their source may be understood later. In psychological terms, such sounds are perceived as a potential threat in that they hang in uncertainty for the perceiver. In *Saw*, we hear much in the way of metal sounds that could possibly be diegetic. They certainly don't sound like a traditional film score. But then there is no indication of any diegetic origin for these sounds. They question the status of the diegesis and, significantly, add to a sense of ambiguity of environment through confusion of sound and image. Similarly, there are regular bass rumbles (almost sub-bass rumbles) on the film's soundtrack. Are these diegetic? That information is never furnished by the film. The potentially disturbing effect of such ambiguous sounds is discussed by Chion, who points to the essential ambiguity of such sounds. Their origins are immediately obscure, although their source might be understood later. In psychological terms, such sounds are perceived as a potential threat in that they hang in uncertainty for the listener.

As an aural counterpart to the rare "non-diegetic insert,"[5] we might wonder if recent cinema is wielding the "non-diegetic sound effect," which likely has the same ambiguity of acousmatic sound, although it sounds like it could emanate from the world on screen yet *cannot* be retrospectively understood and placed in the surrounding (diegetic) world. It indeed has lost its synchronization absolutely, in that there is no possibility of its matching the screen world and thus manifests an extreme of mental confusion and potential threat. The horror genre often has been premised upon the drama of off-screen space concealing the unknown, such as in films like Hitchcock's *Psycho* (1960). However, in *Saw*, these sounds not only are "offscreen," they are also "off world." They are sounds "from nowhere," occupying the same space as the film's non-diegetic music, which also emanates from an obscure space somewhere that is not existentially connected to the world represented on screen. Now, non-diegetic music is purely conventional, and as such does not invite direct questions about its origins. However, sound effects are anchored to screen representations. They provide the spatial and conformational aspects of activities on screen or nearby still in the diegetic world. From time to time, however, sound effects appear to come from outside the diegetic world, most notably in surreal or horror films. For example, in the remake of *The Fog* (2005), as DJ Stevie Wayne (played by Selma Blair) sits in her car, there are deep threatening sounds. Their status is ambiguous – they might be part of Graeme Revell's non-diegetic music, or they could be diegetic sounds of the mysterious fog itself. However, in all likelihood, they are non-diegetic sound effects.[6] This appears literally to be an occult aesthetic, yet such general "ambiences" function to immerse the audience in the film more effectively in sonic terms than might be available as a visual effect. There are highly effective low-volume continuums, such as Freddy Kruger's basement in the *Nightmare on Elm Street* films, or in spaceships such as the Starship Enterprise in the *Star Trek* films and television series. Rick Altman, McGraw Jones, and Sonia Tatroe note that some Hollywood films in the 1930s had continuous low-volume "atmosphere sound" which had a function of "enveloping" the audience in a film's sonic space (Altman, Jones and Tatroe 2000: 352). Such "enveloping" is an effect of the extension of sonic space, which is a characteristic of surround sound but also an effect of the degree of reverberation (or "reverb") evident on any recorded sound. In audio terms, reverb expresses "space" as the equivalent of showing open space visually. Furthermore, the use of electronic reverb, adding a sense of space around a recorded sound, might be seen as a prime signifier of sound as aesthetic in films rather than following any vague attempt to reflect the space represented visually on screen. Philip Brophy notes that, "[p]sychoacoustically, reverb grants us an out-of-body experience: we can aurally separate what we hear from the space in which it occurs" (2004: 108). This inconsistency of sound space represented on the soundtrack and the expected sound ambience that would have emanated from the space represented on screen. This is not only evident in *Forbidden Planet* but also in films such as *Saw*. It illustrates a degree of mental separation emanating from the evident mismatch in *Saw* of expansive, reverb-drenched music and sounds, with an enclosed and circumscribed visual space. We might go further, and approach electronic reverb and echo as a manifestation of a state of mind more than it is a representation of anything. After all, it does not signify diegetic space but something beyond, an emotional and unconscious enveloping of sound. In his discussion of *Forbidden Planet*, Philip Brophy continues,

> Reverb is heavily applied to *Forbidden Planet*'s synthetic sound effects firstly to invoke the expansive opening of interplanetary frontiers, and secondly to invoke an imposing sense of size and space. At least fifteen centuries of European church architecture used reverb to conjure up thundering scale and omnipotent power; sci-fi movies followed suit with their own brand of technological mysticism and God-fearing morality.
>
> *(Brophy 2004: 108)*

So, it is nothing to do with representing the world on screen and more to do with providing an effect and an emotional tone. Annabel Cohen notes that:

> The affective quality [of music] is consistent [with the diegesis]; the acoustical aspects of the music are not. Although the affective associations produced by the music seem to belong to the corresponding images, the sounds that produced those associations do not. Somehow, the brain attends to this affective meaning, while ignoring or attenuating its acoustical source.
>
> *(Cohen 2000: 373–374)*

As registered earlier, the unification of sound effects and music conjoins the distinct psychologies of music and sound effects. The use of electronic echo and reverb marks a *musical* appropriation of sound space, unifying diegetic and non-diegetic sound as a psychological effect more than as a representational counterpart of the images on screen (and diegesis of recorded voices). Sound theorist David Toop points to the "attraction to the synthetic mimicry of resonance, the structural potential of delays and the physicality of sound waves in enclosed space has evolved into a wider exploration of time, space and sound" (Toop 2004: 64). This quotation may have been aimed at a certain tendency in music, but is equally applicable to the use of sound in some films, films that are interested, one way or another, in exploring mental and psychological space. In other words, these films are *about* mental space, enabled by the sonic dimension of the film that is beyond representational functions.

Conclusion

Of course, music and sound effects have always been mixed despite conventional and technological efforts to keep them separate. Film scores have regularly imitated diegetic sounds (as indeed has music intermittently and habitually imitated the sounds of nature). However, in recent years there has been more in the way of radical confusion of score and sound effects. These two aspects of film sound, distinct since the coming of synchronized sound cinema, have converged and crossed what was once a fairly impermeable membrane between these two sonic aspects. The personnel involved in their production often remain as distinct as they had in the heyday of the Hollywood studio system, but techniques and hardware have encouraged a convergence. Developments such as this need acknowledgement from those studying film. The increased depth of aestheticization evident in many film soundtracks since the turn of the Millennium renders many analyses that ignore their nuances little more than naïve descriptions of "what happens" in those films. Narratological concerns should allow for the fact that sound-dominated films are essentially sensual experiences.

Now, on one level, some of this discussion might seem naïve. Austere music might well sound like "sound effects" to the uninitiated. I am aware of this – but there is a tradition of sound effects in film (and television, and video games), and these recent scores/soundtracks engage those traditions more than they come from outside (from art music, for example). However, a number of recent films offer very rich sonic landscapes that work on their own independently of their film. This could be traced to the tradition of programmatic music, illustrating vistas and places through sound, a tradition reinvigorated by certain ambient music and new age music. There might also be an influence from sound art, which has been a burgeoning area of the art world over the past couple of decades. As a concrete instance, one artist relevant for discussion and who has crossed a number of boundaries is Brian Williams (usually known artistically as Lustmord). Starting in left-field rock music, some of his early recordings were of specific spaces (such as the Dunster Abattoir in Bangor and Chartres Cathedral on *Paradise Disowned* [1984]). He worked with experimental rock group SPK when they were using "found" metal percussion and he went on to produce regular recordings that sounded like they were inspired by horror film soundtracks. His 1990 album *Heresy* is seen as inaugurating the "dark ambient" (sub)genre, while albums such as *The Monstrous Soul* make copious use of horror film samples in their nightmarish soundscapes. More recently, Williams worked in Hollywood as a "musical sound designer," usually in collaboration with composer Graeme Revell (with whom he collaborated in SPK in the 1980s). Williams's role in films like *The Crow* (1994) was to provide certain sounds and ambiences that can be used in the film or in Revell's score. This suggests a unified sound design that is "musical" in its origin, as testified to by Williams's screen credit.

It is incontrovertible that the category of music has expanded to include much other sound. For instance, CDs of natural sounds, not just of singing whales, but recordings of natural landscapes, such as the Global Journey CD *Nature Recordings: Thunderstorm*,[7] not to mention the recorded soundscapes of sonic artists such as Hildegard Westerkamp. Such "soundscaping" is perhaps less to do with any attempt to objectively record a sound environment than it is to configure sound "psychogeographically" as personal and emotional landscapes. To a degree, this process might also be identified in some films, which aim to produce a mental and psychological aural landscape, as is the case in *Saw*.

Freed from a functional role, freed from the diegesis, and freely mixing with music, film sound is able to manifest a direct emotion, and a primary psychology. The tradition of sound mixing and construction developed by classical Hollywood and influential the world over was premised upon a solid demarcation of sound effects, dialogue and music, and with a concomitant clarity of purpose for each and the system as a whole. This appears to reflect a sense of clarity of purpose and a solid understanding of the relationships between things in the world that mark protean American cinema of the time. By the same token, the collapse of consensus of sonic clarity might reflect social and political developments – perhaps the cultural confusion is a reflection of or simply emanates from social and political confusion. We can speculate about such "reflection," but what is beyond doubt is that there is a remarkable collapse of the *space* between diegetic sound and non-diegetic music. This manifests a collapse of mental space, between the film's "conscious" and its "unconscious," and perhaps not only between rational and irrational elements in such horror films but also in wider cinema.

Notes

1 When protagonist Kate runs along the deserted underground train, the music consists of a rhythmic loop of treated metallic sounds that are more "sound

effects" than "musical" in origin. This piece has notable similarities with some of Charlie Clouser's kinetic music in the *Saw* films.
2 Such as in other celebrated "sonically based" films like *The Conversation* (1974) or *Blow Out* (1981).
3 Clouser worked in television music with Australian composer Cameron Allen in the late 80s before working with Nine Inch Nails and as a remixer. He worked on show including *The Equalizer* and *Kojak*, ad more recently on *Fastlane* and *Las Vegas*.
4 Ibid.
5 These are the proverbial shots of trains going into tunnels that allegedly implied sex scenes in silent films. They are likely apocryphal stories and the fodder of comedy. Probably the most famous non-diegetic insert is the intrusion of a shot of a bull being slaughtered at the violent riot concluding Eisenstein's *Strike* (1926).
6 A philosophical problem is posed by the notion of the non-diegetic sound effect. The concept of diegetic is itself highly questionable, being dependent on an assumption about the illusory world on-screen, made by an idealized audience member.
7 On Global Journey records, GJ3638, 2001.

Bibliography

Altman, Rick, *The American Film Musical* (London: BFI, 1987).

Altman, Rick, McGraw Jones, and Sonia Tatroe. "Inventing the Cinema Soundtrack: Hollywood's Multiplane Sound System" in James Buhler, Caryl Flinn, and David Neumeyer, eds., *Music and Cinema* (Brunswick: Wesleyan University Press, 2000).

Brophy, Philip, *100 Modern Soundtracks*(London: BFI, 2004).

Burt, George, *The Art of Film Music* (Boston: Northeastern University Press, 1994).

Carroll, Noel, *Theorising the Moving Image* (Cambridge: Cambridge University Press, 1996).

Chion, Michel, *Audiovision: Sound on Screen*, edited and translated by Claudia Gorbman (New York: Columbia University Press, 1992).

Clouser, Charlie, "Interview" at *ign.com*. http://music.ign.com/articles/562 /562509p1.html [accessed 03/12/2004].

Cohen, Annabel J., "Film Music: Perspectives from Cognitive Psychology" in James Buhler, Caryl Flinn, and David Neumeyer, eds., *Music and Cinema* (Middletown: Wesleyan University Press, 2000).

Copland, Aaron, "Tip to the Moviegoers: Take Off Those Ear-Muffs" in *The New York Times*, 6 November 1949, section six.

Kracauer, Siegfried, *Theory of Film: The Redemption of Physical Reality* (Oxford: Oxford University Press, 1960).

Mera, Miguel, and David Burnand, "Introduction" in Miguel Mera, and David Burnand, eds., *European Film Music* (London: Ashgate, 2006).

Prendergast, Roy M., *Film Music: A Neglected Art* (New York: Norton, 1992).

Sacks, Rob, "Charlie Clouser's Scary Soundtrack for *Saw*" (interview with Charlie Clouser) in *NPR's "Day to Day,"* Friday 9 October 2004. http://www .nrp.org/templates/story/story.php?storyId=4132853 [accessed 15/11/2006].

Sergi, Gianluca, *The Dolby Era: Film Sound in Contemporary Hollywood* (Manchester: Manchester University Press, 2004).

Smith, Jeff, *The Sounds of Commerce: Marketing Popular Film Music* (New York: Columbia University Press, 1998).
Toop, David, *Haunted Weather: Music, Silence and Memory* (London: Serpent's Tail, 2004).
Weis, Elisabeth, "Sync Tanks: The Art and Technique of Postproduction Sound" in *Cineaste*, vol. 21, nos. 1–2, 1995, pp. 42–48.
Wierzbicki, James, *Louis and Bebe Barron's Forbidden Planet: A Score Guide* (London: Scarecrow, 2005).

4

MUSIC CULTIZING FILM

KTL and the New Silents

"Cult" film soundtracks can remind us of the fragmented nature of films, pointing to the intersection of film with music culture, which has its own well-developed ideas about "cult" music. While we are used to cult film soundtracks as a component of cult films,[1] film soundtracks that are accorded that status while the film is not are something of a rarity. There are films known almost solely for their music such as *Unchained* (1955), which used music later remade as the hit song *Unchained Melody*, or *A Summer Place* (1959), where Max Steiner's theme from the film later became a staple of "easy listening" music. Some film soundtracks have had cult lives beyond the screen, such as Jack Nitzsche's for *Performance* (1970),[2] Manfred Hübler and Siegfried Schwab's for the Jess Franco film *Vampiros Lesbos* (1971), Alain Goraguer's for *Fantastic Planet* (1973), John Carpenter's for *Assault on Precinct 13* (1976), or Goblin's only partially used score for *Dawn of the Dead* (1978). There is a tendency to "pull apart" these soundtracks from their films, with music such as *La Valleé* (1972, *The Valley Obscured by Clouds*) better known as a Pink Floyd album than a film soundtrack. This chapter is interested in the possibility of the status of music and musicians redefining and cultizing films, altering their sense of cultural value and interest, as well as "opening" them to a new audience. The recent renaissance of silent film has been led by the rediscovery of live music to make the screening of old silent films into special cinematic events rather than remaining akin to the banal normality of watching films on television or in a standardized multiplex. This parallels some developments in cult cinema, from midnight movie origins to festivals and special events which mark out a distinct area of

DOI: 10.4324/9781003299653-4

film consumption. The desire for new and more unique experiences has encouraged the remaking of film as a live event, while technological possibilities have made it easier for small musical ensembles to perform live accompaniment to films, and DVD production has allowed for ease of distribution of the film with its new music. This new phenomenon has opened up the possibility for silent films to be recontextualized through music and related technologies, indeed made into different objects through being associated with strident and original musicians who are unwilling merely to provide music that will have an unassuming role in demurely fitting in with the demands of an old silent film.

New Silents

Silent films are now more prominent than at any time since their supersession by the cinema of recorded sound in the late 1920s and early 1930s. A crucial part of this is that in recent years the provision of new music for these silent films has become a vibrant culture. Many musicians are attracted to the possibilities offered for adventurous music, and the expansion of festivals and "off-mainstream" arthouse screenings, have fostered interest in singular events such as film screenings with live music (Altman 2004: 4). As a counterpart to this, many DVD releases of silent films have new specially-written music for the films while others go out of their way to have an "authentic" score from the time of the film's release.[3]

The current culture of dealing with old silent films on the one hand engages an aim for retaining "original intentions" or "the author's wishes," approaching film as a firmly *historical* entity bound by its own time of production. On the other, there is a profoundly different notion that silent film exists to be "updated" and made into a living breathing contemporary object (Davis 2008; Donnelly and Wallengren 2015). Contemporary music might allow a point of entry for audiences unfamiliar with the conventions of silent cinema, exploiting music as a device to *frame* the film for modern audiences. Addressing one of the first instances of this modernizing impetus, Thomas Elsaesser defended the Moroder version of *Metropolis* in opposition to the obsessive focus on "the phantom 'first night' of archivists and historians" (Elsaesser 2000: 58) For many film aficionados, Giorgio Moroder's 1984 version was "beyond the pale" in accompanying Fritz Lang's enduring dystopic vision with pop songs by Bonnie Tyler and Freddie Mercury amongst others. Blair Davis describes how he found the addition of modern music allowed students to engage more with silent films, as it made the film less alien through its incorporation of music from "their" culture (David 2008: 92). So, on the one hand musical accompaniment to silent films works to "muse-umize" the film, to make it a guaranteed historical object, on the other "novel" scores aim to renew the film as a cultural object and frame it for a new audience. Some films have attracted significant interest from musicians. For instance, Dziga Vertov's *Man with a Movie Camera* (1929) is available on DVD with scores by highly singular composer Michael Nyman (in 2002), the Alloy Orchestra (in 1996), art rock ensemble In the Nursery (in 1999), popular music-inspired The Cinematic Orchestra (in 2002), and Norwegian electronic musician Biosphere (in 1996). Similarly, *Häxan* (1922) was released with a choice of three scores: the late 1960s edit and sound dubbing with author William S.Burroughs's voice and Daniel Humair and Jean-Luc Ponty's music (renamed *Witchcraft through the Ages*), Geoff Smith's hammer dulcimer music or Bronnt Industries Kapital's electronic music. There are also DVDs available with historically sensitive orchestral music by Matti Bye in Sweden and Gillian B. Anderson in the USA, as well as a version by French progressive rock band Art Zoyd which is only available on CD rather than DVD.

The cult reputation of some horror films (indeed, founding films for the genre) has attracted musicians. *The Cabinet of Dr.Caligari* (*Das Kabinett des Doktor Caligari*, [1919]) has had accompaniment from In the Nursery, Timothy Brock, Rainer Viertlböck, dulcimer music by Geoff Smith, a jazz score by Mark Dresser, and Lynne Plowman with the London Mozart Players. Similarly, *The Golem* (1920) has received new music by Aljoscha Zimmermann (chamber score), by guitar player Gary Lucas (which toured internationally), Yegor Zabelob, Betty Olivero, by experimental bands Noize Choir and Wax Magnetic (in Newcastle, England in 2014), and by Black Francis, singer in indie rock group the Pixies; while F.W. Murnau's *Nosferatu: eine Symphonie des Grauens* (1922) has had musical accompaniment from Gillian B. Anderson, Hammer horror composer James Bernard, gothic heavy metal band Type O Negative, and acclaimed "Krautrock" band Faust.

In 2013, the band Red Snapper performed live music to *Touki Bouki* (1973), whilst also retaining the recorded soundtrack to the film from Senegal. Red Snapper produced "acid jazz" dance-based music, mixing beats from club music with acoustic instrumentation throughout the 1990s. Similarly working alongside existing recorded soundtracks, in 2012 Steven Severin added live music to *Vampyr* (1932), which was then released as a CD. Severin used to be the bass guitar player in Siouxsie and the Banshees, one of the original British punk rock bands in the late 1970s and 1980s. He had gradually begun to expand his activities to include producing music for other musicians and became a solo artist in the mid-1990s. As a cult musician and an important member of one of the 1980s-originating "Gothic" bands, it was perhaps no surprise that he went on to write music for films including the horror film *London Voodoo* (2004). What was perhaps more surprising was that he wrote music for some stage dance productions before going on to supply wholly new scores for silent or quiet films. Before *Vampyr*, in 2010, Severin had supplied new music for Jean Cocteau's silent film *Le Sang d'un poète* (1930) and has managed to retain and reinforce his reputation as a cult rather than a mainstream musician. This arguably has been fortified by his soundtrack work and he has only produced music for silent films. Carl-Theodor Dreyer's early sound film *Vampyr* is considered a classic early horror film and has a very quiet recorded soundtrack with no incidental music, which allows for Severin's atmospheric score to be added live. This is not an uncommon facet of new music for silent films, with musicians of a certain cult reputation embracing silent films of a similar cult status. On the one hand, this appears to be a cultural homology in that both film and musician might be non-mainstream, but on the other for the musicians in particular this also appears to be a form of brand protection and reinforcement.

A musician with perhaps even more of a cult reputation, electronic artist DJ Spooky, produced probably the most extreme reworking of a silent classic film. He made performances and released a DVD of *Rebirth of a Nation* (2005), a "remix" of D.W. Griffith's *Birth of a Nation* (1915), which although currently acclaimed as a founding moment in modern cinematic art, has a clear racist agenda. DJ Spooky not only adds a musical soundtrack but also a voice-over commentary on the film's action, perhaps most notably during its sequences lauding the Ku Klux Klan. Yet the remix goes further than this, removing and repeating sections of the film and using superimposed graphics on the screen, all in aid of a critical discourse that becomes incorporated within the film.

These days, old culture habitually is repackaged as "history" or "heritage,"[4] but there is a scope here to remake this straightforward formulation by "cultizing" objects in some way. Musical addition is a clear opportunity to rethink our relationship with the past.[5] Currently, it is often considered a sign of cultural distinction to watch old films rather than recent ones or "consensual" classics. Perhaps the status gets higher once they become black-and-white films and even higher when they are silent films. After all, museums appear happier to screen older films to sidestep any feeling of being part of the fabric of contemporary media culture. Silent films certainly feel as if they hail from, and belong to, another world that's set apart from contemporary mainstream culture. While some films have proven popular for re-scoring, musicians now also attend to less well-known silent films, furnishing them with an alternative life through the addition of cult music, which instantly appears to wrest them from the clutches of cultural preservation and divest them of their sense of historical specificity. Their alternative life comes at a cost - the arguable loss of any sense of historical context – although gains might include new insight into the film and a deeper understanding of its abilities as an emotional and affecting object.

Cult Taste

Cult film culture's characteristic of occasional but repeated viewings[6] translates only vaguely to music. However, the dedication and appreciation accorded to particular filmmakers or actors is certainly similar to the depth of fan appreciation received by certain musicians. While there are distinct similarities between music and film as industries and cultures, there are also significant differences. Music culture is far, far more fragmented than film culture. This has been accelerated in recent years by the increasing possibility of extremely cheap music production and distribution – far cheaper than might be achieved by film. Every music genre has subgenres and further divisions.[7] This means that the spectrum from mainstream to hip obscurity is wider. In some ways this almost adds up to a reformation of what initially looks similar to so-called "elitist" culture, pursued by aficionados who look down upon the more mainstream and popular manifestations and their "undemanding" audiences.

Whilst a notion of cult related to film is not the same as the notion in relation to music, there are some important points of junction. Both require that their audience has a degree of rarefied knowledge and both value their cultural objects beyond the dominant "throwaways" of consumer culture. Indeed, the differentiation from casual consumers has to be defining and suggests a cultural position not too distant from so-called "elitist" minority culture. Indeed, Mark Jancovich notes that the self-identity an audience derives from espousing cult films "emerges from a need to produce and protect a sense of rarity and exclusivity" (Jancovich 2002: 309). The same goes for music. Despite the cultural landscape having reconfigured its earlier high-low elements (Jameson 1991: 3), cult film and hipster music culture have embraced a potentially elitist approach.

In terms of films, experimental and avant garde cinema has become the most marginal possible, although this description is also potentially relevant for films from a different, "low culture" origin. In terms of music, popular classical music (showcased on radio stations such as Classic FM in the UK) has rendered what was once considered the highest musical achievements banal through constant repetition and consumption by mass audiences. Areas of music which were once dismissed as "popular music" now furnish extremely challenging music which is only accessed by a dedicated and committed audience. Since the advent of populism in the academy, it has become unfashionable to champion such minority culture as it is "elitist." Although initially a "populist," I have gradually come to the conclusion that the lack of nuance in the debate threw the baby out with the bathwater. Complex and non-"easy access" culture has been firmly marginalized by academic discourses that have promoted and abetted mainstream consumer culture.[8]

In recent years, the ground has shifted. Live music and small record label releases (particularly on the Bandcamp website or cassette) have provided a fruitful self-conscious alternative to what arguably constitutes an increasingly standardized musical mainstream aimed at mass consumption. Film culture has developed, too, with an increased interest in films from countries previously ignored in Europe and the USA, which now grace specialist festivals, as well as an increased academic interest in "world cinema." In each case, the aficionado is catered for. Cult film is certainly now very much a part of this process. According to Jancovich, Reboll, Stringer, and Willis, despite cult film having a tendency to be "low culture" its opposition to the mainstream furnishes it with "a kind of oppositional and underground culture that it shares with European art cinema" (Jancovich, Reboll, Stronger and Willis 2003: 11). Both art cinema and cult films share a clear sense of valuing of cultural objects in a manner that evades mainstream consumerism's constant run of novelty and fashion (Andrews 2013). Between the two cultural objects of film and music, cult status can be negotiated through a mixture of obscurity and cultural value.[9] Populism and elitism have been reordered along different lines, with the notion of cult film at the heart of this process. The following discussion focuses on an exemplary case of an old silent film being reworked with radical new music, which engages many of these aspects under discussion directly.

The Phantom Carriage

First released in 1921, *The Phantom Carriage* (*Körkarlen* in the original Swedish) was directed by and starred Victor Sjöström. It concerns a self-destructive and aggressive alcoholic, David Holm, who ultimately repents his terrible life after being faced with the possibility of dying and driving the phantom carriage of the film's title. It is an extreme tale of morality, with Holm treating everyone extremely poorly (especially his own wife and child), allowing for a strong redemption at the conclusion. The sense of redemption is evident in one of the film's alternative titles, *Thy Soul Shall Bear Witness*, while another, *The Strike of Midnight*, emphasizes the supernatural. Although predating the strong generic formulation of "horror film,"[10] *The Phantom Carriage*'s depiction of the supernatural using eerie double exposures makes for extremely atmospheric and disturbing passages.

The Phantom Carriage has an extremely respectable status as a classic silent film. It is known to many as the film that inspired Ingmar Bergman to make films (Battaglia 2012), and also has a reputation for its remarkable visual special effects. These involve double exposures allowing for ghostly apparitions including the carriage of the film's title. These two notions can be used as a "frame" for approaching the film, but on its own terms it is a startling experience. The narrative is one of redemption and the principal character David Holm, played by director Sjöström, descends to the utmost depths of depravity in order to ultimately be reformed. Probably the most common musical accompaniment to the film is the score by Matti Bye, a musician who has strong connections to the Swedish Film Institute. His score is historically apt in that it uses a classical chamber ensemble and follows the stylistic musical patterning that was widely accepted as dominant in the early 1920s. This is the most respectable form of film history, enshrining a startling film as high art.

However, while being a respectable cultural object, the film also has something of a "subterranean" reputation. This emanates partly from the film's status as an influential film for the later and less respectable horror genre.[11] While the film was made before the genre had solidified and audience expectations had been set, it contains much that can be recognized and appreciated by contemporary horror film audiences. Furthermore, *The Phantom Carriage* is known – by those who know such things – as inspiration for probably the most memorable and iconic scene in *The*

Shining (1980).[12] Director Stanley Kubrick in effect lifted the whole scene of Jack (Nicholson) taking an axe to a door behind which his wife and child cower. Although he added witty dialogue, the sequence is clearly more than simply inspired by Sjöström's original, where the enraged Holm smashes the door that keeps him from his wife and children. It is a highly striking film which is both shocking and haunting.

Different scores abound, some as cult objects. *The Phantom Carriage* has received DVD releases as different versions with scores by Matti Bye or KTL. Live versions have also proliferated, with Jonathan Richman (who topped the charts with the Modern Lovers in the late 1970s) performing music to it at the 2007 San Francisco International Festival and The Horses (aka Acid Pony Club, consisting of DJs Laura Ingalls and Clement Pony) performing live music to the film at the 2014 JUE Music + Art Festival in Shanghai. On the internet, there are also accessible versions by Gustaf Lindström (electronics and voice), Edward Rolf Boensnes (electronic keyboards), Signal to Noise Ratio (rock 2011), Franz Danksagmüller and Berit Barfred (electronics and voice, Barcelona 2010), Matt Marshall (piano), and the Napa Valley Youth Symphony.

The Phantom Carriage was released on DVD in 2010 with a brand new musical soundtrack provided by experimental group KTL, an ensemble which comprises drone rock guitarist Stephen O'Malley and electronic musician Peter Rehberg. This non-traditional "KTL version" (as it is known) aims at the inculcation of a primal psychological state in a more insistent way than most film scores. In 2009, KTL made performances of *The Phantom Carriage*, which was followed by the DVD release (although there was no CD release of the music). As a statement of intent, rather than including film notes by a film historian, it has some by avant garde filmmakers the Quay brothers. The following year, KTL also performed a live score for Murnau's *Sunrise* (1927), first at the Louvre in Paris. Their film music is much like their non-film music, and is based on droning continuous sound, lacking notable melody or harmonic changes. Its austerity and bleakness are harrowing enough but allied to Sjöström's horrifying film, the effect is most overwhelming. Rehberg and O'Malley both have established avant garde/experimental reputations. O'Malley is most recognized as a member of Sunn0))), the drone avant garde/heavy metal band whose live show aims at sonic effects and is a far remove from concerts of songs by popular musicians.[13] Rehberg is a prolific collaborator and owns the Austrian-based Editions Mego record label which specializes in electronic and experimental music[14] and won the *Prix Ars Electronica* Distinction Award for Digital Music in 1999.

KTL's score reorients the film radically. It is premised upon drones and continuous sound rather than the more traditional process of continual change to match developments on screen. Indeed, they impose their own aesthetic on the film, with the score sounding similar to their albums rather than being compromised by accounting significantly for the film's images. This is not to suggest that the music is indifferent to the film, merely to indicate that it is doing something different from conventional scores by aiming not to be simple emotional support that is hardly noticed, but rather an active and prominent element of the drama. KTL produce a form of avant garde music, although it is a form that has emanated more from a popular music origin than an art music one. Despite sometimes being labelled "avant garde," KTL do not emanate from a traditional art music avant garde background.[15] Technology is paramount to their approach. The ensemble's default sound involves O'Malley's distorted electric guitar sustaining chords seemingly endlessly while Rehberg uses electronic treatment of that sound and bolsters it with complementary electronic sound from either a synthesizer or his laptop computer. One might argue that their sound is "cold" and that this comes partly from their embrace of technology and lack of organic sound.[16] It should also be noted that their sound, while reliant upon digital signal processing, also uses older analogue electronics in the form of O'Malley's thermionic valve-based amplification and the transistor-based signal processing in his board of effects pedals. In live concerts they play though a large rig of the sort that is used for loud rock concerts. While popular notions of digital technology revolutionizing ease of access to music and video material in recent years are incontrovertible, we should also remember that electronic speaker technology has in principle changed little since the 1920s. It is still based on a voltage causing the vibration of a lightweight diaphragm in a speaker cabinet, whether we are discussing a current 5.1 or 7.1 speaker system in a cinema or KTL's non-spatialized rig which aims to overwhelm the audience with sound and obliterate spatial aspects.

KTL are a prime example of avant garde music that emanates from traditions related to so-called "popular music" rather than developing from the traditional fount of avant garde music in art music circles.[17] Rehberg's electronic music background is not in electronic dance music but in recordings and programming, in the complex end of electronic music. Indeed, KTL and Rehberg alone have performed at the Krems festival in Austria which annually showcases challenging and esoteric electronic music. O'Malley, on the other hand, is a more widely known musician although hardly a household name. Sunn0))), the band that he formed with Greg Anderson, came out of extreme metal although they transcended the genre by producing music based on more experimental principles. Inspired by the group Earth, Sunn0))) began making music that was based on sustained tones (on drones) allied to not having a drum beat as a musical component. This is a radical matter indeed, rendering the group an almost deconstructionist anomaly in rock music, and in many ways more closely allied to para-art music such as Glenn Branca or Rhys Chatham. O'Malley certainly has a cult reputation and has been involved in recording with ensembles including the Aethenor, Grave Temple, and Khanate. O'Malley and Anderson also run their own record label (Southern Lord), which supports and showcases similarly left-field bands who occupy the outer reaches of rock music (or post-rock [Reynolds 2004: 358–361], if you would prefer). KTL formed to provide music for a stage show called Kindertotenlieder (Songs for Dead Children) and have produced a number of albums, each named with successive Roman numerals.[18]

The KTL soundtrack to *The Phantom Carriage* is a wholly alien prospect for traditional silent film music, and indeed, conventional film music more generally. Clear differences evident in the KTL version include harsh timbre, regular use of low-frequency sound, using a drone basis with almost no melody, asynchrony, and the cumulative effect of the music's repetitive character. In terms of asynchrony, the music is not closely integrated with the image and often feels like it is proceeding almost irrespective of the film. In terms of cumulative effect, the use of constant drones inspires anticipation in the audience, but is also physically wearing to experience. Furthermore, rather than follow the conventional modes of silent film musical accompaniment, or indeed even taking a recognizably musical (in the traditional sense) approach, the soundtrack adopts experimental musical aesthetics and aspires to a direct articulation of a distinctive psychology, aiming at wreathing the film in a feeling of dread.

The sense of disjunction between sound and image relates to the avant garde aesthetic of distance between image and sound, reminiscent of some of Dziga Vertov's and Peter Kubelka's films. But is this "disjunction" or a less straightforward and far more complex (re)configuration? In Eisenstein's analyses he looked for a common denominator between music and image and alighted at first upon the notion of movement (Eisenstein 1963: 67). His sense of equivalence between film images and music was informed by a sense of structural resemblance at a profound level, allied to a sense of synaesthetic mixing of stimuli and sensation (Eisenstein 1987: 389). Yet in the KTL *Phantom Carriage*, music appears more cyclical than developmental. In musicological terms it embodies *stasis* rather than a sense of movement. Unlike film scoring traditions of "Mickeymousing" (mimicking action) and less crude precise matching of music to action, here, the film *moves* while the sound *freezes*. This is the opposite of Eisler and Adorno's suggestion in *Composing for the Films* that music "breathes life" into the frozen images (Eisler and Adorno 1994: 78). Rather than functioning as a stimulus of movement, KTL's music effects to slow events down.

Altered Status

The imposition of this musical aesthetic changes the film and makes it *theirs*, rather than the group simply writing music that approximates the traditions of music for silent film (as had pop musicians such as Black Francis and Jonathan Richman). This marks the direct importing of avant garde techniques to a place where previously they had obtained no purchase. The overall effect is that the film has been recast as event-centred. Initially, it was a small series of performances and then later DVD releases. This has produced a new context of consumption for *The Phantom Carriage*, aiming at a different audience from the one that was for so long its dominant reception context. So, the film has been moved from being a film "from the archive," which had a reputation as a high-quality example of film art (particularly so in its native Sweden), to one that is able not only to attract audiences more interested in underground/avant garde rock and electronic music but also to attract an audience that is interested in high art performance. Indeed, KTL have performed *The Phantom Carriage* in art music venues rather than mainstream cinemas, and particularly at festivals. For example, the film was performed at the Vienna Gartenbaukino on 7 November 2009, as part of the Modern Festival – with each musician situated on opposite sides of screen (Jones 2009). KTL made subsequent performances of *The Phantom Carriage*, including Bayerische Staatsoper (opera house) in Munich (2 July 2010), Nordisk Film's Imperial Cinema in Copenhagen (29 April 2011), UT Connewitz, Leipzig (2 October 2012), Engineering Museum, Krakow (14 November 2012) and Howard Assembly Rooms, Leeds (1 March 2013). These are isolated events, some in extraordinary venues, and not treated like a musical group on a tour of successive dates or like a film being distributed. *The Phantom Carriage* has been wrested away from film historians. It is an audacious move to take a respected historical object and render it, to a degree, ahistorical through refusing a conventional and historically accurate score.[19]

Is the music more important than the film in this case? A YouTube clip of one of the screenings makes sure that it captures the musicians in action as well as the film being projected ("Filmverstärker #6 - KTL play The Phantom Carriage"). The KTL version begs a question: is the audience "music-led" rather than being composed of "film people"? Without detailed audience research, answering the question convincingly is impossible. Whether it is more about KTL than it is about the 1920s Swedish classic film *The Phantom Carriage*, it is most certainly not simply a new version of the film but in fact constitutes a new film in itself. The soundtrack to the film has not been released as a stand-alone CD but has had two separate releases integrated with the film on DVD. The KTL version initially was released on a limited-run DVD by Tartan [B000UZPMC6 2008], while the later Criterion DVD and Blu-Ray release [B0056ANHCC 2011] includes both Matti Bye's and KTL's scores, putting the KTL version on an equal footing with the traditional version.

Not content with simply making this film an esoteric object, recontextualization has also made it into an intellectual conundrum. The KTL *Phantom Carriage* invokes some fundamental questions of film theory, pertaining to the possibilities of audio-visual disjunction along the lines discussed by Sergei Eisenstein and Nöel Burch in relation to politicized art, and Hanns Eisler and Theodor Adorno in relation to musical integrity in relation to film.[20] The "KTL Version" sets up a number of questions, concerning the role of film historians as custodians of old films and whether such films should be approached as "living art" or "museum pieces." It questions traditional audiovisual aesthetics, most notably the importance of the common-sense tradition of music "matching" action. It invokes questions about technology, where cinema speaker set-ups have trouble with KTL's sounds (especially low frequencies) and cannot possibly duplicate the original version of their live performance in the film theatre. Finally, the KTL version of *The Phantom Carriage* questions just how far film can be conceived as a visual medium, particularly when accompanied by such strident and insistent music.

Music changes the psychological and emotional landscape of films, altering one of the basic perceptual aspects of the unified object. Therefore, different music yields a different film.[21] Film historians have written unproblematically about silent films untethered to musical accompaniment as if they were complete unities, consensual objects. A focus on (radically) different scores suggests that they are not. The soundtrack is more than merely a "bolt-on" to the film but more an essential part of the film experience. Indeed, DVDs with two different soundtracks provide, in effect, two separate films. The audiovisual foundation of film music in human perception and cognition that mixes audio and visual aspects is significant. According to Wolfgang Köhler, "sensory fields have in a way their own social psychology" (Köhler 1947: 20). The key here is not the images (the film) but the music added to make a new film. Music for silent films manifests a debate about how film heritage should be used, and how far silent cinema as an aesthetic medium can be reinvented, or indeed reanimated.

Conclusion

The musicians involved in "recontextualizing" and cultizing silent films are often from a popular music background and have something of a cult reputation. The broader context for this development is not only the expansion of activities available to reputable recording musicians but also the context of "art," which allows these films to be recast as art objects rather than simply "movies," underlined by the isolated success of the novelty silent film *The Artist* (2011). Indeed, silent films are generally accorded a status bordering on art, bolstered by a profoundly different audience from mainstream cinema, who almost always watch these films in a different setting from the multiplex (often "arthouse" cinemas) and bring some degree of contextual understanding to their viewing.

Originally something of a cult film, *The Phantom Carriage*, which for a long time was known as the film that inspired Ingmar Bergman to become a film director, is now known by some as the film with music by KTL. While for some audiences this was through the phenomenon of the live film gig, for most of these people it will have been through the DVD releases, particularly the aficionado's version released by Criterion which contains both KTL's and a more traditional score. In terms of technology, the multi-soundtrack version of films on DVD has enabled such developments, although they are equally driven by a reaction against the banal normality of watching films on television or in a standardized multiplex. This has fuelled a desire for the "organic" evident in live music for silent films, particularly at film and cultural festivals. The irony is that the sense of live organic music in KTL's case exploits electronic technology that now increasingly appears more direct and artistic than standardized media platforms. Cases such as the KTL version of *The Phantom Carriage* augur a changed status for the film; although it remains firmly minority culture it has arguably moved into a different zone of consumption. This might be understood as part of so-called "remix culture" (Navas 2012) but perhaps more profitably approached as part of current processes of historicism and the battle for commercially exploiting and politically controlling the past and its culture.

This process may have had some antecedents in the use of old films and such imagery in popular music since the 1970s but appears to have been a corollary of fragmenting areas of culture, added to the opportunities offered by small ensembles of musicians usually using electronic amplification as well as the possibility of release on DVD. These films are out of copyright and offer a readymade new context for musicians. Cult musicians tend to prefer engaging with and reworking films with more of a cult status. Silent films offer a potential gap between film and music as separate objects. The product of the two allows for a new cult status to be negotiated through a mixture of novel obscurity and traditional cultural value. As a notable instance of silent film being recontextualized through music, the KTL version of *The Phantom Carriage* vividly illustrates the possibility of the status of music and musicians redefining films as cult objects, altering their sense of cultural value and interest, as well as potentially "opening" them to a new audience.

Notes

1 Indeed, Ian Conrich (2006: 115) notes that cult films have similarities with film musicals.
2 See further discussion in Donnelly (2013: 267–272).
3 Silent films have spawned a wide-ranging and successful industry in recent years, with tours of screenings with live music and international festivals, such as Pordenone in Italy, which embrace a sizable number of screenings with live music. There is a degree of vertical integration, with films being toured with musicians and then released on DVD. One flourishing ensemble, the Alloy Orchestra, even has their own "sister company" called Box 5 who restore film prints to be used by them and others. DVD releases have allowed for multiple soundtracks for the same film, sometimes, but not always, stemming from live performances of music to a film screening.
4 Exemplified by the current prominence of media archiving, broadcasters such as TCM (Turner Classic Movies) showing old films and the "constructionist" character of "living museums" (Handler and Gable 1997).
5 It is worth remembering that the phenomenon of isolated scores on some DVDs can make a sound film into a profoundly new experience through promoting the background score at the expense of dialogue and sound effects.
6 The repeated viewing of film is crucial to what Barbara Klinger calls "replay culture" (2010: 3).
7 However, there also can be this degree of fragmentation in cult film circles. For instance, Daniel Herbert (2014) discusses cult video stores exhibiting "taxophilia," an obsession with meticulous categorization of minor subgenres or film types.
8 Studies of culture (particularly Cultural Studies) have been poor at dealing with so-called "high art" (Felsky 2004: 40).
9 This appears to work contrary to the established way of dealing with silent films as historical objects that require "authentic" music from the era of their first distribution. This is what Thomas Elsaesser calls "the phantom 'first night' of archivists and historians" (2000: 58).
10 A sense of "horror films" was not immediate. As Alison Peirse notes, "Certainly in the early 1930s, horror was not consistently or systematically acknowledged as a genre or cycle" (2013: 6)
11 A review on the website *Eat My Brains* goes so far as to proclaim *The Phantom Carriage* "The world's first horror film" www.eatmybrains.com/shownews.php?id=977 [accessed 20/09/2014].
12 For example, see website writing such as Brevett (2014) and Sargent (2014).
13 O'Malley is far from a common rock guitar player. Sometimes billing himself as "Soma," as well as projects with musicians he has collaborated with artists including Italian performance artist Nico Vascellari, French theatre director Gisèle Vienne, Belgian film maker Alexis Destoop and American sculptor Banks Violette.
14 Album *IV* is from around the period of *The Phantom Carriage*, while album *V* has an avant-garde or improvisational feel, yet featuring Icelandic composer Jóhann Jóhannsson orchestrating the track "Phill 2."
15 Although the term "avant garde" is still most often associated with art culture, cultural commentator Greil Marcus used the term to describe British "postpunk pop" in *Rolling Stone* magazine in 1980. Reprinted in Marcus (1992: 108).
16 *KTL V* (released in 2013) expands the sound through the use of an orchestra.
17 Jane Giles discusses interaction between avant garde film makers and more ambitious musicians from rock and pop backgrounds (1995: 44).

18 Apart from five numbered albums, they have also released the *Live at Krems* EP, *The Paris Demos*, and *IKKI*.

19 Some reviews were scathing. *The Fortean Times*'s erudite reviewer David Sutton noted of KTL: "they shouldn't have bothered. ... [the score] is positively distracting, leading this reviewer to watch the film in glorious silence" (2008).

20 Eisler and Adorno state that the radical aesthetic divergence of sound and image is a potentially legitimate means of expression (Eisler and Adorno 1994: 74; Eisenstein 1963: 67–68; Burch 1981: 90).

21 There is a well-known analytical procedure of substituting different music for the same images, which Michel Chion calls "forced marriage" (1994: 188).

Bibliography

Altman, Rick, *Silent Film Sound* (New York: Columbia University Press, 2004).

Andrews, David, *Theorizing Art Cinemas: Foreign, Cult, Avant-Garde, and Beyond* (Austin, TX: University of Texas Press, 2013).

Battaglia, Andy, "Sound: *The Phantom Carriage*: A Most Unorthodox Victor Sjöström Remix" in *Film Comment*, May/June 2012. www.filmcomment.com /article/sound-the-phantom-carriage [accessed 20/04/2014].

Brevett, Brad, "The Phantom Carriage: A 'Shining' Inspiration for Stanley Kubrick" at *Rope of Silicon*, http://www.ropeofsilicon.com/inspiring-kubrick -scene-inspired-kubricks-heres-johnny-scene/ [accessed 12/09/2014].

Burch, Noel, *Theory of Film Practice* (Princeton, NJ: Princeton University Press, 1981).

Chion, Michel, *Audio-Vision: Sound on Screen*, edited and translated by Claudia Gorbman (New York: Columbia University Press, 1994).

Conrich, Ian, "Musical Performance and the Cult Experience" in Ian Conrich, and Estella Tincknell, eds., *Film's Musical Moments* (Edinburgh: Edinburgh University Press, 2006).

Davis, Blair, "Old Films, New Sounds: Screening Silent Cinema with Electronic Music" in *Canadian Journal of Film Studies*, vol.17, no.2, Autumn 2008.

Donnelly, K.J., "Jack Nitzsche's *Performance*" in Mark Goodall, ed., *Gathering of the Tribe: Music and Heavy Consciousness Creation* (London: Headpress, 2013).

Donnelly, K.J., and Ann-Kristin Wallengren, eds., *Making Music for Silent Films* (Basingstoke: Palgrave, 2015).

Eisenstein, Sergei M., *The Film Sense*, edited and translated by Jay Leyda (London: Faber and Faber, 1963).

Eisenstein, Sergei M., *Nonindifferent Nature: Film and the Structure of Things*, translated by Herbert Marshall (Cambridge: Cambridge University Press, 1987).

Eisler, Hanns, and Theodor Adorno, *Composing for the Films* (London: Athlone, 1994).

Elsaesser, Thomas, *Metropolis* (London: BFI, 2000).

Felsky, Rita, "The Role of Aesthetics in Cultural Studies" in Michael Bérubé, ed., *The Aesthetics of Cultural Studies* (London: Wiley-Blackwell, 2004).

Giles, Jane, "As Above, So Below: 30 Years of Underground Cinema and Pop Music" in Jonathan Romney, and Adrian Wootton, eds., *Celluloid Jukebox. Popular Music and the Movies Since the 50s* (London: BFI, 1995).

Handler, Richard, and Eric Gable, *The New History in an Old Museum: Creating Williamsburg* (Durham, NC.: Duke University Press, 1997).

Herbert, Daniel, *Videoland: Movie Culture at the American Video Store* (Berkeley, CA: University of California Press, 2014).

Jameson, Fredric, *Postmodernism, Or, the Cultural Logic of Late Capitalism* (Durham, NC: Duke University Press. 1991).

Jancovich, Mark, "Cult Fictions: Cult Movies, Subcultural Capital and the Production of Cultural Distinctions" *Cultural Studies*, vol.16, no.2, 2002.

Jancovich, Mark, Antonio Lazaro Reboll, Julian Stringer, and Andy Willis, "Introduction" in Mark Jancovich, Antonio Lazaro Reboll, Julian Stringer, and Andy Willis, eds., *Defining Cult Movies: The Cultural Politics of Oppositional Taste* (Manchester: Manchester University Press, 2003).

Jones, Richard Rees, "Viennese Waltz" http://viennesewaltz.wordpress.com /2009/11/18/ktl-3/ [accessed 3/04/2014].

Klinger, Barbara, "Becoming Cult: *The Big Lebowski*, Replay Culture and Male Fans" in *Screen*, vol.51, no.1 Spring 2010.

Köhler, Wolfgang, *Gestalt Psychology. An Introduction to New Concepts in Modern Psychology* (New York: Liveright, 1947).

KTL. "Filmverstärker #6 - KTL play *The Phantom Carriage*" https://www .youtube.com/watch?v=JAxBAz1BrOQ [accessed 20/04/2014].

Marcus, Greil, *In the Fascist Bathroom: Writings on Punk, 1977–92* (London: Penguin, 1992).

Navas, Eduardo, *Remix Theory: The Aesthetics of Sampling* (Berlin: Walter de Gruyter, 2012).

Peirse, Alison, *After Dracula: The 1930s Horror Film* (London: I.B.Tauris, 2013).

Reynolds, Simon, "Post-Rock" in Christoph Cox, and Daniel Warner, eds., *Audio Culture: Readings in Modern Music* (New York: Continuum, 2004).

Sargent, J.F., "6 Iconic Scenes Ripped Off From Lesser-Known Movies" *Cracked*. http://www.cracked.com/article_19826_6-iconic-scenes-ripped-off-from -lesser-known-movies_p2.html#ixzz3CLX35sQH [accessed 12/09/2014].

5

IRISH SEA POWER

A New *Man of Aran* (2009/1934)

In recent years, the phenomenon of musicians providing live music for silent films has become widespread, converting them into singular and often special events. Indeed, silent cinema is more prominent now than it has been since the 1920s. Festivals and archival showings abound, and silent films are part of education, entertainment, and art (Altman 2004: 4). Where there are silent films, there are almost always musical accompaniments. However, there is a smaller subset of this where early sound films have their soundtrack masked and are treated in effect as silent films to be accompanied by live and often new music. A fine example of this is British Sea Power's new score for the celebrated documentary *Man of Aran* (1934). This English rock group has provided distinctive new music for this landmark film, and resembling their own musical output rather than traditional film music. They have since provided a score for Penny Woolcock's *From the Sea to the Land Beyond* (2012) and a new score (a replacement) for the Romanian film *Out of the Present* (originally released in 1999 and directed by Andrei Ujica), both of which are also documentary films.[1] Initially, British Sea Power's *Man of Aran* was a live performance at the film's screening at the British Film Institute in April 2009, which was followed by the CD and DVD release in May. So, how far is this new *Man of Aran* more a musical event than a film? It seems crucial that the DVD comes free with the CD.[2] Music changes the psychological and emotional landscape of films. Therefore, I would argue different music yields a different film, and the new version of *Man of Aran* illustrates this well.

DOI: 10.4324/9781003299653-5

Man of Aran was directed by American documentary filmmaker Robert Flaherty (1884–1951), who had made *Nanook of the North* (1922) in the Arctic, arguably the ur-documentary feature film. Amongst other films, he also directed *Moana* (1926) in Samoa, worked with F.W. Murnau on *Tabu* (1931) in Tahiti, worked with the Korda brothers on *Elephant Boy* (1937) in India, and directed *Louisiana Story* (1948). Flaherty's films inspired the making of ethnographic films and helped found the field of "visual anthropology" as pursued by Gregory Bateson and Margaret Mead in the 1930s, and Jean Rouch in the 1960s. *Man of Aran* was acclaimed and indeed remains a canonical film but has carried with it much controversy.[3] It is now considered "docufiction" or "drama-documentary" in that Flaherty directed locals to act in a certain way, including sharkfishing using a technique that had not been employed on the islands for decades. Set on the stark and waveswept Aran Islands off Ireland's west coast, *Man of Aran* shows hardy islanders growing food in extremely poor conditions aided by seaweed and pulverized rock, catching fish from a cliff and a crab from the rocks, and the lengthy process of killing a massive basking shark with harpoons from a very small boat. Due to the degree of fabrication the film is now often framed by debates about "authenticity" rather than appreciating the poetic imagery and exciting filming, and perhaps quite unfairly ignoring the anthropological value of its depictions.[4]

Music in documentary films can often be seen as manipulative, with its Hollywood patterns and sounds and its clear emotional brief. It is often considered an element that can obscure the veracity of the location images and sounds. Mervyn Cooke notes, "From the earliest newsreel years, sceptical observers questioned the legitimacy of borrowing manipulative narrative techniques from the fiction film ... This concern proved even more troubling when emotively suggestive music was also present" (2008: 267). Flaherty's film was scored by John D. H. Greenwood, a seasoned composer of music for dramatic films. However, Greenwood's score, as noted in a title card at the start of the film, was "based on the original Irish songs of the Aran Islands." In this way, the film's original music appears to add a degree authenticity to the film and indeed asserts as much.

"Silencing Film": Historicism and Reframing

The current, almost frenzied interest in history manifests a cultural trend in the face of rapid change and the destruction of senses of nationality and destiny. We are at a point where much of the recent past is on the verge of being beyond direct memory – which is perhaps why current culture is so pathologically mining images of the past to reformulate it as contemporary entertainment. The remarkable explosion of live music for silent films since the 1990s is a part of the craze for historicism, which involves rediscovering old (sometimes nearly lost) culture, and might be approached as an aggressive colonization of the past as part of a process of cultural renewal. While this marks a different form of "historicism," one that perhaps historians might not recognize, or might even repudiate, it is part of a particularly vehement interest in past culture, evident also in museums and dramatic depictions of the past.

The radical reframing of a film through the addition of new music appears geared explicitly towards a new context of consumption for the film. It is no accident that the increase in live music for films has developed hand in hand with the increase in film festivals that will sanction such showings. This removes old films from the archive and repositions them as "viable" films for contemporary audiences. Some of these novel versions wield a rhetoric of cultural renewal or "updating" in their aspiration to make the silent film a valued object to a wider contemporary audience. Thomas Elsaesser bravely defended the disparaged Giorgio Moroder version of *Metropolis* (1926), an early example of this process released in the early 1980s with a soundtrack of electronic dance music and songs. He suggested that Moroder's modern music allowed the audience to appreciate Fritz Lang's film as again being imbued with a sharp feeling of modernity, which it would have had upon its initial release in the late 1920s (Elsaesser 2000: 58–59). Modern music might allow a point of entry for audiences unfamiliar with the conventions of older cinema, functioning as a *frame* for the film by updating the experience to render a difficult and antiquated work fit for more contemporary tastes.

Returning to *Man of Aran*'s soundtrack, we should remember that the film was not silent but has had its original diegetic sound recording and musical score masked to allow its replacement by British Sea Power's music. This means that the new version violates the original intentions of the filmmakers. However, it does not necessarily mean that the film is made into something of which they, and Flaherty specifically, would not have approved. However, it does detract from the historical value and the integrity of the film as a historical object. Remembering that Greenwood's score is ostensibly based on original Irish songs of the Aran Islands, the issue here is not only that of replacing an original intention but also of replacing an integral component of the film that had an anthropological connection with the culture depicted on screen. The process of "masking" immediately removes respect for the original intention.[5] Music as an addition is able to remove or add to the original intentions of the film significantly. There are some notable historical cases where recorded soundtracks are masked and the original intentions of filmmakers dismissed. For instance, avant garde composer Mauricio Kagel wrote a new score for *Un Chien Andalou* (1929) to replace Buñuel and Dali's stipulation to use discs of Wagner's *Liebestod* from *Tristan und Isolde* and a tango.[6] However, what might be considered more significant is that as a part of the process of making the film ready for new music, its original diegetic sound has been erased. One of the dominant aspects of the original soundtrack is the recording of the sea and wind. The British Sea Power soundtrack includes a fair amount of sea sound, although this has a dislocated quality due to its lack of direct synchronization with the images. This is similar to the extensive and dislocated sea sounds in Flaherty's original. However, these generic sea sounds tend to function as filler material between the main bodies of the British Sea Power pieces of music, or as quiet parts within those pieces. While on one level, these generic sounds constitute a part of conventionalized representation,[7] the sounds also contribute to a misrecognition of what is seen and what is heard, which ultimately problematizes the relationship between the film and the "real world." Another question arises: are these diegetic sea sounds or are they an integral part of British Sea Power's music? While conventionally they appear to be the former, aesthetically they are clearly the latter. This constitutes a seeming mix of non-diegetic music with diegetic sounds.

Many documentaries have proceeded from the position that the music should not detract from nor in any way challenge the primacy of the representations on screen. As a consequence, many filmmakers have eschewed the use of dramatic incidental music as an accompaniment to images and diegetic sound. These elements alone appear to transmit reality very directly while non-diegetic music, particularly in its Hollywood-style score variety, appears the epitome of emotional manipulation and aestheticizing "addition" to a documentary record. However, this is a relatively modern conceptualization (Winston 1999: 71). British documentaries of the 1930s, such as those made by John Grierson and Humphrey Jennings tended to use a fair amount of incidental music. A pair of fine examples of this convention are *Coal Face* (1935) and *Night Mail* (1939, directed by Harry Watt who had worked on *Man of Aran*), both with orchestral scores by Benjamin Britten. Flaherty's film is part of this early documentary tradition, indeed it was produced as a British documentary by Michael Balcon at Gainsborough Studios. As a consequence, it was not considered anomalous to have copious amounts of non-diegetic music.[8] Of course, there is nothing intrinsic to documentary that negates the use of musical scores and in recent years most television documentaries will include incidental music of one sort or another, while even news items on television might find themselves awarded some subtle musical accompaniment. In the case of British Sea Power's score for *Man of Aran* though, the music is prominent almost to the point of dominating the film. This arguably follows a tradition outside mainstream cinema, where occasionally silent films have been accompanied by live music as a more art-based event than regular cinema projection. Gillian B. Anderson suggests that in these situations the music might be conceived as an equal partner with the silent film, but in some cases it manifests *more* than a partnership, designating the film as secondary (Anderson 1988: xv).

It is a critical issue that the British Sea Power version removes diegetic sound, an elimination that perhaps most crucially, erases the characters' voices. The original version of *Man of Aran* has plenty of talking from the characters on screen, in both English and Irish (Irish Gaelic as some would have it). It should be noted that much of it is phatic language with little semantic content (for example, when a bundle is hoisted up a cliff: "Get it up, there!"). Indeed, apart from a few points where minimal narrative information is furnished, the dialogue rather than bearing great semantic content has more of an aesthetic function. The voices are an essential component of the film's sense of authenticity and depiction of the culture of the Aran Islands. Yet it is clear that the sound is almost wholly post-synchronized, making for a "plesiochronous" accompaniment to the images and consisting of sea and to a lesser extent wind noises, along with the Islanders' voices and a few other sound effects.[9] Clearly, the recording of location sound for each shot was too difficult, and the lack of direct synchronization, even of the spoken word and moving mouths at many points, lends the film a sense of dislocation and the feeling of being based upon the principles of silent cinema. As such, British Sea Power's new music is not as disruptive as it might have been.

What is striking when comparing the two different versions of *Man of Aran* is just how different an experience they deliver. Greenwood's original orchestral music, although making much of its authenticity in terms of using Irish song melodies, in fact sounds in many ways a fairly conventional orchestral score for a mainstream film of the period, although it differs in that the amount of music in the film is far larger than was conventional for a British-produced dramatic film of the period.[10] This is no doubt due to *Man of Aran* containing fewer dialogue sequences and more scenes of "silent" action, which call out for some sonic accompaniment. Indeed, this is why British Sea Power's new music works successfully.

Greenwood's score, while including some identifiable Irish song melodies and a couple of dance-based sections, provides some direct support and anchoring to the film's meanings. The opening film titles have some grand and bold music, which suggests something of the nobility of the people of the islands (the "Man of Aran" of the film's title). During the first sequence in the house, which illustrates the animals living alongside the people, Greenwood supplies jaunty, comic music. In contract, in British Sea Power's version, the music is far more tentative and improvisational with a number of instruments making short interjections and the music failing to move into an easily understood piece. Rather than Greenwood's rather ponderous humour, which might almost be construed as laughing at the primitive living conditions of the islanders, British Sea Power's music is darker, perhaps suggesting something of the austere living situation which dictates such a mode of housing. In fact, this is one of the crucial differences between the two soundtracks: Greenwood's score is far lighter, embracing humour on a number of occasions as well as sounding upbeat and jokey, even during the epic shark fishing sequence. As we shall see, British Sea Power's music is less obvious, with humour far less to the fore and indeed the overall character of the music being often unerringly serious.

Sea Power

British Sea Power, as indicated by the group's unusual name, is a distinctive and highly adventurous British indie rock band. Based in Brighton, the group released their first record in 2001, followed by their debut album in 2003. Signed to Rough Trade Records, an archetypal independent record label, they seem to embody an idea of current "indie" music. At the time of *Man of Aran* the group consisted of six musicians: Scott "Yan" Wilkinson (vocals, guitar, and keyboards), Neil Hamilton Wilkinson (bass, keyboards, and vocals), Martin Noble (guitar and keyboards), Matt Wood (drums), Abi Fry (viola), and Phil Sumner (keyboards, cornet, and guitar). Arguably, this was a remarkable and surprising point in the group's career to embark upon producing music for a film. The previous year the third album *Do You Like Rock Music?* had become its most successful, reaching Number Ten in the UK charts and Number Five in the US (Billboard Heatseekers Albums chart). One might have expected British Sea Power to have concentrated its efforts on retaining such top-selling status by focusing on a highly-polished follow-up recording. Instead, it chose to provide music for a film made 75 years earlier. Yet this was not so surprising if the group's concert activities were taken into account. The band has constantly confounded expectations about where rock concerts ought to be performed, preferring individual concert "events" in a variety of outlandish locations to conventional concert tours.[11] Since 2021, the band have shortened their name to simply Sea Power.

British Sea Power is perhaps best known for producing distinctive and original songs that in many cases contain anthemic choruses and build towards a climactic and repetitive statement of these. The group's sound is electric guitar-led and arguably inspired by garage band-type music.[12] There is a desire to sound organic and to avoid elaborate studio effects. Songs are strongly melody-led and insistently memorable, accompanied often by quite basic and disciplined arrangements and little in the way of musical pyrotechnics. This electric guitar-led sound was augmented by the addition of viola player Abi Fry in 2008. British Sea Power tend to use extended melodies, and indeed evince a strong interest in melody, which sometimes are more like traditional folk-style song lines rather than the often simplistic and fragmented ones upon which many contemporary pop songs are based. In dynamic terms, the group's songs often are based on the principle of building up intensity, with much use of repetition and modular elements. Rhythms are certainly insistent but not inspired by dance music and bear more closely a resemblance to the "motoric" 4/4 beat beloved of 1970s Krautrock rather than the snappy traditional backbeat which lifts and emphasizes the second and fourth beats. In a period when popular music is often heavily treated to give a regularity to sounds and performances, British Sea Power revel in a more organic sound based on textural dynamics and live-sounding group performances rather than studio-produced standardization. A sense of musical cohesion across the film is supplied by the ensemble's limited range of timbres and a restricted but effective palette of musical strategies. This includes the dynamic contour of building up the pieces in terms of intensity, the use of regular continuous quaver 4/4 rhythms for energy, and the use of short and repetitive solo guitar arpeggios as ostinato bases. In addition, the music that opens the film is founded upon a repeated ostinato played on single notes on a piano which has a similar structure and character to the guitar arpeggios. The group have translated the essence of their musical oeuvre into an effective accompaniment for film with their score for *Man of Aran*. The sensitive but insistent qualities of their music seem well suited to Flaherty's singular dramatized documentary.

Film and Music: Pulling Apart?

In the 1940s, composer Aaron Copland posited five functions for incidental music. These are: "creating atmosphere, highlighting the psychological states of characters; providing neutral background filler, building a sense of continuity; sustaining tension and then rounding it off with a sense of closure" (Copland 1949: 28). George Burt points to incidental music's many material functions, such as regularly exerting an enormous influence on the pacing of events and "emphasizing the dramatic line" (Burt 1994: 4, 79). British Sea Power's music for *Man of Aran* successfully completes all these functions even though it is not based on the more precise traditions of musical scores for films. Consequently, there is more of a sense of music as at times a semi-autonomous parallel to the images, with the concomitant effect of rendering the film as perhaps a less manipulative medium in terms of concentrated and specific effect on the audience.

The 2009 version of the film has a tendency towards "segmentation." This is less an effect of the structuring of Flaherty's film itself and perhaps more to do with the approach taken by British Sea Power. The 76-minute film is accompanied by distinct musical pieces, often with sea sounds between them. The CD divisions and titles reinforce this, as do the DVD divisions which are based largely on the musical pieces. Almost all of the group's musical pieces are extended and repetitive, based on gradual unfolding and often building up in intensity. They are thus long pieces and tend to cover substantial sections of the film where certain activities are depicted. So, rather than matching the momentary dynamics of events on screen, the music provides a blanket, unifying and furnishing a general ambience to the (often dramatic) events recorded by the film. Indeed, the score consists of a number of "grooves," which in some cases prove highly uplifting in their dynamic build-up. Interestingly, the DVD cover publicity for *From the Land to the Sea Beyond* calls the film itself "uplifting." I was not convinced that the film deserved this description. However, British Sea Power's music certainly has that quality, and in abundance at certain points in Penny Woolcock's film. The same goes for the earlier *Man of Aran*, with the music lifting the sense of pace and excitement, particularly in comparison with some of the same sequences scored by Greenwood.

British Sea Power's music for the film tends to work on repetition and cumulative effect, rather than variation or alternation of material. A few pieces in the film had originally been conceived as songs and the film includes a song in the score which appears as an isolated instance.

Certain characteristic *timbres* and mixtures tend to dominate their score. There is a good amount of guitar notes played with an e-bow, a magnetic device that vibrates the strings giving a quality similar to bowing them. This is often added to the string instruments (viola and some cello). Another notable strategy is the use of regular quaver (eighth note) pulses, led by guitars strumming chords but often supported by viola. This encapsulates one of the characteristic sounds of British Sea Power, and at times here it becomes their default sound, which they wield highly effectively. Indeed, there is a preponderance of regular quaver pulses in each piece that builds up gradually, with the focus of the rhythm and the full involvement of the drums bringing the music to higher levels of intensity. Rather than simply leaving this up to the drums, or the guitars, which should have been a fairly conventional approach, British Sea Power often uses the viola as a rhythm instrument, too, in an extremely unconventional move. The often subtle and atmospheric music partners the film effectively, although there are almost no clear synch points or moments where the music changes its dynamics precisely to match screen activity.

The film opens with title cards that slightly precede the inauguration of the haunting opening piece of music. With the main title card, a piano arpeggio starts slightly tentatively, locking into a high-register eight-note ostinato which runs throughout the whole piece, which lasts for over three and a half minutes. It sounds echoed, perhaps with some electronic reverb but mostly though being played with the sustain pedal depressed and recorded in a room with reflective surfaces.[13] The piano motif simply repeats *ad infinitum* without development, although at certain points it is apparent that it is manually produced as its speed and fingerfall varies. Over the top of this, e-bowed electric guitar and strings in unison make extremely slow sustained rising pitches on an A major scale (from C sharp to G sharp and then downwards).[14] This makes for a slow melody, indeed so slow that it hardly registers as one at all, and has more of an effect of simply rising pitch, and enhancing the effect of it being organic music. This piece has no real dynamic connections with the images of *Man of Aran*, accompanying first the opening title cards of the film (including, of course, the one that credits John Greenwood's music based on Aran Island songs). After this, the images depict Michael, the boy of the central family, catching a crab from a rock pool. During this activity, the rising melody disappears leaving only the piano arpeggio, which then returns and the piece concludes with sea sounds. These sounds have a stylized quality to them; indeed, they sound remarkably like some of the sea sounds on Flaherty's original soundtrack, and similarly have a slightly dislocated quality to them. A different version of this piece appears towards the conclusion of the film, accompanying images of a school of basking sharks in the sea, boats going out to them, and the woman at the boiling cauldron.[15]

The four-minute sequence illustrating the laborious process of grow-ing food begins with sea sounds accompanying dramatic images of the raging sea, leading into a song. The singing starts over one of the film's iconic images, of the woman with a gigantic cargo of seaweed strapped to her back in a basket. The song has an interesting genealogy. *Come Wander with Me* is a pre-existing cult song, written by film and television composer Jeff Alexander with words by screenwriter Anthony Wilson, and had appeared in an eponymous episode of the television series *The Twilight Zone* (season 5, first broadcast in 1964).[16] British Sea Power only uses the chorus of the song, a folk-inspired melody which simply repeats, with lyrics referring to someone who "came from the sea," and are sung by a male voice doubled by a female voice. The instrumental backing is subtle and understated, with guitar arpeggios marking the chord changes, some viola scrapes, and a drum kit played quietly with brushes. The song does not sound out of place in that it has a folk quality that perhaps dis-tantly owes something to Irish folk music, while its plaintive tone and potentially ambiguous invitation to "come wander with me" provides a serious and slightly morose cast to the events on screen.[17] This is under-lined by the home chord of A minor having its fifth augmented (from E to F) in alternating chords at the conclusion of each verse. After the sung verse the melody again is stated by cornet and morose wordless vocals before concluding with sea noises. The use of a song like this is not a traditional form of accompaniment and appears to suggest the primacy of British Sea Power's music over the film.

The whole shark fishing sequence lasts over 20 minutes and is the centrepiece of the film. As a film sequence, it not only concentrates on the men in the boat confronting the shark but also includes sections dealing with the woman and boy on land. It embraces three different pieces of music by British Sea Power which aim at atmospheric effect rather than musical cohesion. After extensive shots of the boy climbing down the cliff and looking downwards, the appearance in shot of what the boy is beholding inspires momentary silence in the soundtrack. The startling close-up shots of the gigantic basking shark are then accompanied by isolated single-note metallic-sounding electric guitar wails, using electronic distortion and reverb. This sounds reminiscent of whale singing. It appears not only representative of the "otherworldliness" of this monstrous but passive shark but also of the agony of the fish being brutalized and killed. It is also representative of the process of close-quarters combat with it, where the Aran men have their boat tied to the basking shark in a bid to weaken and kill it. The guitar wails become more frantic with the screen activity, now doubled by a heavy drumbeat alongside synthesizer and guitar outbursts. The drums enter at the point where the men have managed to tether the shark to the boat. Taking some time to building into a riff, the chaotic montage is accompanied by a heavy 4/4 tom-tom beat. As the battle becomes more frenzied an exciting tremolo-picked guitar lead enters, racking the intensity further. While the strings make a regular quaver pulse on the same notes, the guitar playing includes Jimi Hendrix-style wails. At the point where the shark is dramatically harpooned, the music has reached a cacophonous crescendo. This is in effect a lengthy montage sequence with a wealth of dramatic shots edited together.[18] Despite the fact that the music is not aimed at making strong points of synchronization with screen activity, the shark is harpooned on an emphasized first beat of a bar, redoubling the effect.

A screen title card informs the audience that it took two days to "win the shark's oil for their lamps." Immediately another, different repeated solo guitar arpeggio with a little electronic reverb giving it some space and atmosphere begins as the foundation of the succeeding piece of music (*Conneely of the West*). This guitar figure is related only distantly to the earlier one (*Boy Vertiginous*). In effect, it gives the impression of three falling notes with the final note each time sustaining for a bar to leave space for breath in the continuing concentration of shark fishing on screen. This time-consuming operation is emphasized by the intercutting of shots of the woman and boy now in the house waiting anxiously. The music is far calmer than before and lends an air of resignation to the proceedings, suggesting that the battle is won but patience is still required.

To accompany two other boats going out to help bring in the defeated shark, the music begins a new piece (*The North Sound*), with yet another unaccompanied guitar arpeggio (again with descending high notes, chromatic, same lower string notes), which forms the foundation for the piece and builds in energy, despite the images suggesting that the main work is completed. Despite some outlandish echoed sounds this is perhaps the most conventional rock piece, as it exploits energy to express something of the excitement of the community about the killing, with a chain of people pulling the fish carcass ashore with a rope while the woman protagonist boils a cauldron. Deep ominous booming notes signal that this is not quite the victory it appears, indicating the possibility of the music's comment framing a new interpretation of the 1932 images.

Man of Aran concludes with some startling and stylized images. Flaherty clearly wished to leave a strong and emotional impression of the family, using some iconic but mannered static images of the boy in close-up looking to the side and a long shot of the family along with harpoon in dramatic silhouette. The music during this sequence begins in a similar manner to some earlier pieces with a motif based on three guitar arpeggios, which later develop into strong rhythmic movements based around chord changes and with prominent cornet.[19] Flaherty's shots of the sea are absolutely astounding and their intermittent regularity gives the film its central visual character. Another version of this piece of music had already appeared on the British Sea Power album *Do You Like Rock Music?* (2008) as *The Great Skua*.[20] The music closely resembles a song, built around a guitar arpeggio based on three chords (G–D6–CM7). It has a cornet melody and a section that alternates two chords (C–F) and then, as it builds to a dramatic and uplifting climax, the chords change to a progression of C–D minor–F for the conclusion. Yet it was not a song originally but an instrumental piece. If the original recording was intended to convey something of the soaring seabird, then it also appears perfectly to fit Flaherty's highly evocative and pyrotechnic closing stages of the film, showcasing a montage of towering waves breaking on dramatic barren cliffs and shots of the heroic central family. The climactic conclusion of the song coincides with dramatic static close-up shots of the man and the boy, interspersed with images of the waves, and then one of the family unit in silhouette. This proves a far more dramatic finale for the film than in the original 1934 release, and the increase in drama comes not only from the music's effective partnering with Flaherty's poetic and life-affirming imagery but also from the dynamic materiality of the music itself.

Conclusion

Man of Aran is a startling film, with poetic images in abundance as well as dramatic and exciting sequences. Such films are able to bear the weight of substantial musical addition, and this is proven by British Sea Power's new version of the film. The new music has a number of effects on Flaherty's film. One is that the music *emphasizes* the veracity and age of the images, through a process of "framing." This is clearer than in the original score. Freed from music that underlines the reality of the images (Greenwood's music based on Irish melodies), the new music is able to express an inner emotion and empathy for the islanders not available earlier. Furthermore, it is able to do this using a more contemporary musical language. While this might well make the film more accessible for a contemporary audience, the new music's framing of the images also, I would suggest, makes them seem more "past." In the process of "renewing" *Man of Aran*, British Sea Power's music adds a sense of doubtful "historical status" to its existing doubtful authenticity. Yet these additions might not be important. The film certainly "documents" the reality of the location if nothing else, and as such it is a valuable documentary record of past events, no matter how "authentic" they might or might not be. New music, while detracting from the past-ness of the event depicted, aestheticizes the film, in a way matching Flaherty's dramatically aesthetic approach to *Man of Aran*. The film embodies the notions of manipulation, reconstruction, and inauthenticity with respect to documentary film. Does British Sea Power's music reproduce Flaherty's folk culture romanticism, embellish it, or even comment on it? There certainly is a distinct romanticism in British Sea Power's desire for an organic rock sound, not to mention their eccentric choice of locations for concerts. Their music for the film certainly does not "speak down" to it, or comment in any knowing or negative manner. There was already a quality in British Sea Power's songs that has enabled their music to make an effective transition to the scoring of moving images.[21] This is primarily down to mood and energy and while proving the band's versatility also confirms the versatility of certain films for musical retrofitting.

This process of masking an original soundtrack and rescoring the film illustrates a profound difference in conception of film: on the one hand, seeing them as historical documents, works of art essentially imbued with the period of their production and on the other, seeing them as living objects that have new life breathed into them by the new moment of the film's experience with novel music. The former approach represents the important current notion of the cultural museum while the latter represents the vertiginous possibility of reappropriation, which can produce startling novelty but, in some cases, involves the crude co-opting of existing culture into something of questionable value. Yet the British Sea Power version of *Man of Aran* is a highly effective film, removing the dialogue that lacks direct synchronization with the images and Greenwood's jaunty "telegraphing," wall-to-wall orchestral score in favour of a darker musical framing of the film. British Sea Power certainly took the film seriously, as their music gives a more solemn cast to the images throughout, as well as the extremity of events depicted being subject to the band's keen sense of musical dynamics, which build up to startling musical climaxes that not only complement Flaherty's dramatic images but also create a much wider sense of mood and excitement dynamics for the film. British Sea Power's *Man of Aran* is in effect a new film rather than simply an amended version, although the prominence of the music perhaps helps remove the film from its documentary context and toward status as more of a musical event.

Notes

1 Although also a documentary with music by British Sea Power, *From the Land to the Sea Beyond* appears a wholly different prospect. British Sea Power were brought onto this documentary project through the producers being fans of the group's music and wanting a live performance by the group at the Sheffield Documentary Festival. This was conceived much more as a collaboration between the group and director Penny Woolcock and British Sea Power used a number of existing songs that had appeared on earlier records, which they rearranged as well as incorporating new material. Cf. Making *The Sea and the Land Beyond* documentary extra on the *From the Sea to the Land Beyond* DVD (BFI 2012).

2 The DVD includes a number of different soundtrack options to accompany the image track. These include "Studio," "Studio 5.1," "Live," "Live 5.1," and "Bonus Soundtrack" (which is almost wholly ambient and electronic and assembled by the group's principal singer Yan).

3 Upon its initial release, Flynn and Brereton attest that, "When the film was first seen by the political elite [in Ireland], it was said that Eamon de Valera – the leader of the Fianna Fáil political party who above all others helped define a post-Civil War identity that continued well into the 1950s – wept at its heroic portrayal of Irish people. The film reflected a preoccupation with the West as defining a pure strand of Irish identity and was marketed internationally as a realist document of life in that period" (Flynn and Brereton 2007: 259). Ruth Barton sums up its current status: "*Man of Aran* now occupies a troubled position within Irish cultural life, representing for many the falsification of Ireland by the many cultural invaders who plundered it for its transformative powers, and of local Irish willingness to collude in this process. Since its release, it has become a marker of both artistic excellence and compromise" (Barton 2004: 48).

4 The film is now seen as a "fictional documentary," using reconstruction of practices that had ceased years earlier and depicting a central nuclear family who were in actuality not actually related to one another. See George Stoney's documentary *How the Myth Was Made* (1979) and Mac Dara Ô Curraidhin's *A Boatload of Wild Irishmen* (2011).

5 In recent years, Steven Severin has added live music to *Vampyr* (1932) and Red Snapper to *Touki Bouki* (1973), but both retaining the original soundtrack as well.

6 This was composed and recorded despite the tradition that the film should be accompanied by discs suggested by the directors.

7 Indeed, current television convention means that documentaries using silent film footage almost always accompany them with some sort of spurious diegetic sound.

8 John Greenwood (1889–1976) scored almost 50 films, including *Elephant Boy* (1937), *The Drum* (1938), *Pimpernel Smith* (1941), *San Demetrio, London* (1943), *Hungry Hill* (1947), Eureka Stockade (1949), Quartet (1949), *The Last Days of Dolwyn* (1949), and *The Gentle Gunman* (1952). Huntley points out that Greenwood was a symphonist and conductor and wrote a vast number of film scores (Huntley 1947: 206–207).

9 The voices sound as if they were recorded in a different, more enclosed space as well as synchronizing precisely only occasionally. For more discussion of such plesiochrony and its use in documentaries, see. Donnelly (2013: 181–183).

10 I already noted that *Man of Aran* was what must have been one of the first symphonic scores, certainly for a British film. Indeed, it is more "wall-to-wall" than was standard for British films throughout the later 1930s (Donnelly 2007: 18).

11 For example, Carnglaze Caves in Cornwall, Grasmere village hall (2005), the Scillonian club on the Scilly Isles, the Czech Embassy in London, the Monaco Hotel on Canvey Island (which was broadcast on BBC2's *The Culture Show*), appeared on *Later With Jools Holland* (BBC, Feb 2008) alongside Cumbrian wrestlers and the London Bulgarian Choir, Berwick village hall (East Sussex 2011), Jodrell Bank Observatory (2011), at the CERN physics lab in Geneva, at the Centenary Gala for Poet Laureate Sir John Betjeman in 2006 (Prince Charles was guest of honour, Nick Cave and Dame Edna Everage also appeared), on the Great Wall of China, the Chelsea Flower Show, the Natural History Museum in London, and on an island in the Arctic.

12 Perhaps at times reminiscent of the Velvet Underground, or more recently Stereolab, in that the guitars usually provide continuous rhythm and will move through a handful of chords rather than articulating repetitive riffs as a foundation for the music.

13 The piano arpeggio is reminiscent of Harold Budd's echoed piano on his collaborations with Brian Eno, *The Plateau of Mirror* (1980) and *The Pearl* (1984).

14 Which might be understood bitonally as a rising Phrygian scale on C sharp to its fifth and back.

15 The opening track is called *Man of Aran* on the CD and the reprise is called *Woman of Aran*.

16 In the episode, it is sung by actress Bonnie Beecher and has a supernatural function while enchanting a singer in search of a song to record. The verses of the song are added to throughout the episode, inexplicably fitting recent events and foretelling future ones.

17 British Sea Power only use some of the song words from the original: "He came from the sunset, he came from the sea. He came from my sorrow and can love only me. Come wander with me love, come wander with me. Away from this sad world, come wander with me."

18 These include long shots and close-ups of the boat, the shark thrashing in the water, the woman and boy watching from the shore, the boat being taken on a "Nantucket sleighride" (being pulled along by the speared shark).

19 The track is titled *No Man is an Archipelago* and runs for 04:49.

20 And indeed, two other pieces had already appeared in different versions as *North Hanging Rock* and *True Adventures* on the band's album *Open Season* (2005).

21 Indeed, this quality is evident in an effective fan video for *North Hanging Rock*, which accompanies the song with a short German silent film from the early years of the 20th century (*Lights and Shades on Bostock's Circus Farm*). The film depicts a farm of "pensioner' animals," including an elephant that dies and is moved with great effort and its body burned.
www.youtube.com/watch?v=7sRaN209ARs [accessed 10/1/2014].

Bibliography

Altman, Rick, *Silent Film Sound* (New York: Columbia University Press, 2004).

Anderson, Gillian B., *Music for Silent Films 1894–1929: A Guide* (Washington, DC: Library of Congress, 1988).

Barton, Ruth, *Irish National Cinema* (London: Routledge, 2004).

Burt, George, *The Art of Film Music* (Boston, MA: Northeastern University Press, 1994).

Cook, Mervyn, *A History of Film Music* (Cambridge: Cambridge University Press, 2008).

Copland, Aaron, "Tip to the Moviegoers: Take Off Those Ear-Muffs" in *The New York Times*, 6 November 1949, section six.

Donnelly, K.J., *British Film Music and Film Musicals* (Basingstoke: Palgrave, 2007).

Donnelly, K.J., *Occult Aesthetics: Synchronization in the Sound Film* (New York: Oxford University Press, 2013).

Elsaesser, Thomas, *Metropolis* (London: BFI, 2000).

Flynn, Roderick, and Patrick Brereton, *Historical Dictionary of Irish Cinema* (Lanham, MD: Scarecrow, 2007).

Huntley, John, *British Film Music* (London: Skelton Robinson, 1947).

Winston, Brian, "Documentary" How the Myth Was Made" in *Wide Angle*, vol. 21, no. 2, March 1999.

6

THE CLASSICAL FILM SCORE FOREVER?

Batman, Batman Returns, and Post-Classical Film Music

Since the 1930s, music has not only been a significant component of narration in mainstream films but also has been organized as a coherent and discrete discourse within them. *Batman* (1989) and its first sequel *Batman Returns* (1992) highlight the ways post-classical Hollywood employs and orders music, both in terms of using classically inspired forms and more recent procedures. It is possible to see the musical strategies of contemporary films in the light both of continuity and of discontinuity with those of classical cinema.

Music was and continues to be an integral part of the multimedia phenomenon of Hollywood blockbuster films. This is highly evident in the *Batman* series of films. Danny Elfman wrote the musical scores for *Batman* (1989) and *Batman Returns* (1992), and they provide continuity across the films along with director Tim Burton and Michael Keaton as Batman. Elfman's music had a significant impact and elevated his reputation for engaging and effective film scores. In some ways, these two *Batman* films are representative of the contemporary trends in expensively produced Hollywood blockbuster films – *Batman* was ranked in the Top Ten grossers of all time[1] – although both films also have interesting and unusual aesthetic strategies.

Classical and Neoclassical Film Music

In some ways, these two Batman films are representative of the contemporary trends in expensively produced Hollywood blockbuster films – although they have interesting and unusual aesthetic strategies. While

DOI: 10.4324/9781003299653-6

superficially, films have changed a great deal since the 1930s, in some ways their underlying structures and assumptions are similar. In terms of film scores, what Claudia Gorbman refers to as "classical film scoring" (1987: 70) and Kathryn Kalinak to "the classical film score" (1992: xv–xvi) dominated mainstream Hollywood films and its principles may have persisted although some went out of fashion. The use of a loud orchestral score especially written as fragments and appearing as an almost continuous ("wall-to-wall") musical fabric, became less dominant in the 1960s, although it became resurgent from the late 1970s.

The assumption of the classical film score was that music should "underscore" the visuals, creating emotional and dynamic effects, homologizing visual activity, and providing information and atmosphere for the film's narrative development. Kathryn Kalinak, in *Settling the Score*, suggests that contemporary Hollywood film music proves the persistence of the musical blueprint established by classical cinema (Kalinak 1992: 189), suggesting that the style and assumptions behind film music have changed little. Her declaration of the seeming permanence of Hollywood film music's form directly matches Bordwell, Staiger, and Thompson's claim for the persistence of the classical mode of film production (1985: 368). Kalinak points to the prevalence of pop songs as scores in the late 1960s and early 1970s as something of an aberration, indeed an opposition to classical principles through which the process of "classical scoring" has managed to endure (Kalinak 1992: 187). Yet although many contemporary scores bear some resemblance to studio-era film music, industrial imperatives and aesthetic concerns have not remained static, mitigating against the notion of a direct continuity between contemporary film music and that of classical cinema.

While films like *Easy Rider* (1969) and *American Graffiti* (1973) forewent especially written musical scores in favour of a succession of pop songs, many contemporary Hollywood films use both in some way. In addition to this, instrumental forces changed. The sound of the romantic large-scale orchestra, which had been introduced to films from the classical concert hall and was ubiquitous from the early 1930s onwards, declined in the 1960s and 1970s. There were more sparse scores, both in terms of the amount of music and the number of instruments used. Also evident was the use of a more discordant musical language imported from more recent concert music. Prime examples of these styles are Richard Rodney Bennett's score for *Figures in a Landscape* (1970), Jerry Fielding's music for *Straw Dogs* (1971), and Jerry Goldsmith's score for *Chinatown* (1974). In 1970, composer Ron Goodwin declared:

> I think there was once an attitude, very firmly adopted, that "if it's film music, it's got to be big," but that has certainly changed in the last

couple of years ... the main thing [now] is that "wall to wall" music isn't necessary. You must give the film room.

(Cooper 1970: 3)

Kalinak points out an explicit return to the style and sound of the classical film score in the wake of John Williams' music for George Lucas' *Star Wars* trilogy (*Star Wars* [1977], *The Empire Strikes Back* [1980], and *Return of the Jedi* [1983]). These films use a lot of music, and the Batman series of films includes scores of more than an hour's duration, marking a return to the wall-to-wall *bravura* orchestral music that had seemingly drifted out of fashion.

Orchestral music in the two Batman films certainly draws on the classical Hollywood tradition, yet rather than being simply a return to the styles of studio-era scores, it manifests specific allusions to particular stylistic aspects of studio-era film music. Kalinak's use of the term "persistence" presupposes direct continuity – "revival" might be a more appropriate description. After all, recent Hollywood films differ in many ways from those of the studio era.

In industrial terms, the mode of production for film music in contemporary cinema is very different from that of classical cinema. There is no more film music "production line" (Darby and Dubois 1982: 486), where there were rosters of composers, arrangers, and musicians all under one roof and on the permanent payroll. This has meant that there is undoubtedly less of the standardization that characterizes the music of classical cinema. Now there are even a few film composer superstars with names known by the general public, figures like Ennio Morricone, Jerry Goldsmith, and Hans Zimmer. Some musicians producing music for films have also had an eye on commercial success outside films. Indeed, there are significantly different imperatives, most notably tied-in musical products – namely singles but more importantly soundtrack albums of both orchestral scores and pop songs. In fact, there have been musical tie-ins with films since the silent days, for example, Fats Waller's *The Sheik of Araby* was sold as a sheet music tie-in for the Rudolph Valentino film *The Son of the Sheik* (1926), while the development of the film musical gave great opportunities to the sheet music industry. Yet since the late 1950s, with the advent of rock 'n' roll and the saturation development of the record market, there has been a proliferation of tied-in songs and films.

Batman

Batman's high-profile release in 1989 was complemented by the release of two soundtrack albums: Danny Elfman's large-scale orchestral score and Prince's song cycle. The second one gave a large profile to the film through association with one of the world's top music stars of the time. At this point, Elfman was a relatively minor name on the film composing circuit, having scored Tim Burton's previous films *Pee Wee's Big Adventure* (1985) and *Beetlejuice* (1988). Prince, on the other hand, had become one of the best-selling pop artists of the 1980s with albums such as *Around the World in a Day* (1983) and *Sign o' the Times* (1987), as well as writing the music for and starring in the film *Purple Rain* (1984) and providing music, starring in, and also directing *Under the Cherry Moon* (1986). *Batman* involves an uneasy cohabitation of Elfman's score with Prince's songs. Although the songs are marginalized and indeed much of Prince's album does not grace the film, it manifests an extension of the text beyond its traditional boundaries to include intersecting aesthetic products.

During the 1980s, the term "synergy" gained currency as a description of the simultaneous promotion of a franchise product (Denisoff and Plasketes 1990: 257), tying in products from the music industry with the film industry to create a compound package. Thomas Schatz cites *Batman* as characteristic of the multimedia nature of contemporary film production (Schatz 1993: 32). The existence of two soundtrack albums for *Batman*, indeed the existence of Prince's music tied to the film, is an example of the synergy of Warner Brothers' recording and cinematic arms. *Batman*'s producer Jon Peters commented on the high-profile extensions of the film: "The album and the film are separate works ... in two different media, complementing and supporting other" (Denisoff and Romanowski 1991: 694). It seems that Peters was instrumental in the release of Elfman's

album, the music of which was originally to appear only as a track or two on the Prince album (Burlingame 1990: 21; Schweiger 1992: 19).

Soundtrack albums provide a space for the plenitude of music; what may have been a few seconds and hardly noticed in the film can be enjoyed as an aesthetic object in its own right, its own logic undiluted by the exigencies of the film. *Batman* was the first film to institute the release of two soundtrack albums, a strategy that become common in its wake, examples being *Dick Tracy* (1990) (three discs), *Addams Family Values* (1993), *The Crow* (1994), and *Forrest Gump* (1994) (two discs, one of them double). In each case, these soundtracks reveal a division of the films' music into orchestral score and song compilation. One reviewer commented about *Batman*'s dual soundtracks: "both [albums are] excellent accessories for the further enjoyment of the biggest movie of the year" and suggested, "Buy the Prince album to get in the mood for the movie. Then go see it and whistle Elfman's haunting theme on your way back home to Prince" (McIlheny 1990: 108).

Prince's album forms an intersection with the film, aesthetically, commercially, and in narrative terms. It not only includes some dialogue from the film but bizarrely is conceptualized as a coherent narrative with dialogue apparently sung between the characters. It comprises its own narrative of sorts, with Prince singing various character parts: Batman in *The Future*, Joker in *Electric Chair*, Vicki Vale and Bruce Wayne in *Arms of Orion*, Joker in *Party Man*, Bruce Wayne in *Vicki Waiting*, Joker in *Trust*, Vicki Vale in *Lemon Crush*, Batman in *Scandalous*, and all of these characters in *Batdance*. This final song is the culmination of the dynamics and the narrative of the LP *Batdance* comprises an "operatic" interaction between Joker, an obscure character called "Gemini," Vicki Vale, Bruce Wayne, and Batman. While Joker and Batman interject samples of dialogue from the film (such as "I'm Batman"), the sleeve notes also ascribe voices within this song to "choir," "Joker's Gang," "Bat Dancers," and even "Prince" himself.

Batdance was the scout single from the package, released before the film to precede it as an advertisement. It became Prince's equal most successful single in the UK and was the forerunner to two other UK Top 30 singles from his soundtrack (*Party Man* and *Arms of Orion*), with the film seemingly having driven his LP's success (Denisoff and Romanowski 1991: 697). *Batdance* provides an interface with the past, announcing the new *Batman* film through referencing the chorus vocals from Neal Hefti's theme for the camp 1960s television show. This provided a musical bridge between the previous representation of the character and the oncoming film. *Batman* presents all the songs as diegetic music, that is, it grounds them all as appearing "realistically" within the diegetic film world. *Party Man* is foregrounded, played on a ghetto-blaster by

Joker when he indulges in some art terrorism, while *Trust* materializes at the carnival and some Prince songs appear as ambient music at Bruce Wayne's party (*The Future*, *Vicki Waiting*, and *Electric Chair*). Thus, the film ties the songs to the mundane everyday "reality" of the film, while Elfman's more prominent orchestral score functions as the film's "heavenly voice," appearing from nowhere. Despite the bipartite nature of the music in the film, there is one point of union between the two. The Prince song *Scandalous* appears for a portion of the end credits while some of its music, rearranged by Elfman, appears earlier in the film, albeit fleetingly. Generally, Prince's music appears obtrusively but only occasionally, while Elfman's orchestral music is virtually continuous throughout the film. The music as a whole is constantly foregrounded in a non-classical fashion, with musical logic often overriding narrative logic.

Reviewers noted the film's musical strategy, that of Elfman's wall-to-wall studio era-styled score plus the foregrounding of Prince's music in the fringes of the film: "Prince's songs, which interrupt an outstandingly old-fashioned score by Danny Elfman … only get gratuitously in the way during two scenes" (Newman 1989: 269). Prince visited the set during production and was inspired. He reportedly said, "I can hear the music." (Denisoff and Romanowski 1991: 693) But sadly for him the final product turned out to have Danny Elfman's music rather than his own.

Elfman's orchestral score dominates but is not as well integrated with the film as it initially appears. This is at least partly accounted for by Elfman's relative lack of experience in film music but also his lack of experience in orchestral music. Elfman is from a rock background, having been the singer in the experimental rock band Oingo Boingo in the 1980s. At times his *Batman* score is obscured by sound effects rather than take them into account, and the internal musical logic of many pieces outweighs their logic in the filmic environment. For example, when Joker first sees a picture of Vicki Vale, the refrain of *Beautiful Dreamer* appears, and dialogue continues, the music lacking any direct interface with the action. At this point, the music does not bow to the image track through matching the momentary dynamics of the action; rather its time scheme carries on regardless of the film. Much in the same way that pop songs are often forced to in films, here the music retains its own full integrity rather than being forced to bend itself to fit momentary changes in the action. Songs usually have their own regular rhythmic and standardized temporal structure (set by tempo and repeating structures like verse and chorus), which means that when they are foregrounded, action must be cut to their requirements, unlike the flexible orchestral underscores which have traditionally been built around the requirements of the processes of filmic narration. So, while there are songs by Prince, Elfman's score also adapts an older form of popular song, which follows similar patterns in its relationship with moving image events.

Elfman's music distinctly resembles scores from classical Hollywood films.[2] His score not only uses an extremely large orchestra, up to 110 instrumentalists, but also *leitmotifs*, musical themes associated with characters or other things, a central strategy of musical scores in classical cinema. There is a repeated Batman theme, while Joker has a foregrounded musical theme associated with him, the melody from the old Stephen Foster song *Beautiful Dreamer*. In addition to these, a rearrangement of Prince's *Scandalous* appears twice, associated with the love of Wayne and Vale. These themes interact at times, forming a direct union between musical and narrative processes. At the film's conclusion, for example, the *Batman* theme and the *Scandalous* melody (the love theme) alternate in quick succession, suggesting a union of Batman and Wayne's love for Vale, the two halves of the protagonist's schizoid character. Yet the film's climactic triumphant fanfare, which owes more than a little to Richard Strauss' *Also Sprach Zarathustra*, immediately supersedes them and asserts the superhero himself as we then see Batman alone on the rooftops.

The theme for Batman himself codes the Gothic at its opening, with deep solemn strings and brass then becoming martial in a pounding march with snare drum and brass punctuation. It functions directly as a fanfare for Batman, announcing his presence while being associated solidly with both film and character. Consequently, along with the overall style of the film's music, it also works outside the film's context. It was prominent in the trailer for the film and reappeared in the first sequel, *Batman Returns* (1992). Despite the wide usage of the theme, *Batman Forever* (1995) and *Batman and Robin* (1997), in keeping with other changes from the previous films, instituted a new theme for Batman, the musical score being written by Elliot Goldenthal rather than Elfman. Along the same lines, one-time Elfman orchestrator and conductor of the *Batman* score, Shirley Walker, wrote the music for the film derived from the animated television series, *Batman: Mask of the Phantasm* (1993), and declined to use Elfman's Batman theme. However, the distinct flavour of Elfman's music is so centrally associated Batman that both Goldenthal's music for *Batman Forever* and Walker's for *Batman: Mark of the Phantasm* have retained its broad style.[3]

A key characteristic of Elfman's score is the use of massed and strident brass instruments. The score for *Batman* is characterized by parallel harmonies, chords that move up and down by a semitone, a staple of music in the horror genre. Like pop, rock, or dance music, Elfman's score is underlined consistently by a strong rhythmic impetus, a pulse or beat that is at the heart of many of the film's pieces of orchestral music. This beat gives the music a highly purposeful edge as well as propelling the action. For instance, when Batman with Vicki Vale drives the Batmobile to the Bat Cave, the music is portentous and compensates for the lack of dialogue. A vocal chorus provides stabbing rhythmic notes, reminiscent of Carl Orff's *Carmina Burana*. The choir keeps a regular rhythm in operation, which builds and paves the way from the *Batman* theme's climactic entrance, and while this provides an aural zenith for the sequence, it is surmounted by the visual *coup de grâce* of the Batmobile not slowing to enter a hatch in a sheer rock wall.

Elfman's music in *Batman* is pure Gothic melodrama at its opening, using a large, dark, and Wagnerian orchestral sound. Some reference points apart from Wagner might include Saint-Saëns' *Danse macabre* and horror film music that has formalized Gothic musical traits. Indeed, it signifies directly to the audience through the use of recognizable musical forms and styles. It uses the melody of *Beautiful Dreamer* for its many extra-textual connotations of wistful nostalgia. The arrangements of the tune underline this, coding childlike innocence and having an air of irony since that counterposes Joker's real intentions with respect to Vale. The score is also replete with waltzes of all kinds, which are also associated with Joker. These. include a circus-type waltz when Joker first reveals himself and kills crime boss Grissom and later a mock-Strauss waltz when he dances with Vale. Elfman's arrangements include some very distinct instrumental sounds, such as the celesta and the Ondes Martenot. The celesta's delicate bell-like sound is probably most widely known for its use in Tchaikovsky's *Dance of the Sugar Plum Fairy* from *The Nutcracker*, while the Ondes Martenot was an early electronic musical instrument used for its otherworldly sound in some film scores of the 1940s such as Miklós Rosza's for *Spellbound* (1945) and *The Lost Weekend* (1945). At the denouement in Gotham's deserted cathedral the score uses a Phantom of the Opera-style organ, referential strategy that Elfman also followed in his score for *Darkman* (1990).

At times, *Batman* uses music as a direct communication. The Flugelheim art gallery sequence is explicit in its use of the audience's mental library of musical styles and genres. It contains in succession Mozart's *Eine kleine Nachtmusik* (a token of high art culture), Prince's *Party Man* (pop song), and the theme from *A Summer Place* (cheap Mantovani-style arrangement of a worn-out romance tune, originally a film theme by Max Steiner). Audiences are extremely musically literate and the music in the film gears itself precisely towards this. Also, while Joker and his gang perform their art terrorism in the gallery, the foregrounded song *Party Man* flaunts its self-consciousness through being explicitly about Joker and indirectly about Prince. ("All hail, new king in town. Young and old, gather round. Black and white, red and green, the funkiest man you've ever seen.")

In the *Party Man* sequence, the beat of the music is the central temporal process, underlined by some cuts taking place on emphasized beats (the first beat of the bar). Joker and his gang's actions directly reflect the rhythmic impetus of the song through their dancing. Musical logic dominates visual and narrative logic. This bears out Kalinak's point about pop songs disregarding the dynamics of films (1992: 187), yet in this case the song is articulating and creating the dynamics of the action in a way reminiscent of song sequences in film musicals. In any case the aesthetic evident in this sequence is certainly an anomaly in the dominant form of mainstream narrative cinema, where music regularly takes a back seat to other elements of the film, and traditionally is rarely foregrounded in this manner.

Prince's songs are notably associated with Joker: *Party Man* at the Flugelheim gallery and *Trust* at the Gotham street carnival. These and *Beautiful Dreamer* tend to keep their integrity, their musical logic ... one could almost say that Joker represents the triumph of musical logic over cinematic logic, while Batman represents the subordination of musical logic to cinematic logic, his image consistently invoking his musical theme.

Batman Returns

If *Batman* demonstrates a situation where commercial logic has foregrounded aspects of the film's music, the first sequel displays a qualitatively different scenario – or at least a development from the musical strategy of the original film. *Batman Returns* has a similarly large-scale orchestral score using a language derived from classical cinema while relegating pop music's role to some short-lived music at a party and an end title song. It has one featured song, *Face to Face* (performed by Siouxsie and the Banshees), although it briefly uses Rick James' *Super Freak*. *Face to Face* was co-written by Elfman and attains a degree of continuity with the orchestral score through using musical elements from the film's character themes (*leitmotifs*). It appears for the end titles and as diegetic ambient music in the party sequence where, literally face to face, Bruce Wayne (Batman) and Selina Kyle (Catwoman) recognize each other's alter egos. *Batman Returns* certainly contains less in the way of pop music than its predecessor, with the film's soundtrack album consisting of Elfman's score and the one featured song. According to Elfman, "Tim Burton was very clear that there wouldn't be Top 40 songs dropped in at random" (Schweiger 1992: 19). Recorded by Siouxsie and the Banshees, who had been most prominent at the end of the 1970s and start of the 1980s, the song was merely used by the film sufficiently to justify its tied-in status while in conventional fashion the music video for the single incorporated images from the film.

Batman Returns' preponderance of scored orchestral music demonstrates film logic dictating musical logic, following the modes of the prestige orchestral scores of the 1930s and 1940s. The music is tethered directly to the screen action. So, the film's principal characters all elicit the appearance of their respective musical themes: Batman has his own heroic theme that survives from the first film, a four-note figure, and a deep plodding melody represent the Penguin, while Catwoman has scratchy string glissandi and a full string melody. My rudimentary descriptions of the respective musical themes ("scratchy" like a cat, "plodding" like a penguin) bear out the use of musical clichés. Elfman confirms this: "whenever he walked on the stage, I saw the Penguin as an opera singer who was about to deliver an aria. I gave his melodies a grand, overblown quality" (Schweiger 1992: 18). All three *leitmotifs* appear in quick succession when Batman accosts the Penguin "surveying the riot scene," which intercuts with Catwoman's acquisition of a whip in a department store. Here the music moves from one character theme to the next, subordinating itself to the film's action. Classical Hollywood composer Max Steiner said of his score for *The Informer* (1935): "A blind man could have sat in a theatre and known when Gypo was on the screen" (Prendergast 1977: 42). Steiner means that whenever the film's protagonist appeared, he was doubled by the appearance of his own *leitmotif*, and this is much like sections of *Batman Returns*. Elfman's orchestral score is, however, paradoxical in that it follows very precisely the modes of classical scores, using thematic techniques to build a wall-to-wall fabric in the same way that Steiner and Erich Wolfgang Korngold constructed their scores in the 1930s and

1940s. It is paradoxical in that it copies explicitly the musical techniques of classical cinema, yet the effect is overblown and parodic. Elfman's distension of classical principles led to a startling score that provided a very large and antiquated texture for the film. This ties obliquely to the notion of "retrofuturism" which is evident in *Batman Returns'* design, perhaps more so than in the first film. The film appears to be representing a different time trajectory, as if things had developed differently in the 1940s, and the music is an integral part of this.

How far can post-classical film music revive the musical modes of the studio system, where the industrial base is no longer in place? The *Batman* scores seem quite literally to be "speaking in a dead language' to use Fredric Jameson's phrase (*Postmodernism*, 1984: 65). Arguably the language of classical film scores was already a dated if not outmoded musical language in its studio system heyday since nineteenth-century concert hall music provided the musical language of classical cinema. The *Batman* scores do not fully comply with Jameson's description of pastiche, which he distinguishes from parody. While parody uses and exaggerates language with an ulterior (often comic) motive, pastiche involves the neutral reuse of an antiquated or obsolete language.[4] It is rather that the *Batman* scores contain a degree of parody corresponding with the generally hyperbolic and self-conscious character of the films themselves. They take the techniques of the classical film score and elevate them to the level of cliché. The music is melodramatic, lacks subtlety, and foregrounds clichés with which the audience is familiar, or rather overfamiliar.

Elfman's *Batman* scores contain a degree of parody corresponding with the generally hyperbolic and self-conscious character of the films themselves. We could see the score's "revivalism" in terms of the art music (and art history) concept of the neoclassical, where composers "revived the balanced forms and clearly perceptible thematic processes of earlier styles ... [while] the prefix of 'neo-' often carries the implication of parody, or distortion, of truly Classical traits" (Whittall 1984: 104). The *Batman Returns* score is certainly excessive in comparison with the scores in classical cinema, despite its obvious referencing of that style. It uses the principles and form, the surface of studio-era scores, yet these appear distorted by the music's distinctive character and its conspicuousness in the film. Elfman verifies this process: "Though I try to reflect the spirit of Korngold and Rózsa when I write traditionally, the music still goes through some funny circus mirrors in my head. So it comes out far more twisted than those great old scores" (Schweiger 1992: 17).

John Williams' film music is also an essential reference point (in fact the *Batman* music bears a passing resemblance to Williams' music for Brian De Palma's *The Fury* [1978]), yet Elfman's music is much more arch and based more upon exaggerating the tenets of musical style in classical cinema. However, both composers could to some degree be dubbed "neo-classical" in that they value the classical and use it as a model while also differentiating their music from it. The architectural resonance of the term neoclassical ties the music of the *Batman* films with the startling set designs of Anton Furst (*Batman*) and Bo Welch (*Batman Returns*). Both music and set design situate the films in what seems to be an alternative present, one projected to now from a 1940s past. This resonates with Jameson's description of earlier representations of the future having "turned out to have been merely the future of one moment of our past'" (Jameson, "Progress Versus Utopia," 1984: 244).

Elfman's music then, seems to be a future version of the Classical Hollywood film score, but one that has followed a different and more direct line of development, although not quite the same one as John Williams' film music. While both composers' music could be characterized as neoclassical, John Williams' work is best described as a pastiche of classical film scoring, and Danny Elfman's music for the *Batman* films as a parody of the film music of the past. However, Williams was instrumental in the renewal of classical Hollywood-inspired film scores. It is striking that Thomas Schatz identifies *Jaws* (1975), the film that established John Williams as one of Hollywood's pre-eminent composers, as the film that heralded the "New Hollywood" (Schatz 1993: 17). While *Jaws* has a prominent musical score, the music in classical films more directly inspired Williams' music for *Star Wars* (1977). Kathryn Kalinak writes that "Through Williams' example, the epic sound established m the thirties once again became a viable choice for composers in contemporary Hollywood" (Kalinak 1992: 189). Williams' music for *Superman* (1978) and *Raiders of the Lost Ark* (1981) are characteristic of this style, as is Alan Silvestri's for *Back to the Future* (1985). The epic sound and style of the studio-era classical score is clearly evident in *Batman Returns*. Elfman is plain about his admiration for the scores of classical cinema, particularly Hugo Friedhofer's score for *The Best Years of Our Lives* (1946), and decries modern film music. He said: "To me, contemporary film scoring doesn't enhance the action, all it does is provide pretty 'wallpaper.' Old-fashioned film scores were much more dynamic" (Deutsch 1993: 9). Elfman's music is certainly dynamic, but while it exhibits massive variation in texture as well as temperament, much of the rise and fall of the music's intensity is dictated solely by the film's visual track.

In *Batman Returns*, the music is tailored directly to the film's momentary dynamics. At times it even "Mickeymouses" – mimics screen action – yet it is not pleonastic, it is a central component of the film's identity and of its narration. The music sounds like an overblown, impossibly large, and prestigious classical symphonic score. It sounds rather like a spoof, a distortion of studio-era film music, but this is due to the use of culturally coded (or, more precisely, overcoded) instrumental timbres and styles, like the use of deep Gothic brass, chiming celesta, and Grand Guignol organ. These are musical clichés, and Elfman's awareness of this means that it is foregrounded as an effect. This procedure is far more pronounced than in *Batman*, forcing the music explicitly into the realms of parody. The sheer volume of music, added to the world that the film creates, is reminiscent of the stylized world of the film musical, such as *The Pirate* (1948) and *Seven Brides for Seven Brothers* (1954), where design and music coalesce into a world of dazzling visuals and explosive musical sound. This style also relates to cartoons and, like cartoons, *Batman Returns* constructs its own world rather than directly copying our own, while the preponderance of Mickeymousing (which, of course, was named after cartoon music) can be accounted for with reference to the *Batman* films' cartoon qualities, inherited from their origin in comics. Elfman supplied the theme for the television cartoon series *The Simpsons*, and there is a correlation between his style, and the dramatic and quick musical changes, quotation, and parody established by cartoon composers such as Carl Stalling and Dick Bradley.

Elfman is highly conscious of his music being something more than simply a silence-filler: "I would love some day to have people hear the two *Batman* scores while looking at the image, but without the sound effects" (Deutsch 1993: 9). The relationship of music to image in *Batman Returns* often resembles that of a ballet, in the way that the continuity of the music interacts with, but is not necessarily subordinated to other elements. Film composer Dimitri Tiomkin wrote: "There is a much closer affinity between ballet and movies than casual thought suggests ... Sometimes I think a good picture is really just a ballet with dialogue" (Tiomkin 1974: 58). This perspective, also verified by sound designer Walter Murch (Paine 1985: 356), is at times explicitly borne out by *Batman Returns*. Its opening gives Elfman a showcase for his music, with the first five minutes of the film containing just two words of dialogue, thus allowing the music a major role in the articulation of action. The opening of the film resembles silent cinema music in that it is continuous and proceeds without the inconveniences of the spoken word or excessive sound effects. The music replaces both asserting itself as a major component of the film and retaining its own internal logic despite its close marriage with the image and storytelling processes.

Batman Returns starts with a slow version of the *Batman* melody as snow falls over the Warner Bros. logo. As this changes to an urban exterior scene, Gothic organ presents the short four-note musical figure associated with the Penguin throughout the film. The camera cranes upwards and across to a large Gothic house that has a light and shape at the window in a visual homage to *Citizen Kane* (1941). Cut to the interior of the house and a birth offscreen. Next, a caged infant attacks a cat as its parents look on, and the music here features the celesta and plays a short ballet-styled piece to counterpoint the comic violence. The next cut moves back outside, following the parents pushing their cage-like baby carriage through a snowy park, and culminating in them throwing it into the river Here the music is a corruption of clichéd Christmas music featuring sleigh bells and a wordless choir singing Disney-style. Elfman's interim project, *Edward Scissorhands* (1990), was undoubtedly influential, with *Batman Returns* using beautiful and overwrought fantasy-invoking choirs more than *Batman*. This walk to doom features the first appearance of the full melody associated with the Penguin, anticipating the child's rebirth. Upon the baby carriage's impact in the water and disappearance down a drain, the music punctuates the seeming finality of the act with a tubular bell toll. The camera then closely follows the baby carriage down the river, while the music starts a solid 4/4 rhythm and begins tentatively to offer excerpts from the *Batman* theme. Upon the appearance of the main title (with bats flying through it), the music reaches a climactic chord and then proceeds with the full *Batman* theme that it has been withholding from the audience. The thumping beat persists along with an arrangement of the theme that has changed little since the first film, as the camera follows the baby carriage floating along the sewer finally coming to rest inside the Penguin house at the zoo. It is a highly melodramatic opening to a film, with massively telescoped action in temporal terms. This sequence is a rebirth sequence, the Penguin going from human birth to symbolic rebirth through the sewer into the zoo. Radical changes in the character of the music mark each step of the way. It involves Mickeymousing, articulating changes in the image track, and providing narrative information (themes for Batman and the Penguin, the Christmas setting, the film's mixture of moral darkness and quirky humour). *Batman Returns'* opening sequence provides remarkable scope for Elfman's music, indeed an opportunity rarely available for composers in contemporary cinema.

Conclusion

In summary, the first two *Batman* films demonstrate two strata of Hollywood's musical strategies developed in the 1980s and 90s. *Batman* exhibits a cohabitation of orchestral score and tied-in pop songs, while *Batman Returns* uses only one tied-in song and has a large-scale score inspired more directly by the music of classical cinema. They both use classically inspired forms recast by more recent procedures. The fragment-ing of the Hollywood studio system had a significant effect on the pro-duction of music for films, and there have also been important changes in film music due to cultural developments outside the cinema. With film production becoming a component of multimedia industries, films themselves have increasingly become vehicles for tied-in pop music, as can be verified by any visit to a CD or vinyl retailer. Musical tie-ins were important for film production during the studio era and they directly affected film form: they spawned the musical film. With the recession of the musical genre, this impetus has moved into dramatic films, as witnessed by the use of Prince in *Batman*.

Yet, tie-ins can equally include the film's orchestral score as well as songs. The mere existence of two soundtrack LPs suggests that music has a more important position in films than it had in the past. It is not unreasonable to suggest that the dual function of music – as both film element and object in its own right – has had an effect on the character of the music itself. Music's status in films has become elevated and this has removed the orchestral music from the alleged position of "unobtrusiveness" which it occupied in classical cinema and into a more conspicuous position.

Although it initially seems to resemble the film music of the 1930s and 1940s, the orchestral music in the two films signifies in a fundamentally *different* way from classical film scores. Both of the films are premised upon the existence of a sophisticated cultural literacy among the audience. This assumes that the unprecedented access to images and narratives has supplied a knowledge of the Batman figure, Gothic imagery, and so forth, largely made available through contemporary audiovisual culture's principle of recycling. The music works in exactly the same way, relying on the audience's musical literacy for its signification. Particularly in *Batman Returns*, the music goes beyond the generic music and forms used in classical cinema. It works through the use of archetypal sounds and musical styles, burlesquing certain musical forms under the umbrella of its parody of the classical film score.

The orchestral music in the *Batman* films matches the mixed construction of period in the films, blending both the historical (1940s design, the classical score format) with parodic and contemporary aspects. Post-classical cinema seems to display a proliferation of music that is unified at the point of the film as both text and as commodity. Indeed, Tim Burton, director of the first two *Batman* films allegedly asked, "Is there a movie here, or just something that goes along with the merchandising?" (Schweiger 1992: 19) Yet *Batman* and *Batman Returns* can hardly be accused of being fully determined by the requirements of tie-ins. The music in the films is testament not only to the pressure to use marketable pop music in films, but also to the ongoing significance of several aesthetic traditions and strategies which incorporate such music in a variety of ways.

Notes

1 "All-time Top Ten grossing films at North American Box Office" in *Variety*, 20–26 February 1995, A54.
2 Janet K.Halfyard notes a superficial similarity between Elfman's score and classical film scoring (2004: 62).
3 Although Eliot Goldenthal praises Danny Elfman's music, he asserts that his music never looks back to it (Singer 1997: 125).
4 Jameson ("Postmodernism," 1984: 65). The term comes from "Pasticcio," which was used to describe operas that consisted of arias from disparate sources and "faked" bridging parts.

Bibliography

Bordwell, David, Janet Staiger, and Kristin Thompson, *The Classical Hollywood Cinema Style and Mode of Production to 1960* (London: Routledge, 1985).
Burlingame, John, "Danny Elfman on the Move" in *Soundtrack!*, September 1990.
Cooper, Rod, "Beating the Drum for the Music Makers" (Interview with Ron Goodwin)" in *Kinematograph Weekly*, vol. 634, no.3279, 15 August 1970.
Darby, William, and Jack Dubois, *American Film Music: Major Composers, Techniques, Trends 1915–90* (Washington, DC: McFarland, 1982).
Denisoff, R. Serge, and George Plasketes, "Synergy in 1980s Film and Music: Formula for Success or Industry Mythology?" in *Film History*, vol. 4, 1990.
Denisoff, R. Serge, and William D. Romanowski, *Risky Business: Rock in Film* (London: Transaction, 1991).
Deutsch, Didier, "Interview with Danny Elfman" in *Soundtrack!*, December 1993.
Gorbman, Claudia, *Unheard Melodies: Narrative Film Music* (London: BFI, 1987).
Halfyard, Janet K., *Danny Elfman's Batman: A Film Score Guide* (Lanham, NJ: Scarecrow, 2004).
Jameson, Fredric, "Postmodernism, or the Cultural Logic of Late Capitalism" in *New Left Review*, no. 146, July/August 1984.
Jameson, Fredric, "Progress Versus Utopia, or, Can We Imagine the Future?" in Brian Wallis, ed., *Art After Modernism: Rethinking Representation* (New York: New Museum of Contemporary Art, 1984).
Kalinak, Kathryn, *Settling the Score: Music and the Classical Hollywood Film* (Madison, WI: University of Wisconsin Press, 1992).
McIlheny, Barry, "Review of Elfman and Prince Soundtracks" in *Empire*, 1990.
Newman, Kim, "Review of Batman" in *Monthly Film Bulletin*, vol. 56, no. 668, September 1989.
Paine, Frank, "Sound Mixing and *Apocalypse Now*: An Interview with Walter Murch" in Elisabeth Weis, and John Belton, eds., *Film Sound: Theory and Practice* (New York: Columbia University Press, 1985).
Prendergast, Roy M., *A Neglected Art: Film Music* (New York: New York University Press, 1977).
Schatz, Thomas, "The New Hollywood" in Jim Collins, Hilary Radner, and Ava Preacher Collins, eds., *Film Theory Goes to the Movies* (London: Routledge, 1993).

Schweiger, Daniel, "Danny Elfman Returns" in *Soundtrack!*, September 1992.

Singer, Michael, *Batman, and Robin: The Making of the Movie* (London: Hamlyn, 1997).

Tiomkin, Dimitri, "Composing for the Films" in James Limbacher, ed., *From Violins to Video* (Metuchen, NJ: Scarecrow, 1974).

Whitall, Arnold, entry in Stanley Sadie, ed., *The New Grove Dictionary of Music and Musicians, vol. 2* (London: Macmillan, 1984).

7

HEARING DEEP SEATED FEARS

John Carpenter's *The Fog* (1980)

When my mother was young her household was plagued by a poltergeist. I have always been intrigued by the story, not least hearing about how the phenomenon was nothing like "special effect" ghosts in films but had a sonic presence rather than a visual presence. Indeed, paranormal happenings seemingly often involve noise, particularly of the infrasonic and ultrasonic variety. My mother's poltergeist activity exhibited an early warning on each occasion through the family dog becoming frenzied in clear reaction to sounds outside the range of human hearing, before the onset of a spate of audible banging and scraping sounds. Sounds can be disturbing, and one might argue that films can often have scarier and more disturbing sounds and music than their visuals.

There is something primal about affecting sounds. Acoustic ecologist R. Murray Schafer has speculated and experimented concerning ambient sounds that are internalized unconsciously. He has been concerned about mains hum, also known as power line hum:

> in countries operating on an alternating current of 60 cycles, it is this sound which now provides the resonant frequency, for it will be heard (together with its harmonics) in the operation of all electrical devices from lights and amplifiers to generators. Where C is tuned to 256 cycles, this resonant frequency is B natural. In ear training exercises I have discovered that students find B natural much the easiest pitch to retain and recall spontaneously. Also during meditation exercises, after which the whole body has been relaxed and students are asked to sing the tone of "primary unity" – the tone which seems to arise

DOI: 10.4324/9781003299653-7

naturally from the center of their being – B natural is more frequent than any other. I have also experimented with this in Europe where the resonant electrical frequency of 50 cycles is approximately G sharp. At the Stuttgart Music High School I led a group of students in a series of relaxation exercises and then asked them to hum the tone of "primary unity." They centered on G sharp.

(Schafer 1994: 98–99)

On the standard equally tempered scale, 60Hz is slightly flatter than B natural and is in fact pretty much halfway between A♯ and B (two octaves below Middle C).

Droning tones dominate John Carpenter's electronic music for *The Fog* (1980). Qualitatively, they are an analogue of mains hum, delivering a sound that embodies the electric essence of the synthesizer as instrument. There is something primal about the film's music. While perhaps *The Fog*'s music *should* have centred on a (slightly flat) B natural drone, its opening music centres on A natural. (It is in the key of A minor, which is easier to play on keyboards, in essence consisting of white keys only.) Some of the later drones in the film, however, centre on B and a slightly flatter pitch. While we should remember that analogue recordings on tape often raise or lower pitch through changing the speed of the tape, we should not discount a direct connection between these sounds and the frequency of mains electricity, particularly as electronic music embodies an essence of electricity and non-organic music making. Philip Brophy's discusses Carpenter's music for *Escape from New York* (1981):

Played by synthesizer banks triggered by sequencers, the pulse is exceedingly inhuman ... it is the product of electrical energy – always stated and presented as such and never allowed to "become music" ... [T]he synthesizer's innate capacity for "inhumanness" is exploited to conduct (literally) energy and channel it through the score.

(Brophy 2004: 99)

This account relies on the character of analogue synthesizer music as an emanation from technology and particularly electricity, a characteristic of Carpenter's music in the 1970s and 1980s which is evident across his films.

A fairly straightforward horror genre film, *The Fog* concerns a mysterious eponymous fog that descends upon a coastal town, containing the revenge-seeking ghosts of those who were robbed and killed to enable the foundation of the town. The film's director, John Carpenter, usually creates his own incidental music, utilizing primarily 1970s keyboard synthesizers.

On the face of it, his music bears more resemblance to his popular contemporaries Jean-Michel Jarre or Vangelis than electronic experimentalists such as Vladimir Ussachevsky or Pierre Henry. Carpenter's film scores tend toward the basic and highly repetitive with clear textures, carrying an influence from minimalism, which is also evident in that the listener can hear and follow the developmental processes. The music regularly consists of a couple of basic themes, and extended pieces that are based on drones or *ostinati*, which provide stark tension and tend to grace the moments of climax in Carpenter's films. This procedure is perhaps most clearly illustrated in his breakthrough film, *Halloween* (1978), which established the highly distinctive style of Carpenter's film scores. Being electronic and premised upon spare texture and repetition, the scores initially appear characterized by musical primitivism. Burnand and Mera noted that "The obvious features of Carpenter's scores are obsessive repetition, primitivism and minimalism, and an improvisational approach that works at the most basic level of musical communication" (Burnand and Mera 2004: 65). His music, particularly in his earlier films, appears to revel in its "lo-tech" sound and what might be called a "homebrew" status. In other words, this film music emanates from outside the established industry for producing incidental film music, indeed standing in distinct contrast with modes of traditional mainstream film scores. Indeed, Carpenter's music provides a distinct contrast with modes of traditional mainstream film scores. Classical Hollywood film composers "operated within a paradigmatic range of classical norms. The combination of these stylistic parameters yielded a remarkably uniform group style among Hollywood composers that emphasized leitmotifs, theme writing and symphonic orchestrations" (Smith 1998: 6). Jeff Smith's succinct stylistic summary of classical cinema's incidental music might well be applicable to the overwhelming majority of contemporary film incidental music (Bordwell and Staiger 1985: 367). Carpenter's score for *The Fog* does include a number of traditional horror film score elements. Apart from the identifiable, repeated "themes" (leitmotifs), the film contains music for direct atmosphere rendering, intermittent bursts of music ("stingers") to accentuate violent action, pulses that bear some resemblance to heartbeats and repeated loops of musical material (as either *ostinati* or sustained droning tones).

Carpenter's score contains two repeated musical themes, but their placement appears not important structurally and not particularly interesting from the point of view of analysis. It is hardly surprising that the score's structure and unity are minimal; it revels in its fragmentary and repetitious in nature. Rather than being written to fit the film Carpenter's music arises more a part of the genetic make-up of the film – in its DNA. As the film's director, Carpenter occupies a profoundly different position from most film composers, where he includes music as an essential component of the overall conception of film as organic an object, and therefore as an integrated part of film sound design. Carpenter's style regularly involves minimalist camerawork and lighting, and although he often uses Panaglide (a variation on the Steadicam device) there tend to be few ostentatious visual flourishes, despite shooting all his films in widescreen (anamorphic 2.35:1).[1]

After being dissatisfied with the film once it was finished, Carpenter decided that the film needed redevelopment. Some set pieces were shot and added, and many of the sequences of impact violence were made more explicit with additional "gore" shots. The added scenes included the prologue and the attack on Stevie Wayne on the roof of the lighthouse.[2] While the film might have sacrificed some of its subtle atmospheric intention for bludgeoning action, it remains a haunting film.[3] It is highly likely that the music and sound effects were also bolstered and expanded, following the common assumption that music can save a failing film. This is evident at times in the superimposed sounds of "stingers on top of stingers" to give a massive sonic shock at precise moments of *The Fog*. For instance, at 16:32 when the first stabbing impact of the film takes place (on the Seagrass) the stinger is treated with electronic echo to enhance its force, while at 1:18:12, when the ghosts threaten Stevie Wayne on the roof of the lighthouse, an electronic stinger is augmented by the sudden and simultaneous onset of an organ chord.

The film's prologue has the character of an entirely separate scene in that it entails a cameo from John Houseman, who narrates a ghost story to a group of children around a campfire. Houseman had been a part of the Mercury Theater with Orson Welles, worked on *Citizen Kane* (1941), and enjoyed a long and distinguished career as a film producer and character actor. In terms of music, this sequence remains isolated in that his voice has accompaniment from a piece of music which does not emerge again in full, only in fragments. The relationship of music and voice has something of the operatic aria about it, with an interplay of dynamics and phrasing taking place between the two. It is preceded by a screen card quoting the conclusion of an Edgar Allan Poe poem (*Is All We See and Seem but a Dream Within a Dream*) which cues regular pulsing notes on the piano along with the subtle appearance of the deep drone that becomes ubiquitous throughout the film. It is accompanied initially by the ticking of a pocket watch that dangles at the right of the frame until the snapping shut of the case alongside a shock stinger. It appears alongside a sequentially descending melody on the piano (in A minor with an A pedal), which appears only intermittently in this pre-credit sequence. The melody opens the film over the Poe title card and then appears in the opening sequence when the camera alights on Andy among the children listening enrapt, which suggests the possibility that the ensuing film might be read as his fantasy. The opening melody is then subjected to a blockage, where the music remains as the opening three notes and refuses to run to the full 12 notes of the theme apart from on isolated occasions. The structure of the music in this sequence follows an alternation between this melodic line on piano that is based on a descending minor key chord pattern over a synthesizer drone, and a section of more sustained piano notes which is more dramatic and less melodic than the previous motif.[4] The other section involves a so-called "drop out," where the existing melodic and harmonic structure dissipates to be replaced by sustained notes on the piano that cohere into sustained chords. The characteristic aspect here is the drop by a minor 6th in the bass, causing an unusual underlying chord change (A minor to C♯ minor, then C♯ minor to F minor). These piano chord changes that stress rising pitch function as powerful emphases, adding further drama and tension to Houseman's story. The conclusion of the narration involves a succession of the slow chord changes on the piano in sequence. The mix of timbres has the ethereal synthesizer representing the unknown counterposed with the organic sound of the piano that marks the familiar. These

coordinate points place us into an "in between" state, emphasizing the "spooky" music as the sonic equivalent of a ghost story.

During this narrated sequence the music is highly effective and manipulative. The second section of the two alternated sections of musical material punctuates the scary story most dramatically with its sustained tones and pitch ascents, some of which occur between the cadences of Houseman's voice. The first section, in its quiet but insistent droning and repetition, soporifically lulls the audience into a dream state. The falling pitch (by sequence) and repeated melody depict the entry to a vortex and invoke fatality, and the inevitability of the story of the demise of Blake and his fellow lepers at the hands of a conspiracy returning to find justice in Antonio Bay. The sequence ends with the closure enabled by the equivalence of sound fading. The camera moves upwards and away in a classic concluding visual cadence, and simultaneously displacing the sound of the electronic drone with a fading-in radio tone. The structure of the music in this pre-credit sequence boosts the sense of inevitability and the importance of time invoked from the outset by the ticking clock. The sequence concludes with music accompanied by another iconic diegetic sound: a tolling bell, which often signifies impending doom.

Carpenter played in a band called The Coupe de Villes, which also included the film's editor Tommy Lee Wallace and cinematographer Nick Castle. One of the group's songs appears in Carpenter's comedy *Big Trouble in Little China* (1986) and they even made a pop promo to accompany the single release. One of their songs graces the soundtrack of *The Fog*. Disc jockey Stevie Wayne introduces it (although fails to give it a title) and dedicates it to the crew of the Seagrass, shortly before they are attacked by the ghostly ship.[5] Indeed, the film has a prominent unifying device in the town radio station (KAB Antonio Bay), which Andy's mother Stevie Wayne mans alone, playing a constant run of records. A sonic and conceptual opposition between the records played on the radio and the film's electronic incidental music structure the film's soundtrack.[6] Michel Chion points to the importance of the radio station certain sections of *The Fog*, where it remains constant and ubiquitous, traversing the diegetic locations of the film. He notes that the compassionate disembodied voice of Wayne unifies and saves those under threat despite her isolation (Chion 1999: 118–119). Her voice marks certainly a significant aspect of narrative development, interspersed with a selection of banal recordings, verging on Muzak.[7] However, the music on the radio also serves a notable function, one that makes for a complex relationship with *The Fog*'s incidental score. The diegetic (but off-screen) and non-diegetic music form a matrix of sorts. A notable opposition exists between the two musical formats, each with different functions, qualities, and effects. However, the associations reverse, where the music on the radio, originally conceived as

emotional or sentimental, finds its function converted to that of emotionless music. As part of this process, the film's electronic underscore, which
uses sounds that traditionally have not been accorded sentimental status,
becomes the chief sonic emotional element.

Radio records	Electronics
Diegetic	Non-diegetic
Mostly jazz recordings	Functional incidental music
Cheap sentiment	Emotionless
"Background noise"	Affecting sound

The broad schematic division of the two different musical discourses in
The Fog not only illustrates their radically different characters but also
differentiates their functions and effects within the film. The radio's music
embodies the human: organic, weak and fallible in contrast with the synthetic sonic embodiment of the supernatural, killing machines, which
appear to be highly efficient (perhaps like the "machines" of the synthesizers). Furthermore, the pieces of music on the radio are compromised,
existing in the film as fragments without their fullness.[8] While musical
underscores traditionally have been thought of as simply "background"
or "wallpaper," *The Fog* includes music on the radio as precisely the sort
of banal background music which might have been related to film music of
the most undistinguished kind. Indeed, Claudia Gorbman noted the similarities between film incidental music and Muzak (1987: 56–59). While
the radio music is associated with sentiment, its use in the film is without
sentiment: precisely as an absence of emotion. Conversely, the synthesizer
music of the underscore, a type of music which is normally associated
with the mechanical and unemotional, works in the film to make direct
emotional effects.

The processes that govern the use of these two musical discourses
in *The Fog* are dominated by superimposition and displacement, where
the electronics override records (and vice versa). These are not traditional "musical" developments. Indeed, David Burnand and Miguel
Mera point to there being little "musical" development in Carpenter's
music (Burnand and Mera 2004: 60). Instead, one might argue, these
procedures emanate from the recording process, an aspect at the heart
of film scoring even if it is rarely acknowledged by film music composers or scholars. While broadly speaking Burnand and Mera are correct,
Carpenter's music forms a complex dialogue with diegetic music and
diegetic sound effects. Indeed, diegetic music can take on a dramatic
significance in the occasional absence of underscore. The sequence of
weatherman Dan being killed by the ghosts at the weather station has

no incidental music but instead the anempathetic music from the radio station.[9] The anodyne character of the music functions particularly effectively in this situation, and in the aftermath of the attack continues without inspiring pity.

The records played on the radio throughout the film include swing, cool jazz, jazz-funk, Dixieland jazz and other pieces, all of which take on something of the generic in their character. It all comes across as emotionless, soporific music, what might be deemed "sound filler" or aural wallpaper. Of course, this is precisely the sort of pejorative description that has been levelled at incidental music in film over the years. I find it impossible to regard the music as distinct pieces, which, I would argue, is precisely the intention of the film: to create a bland and soporific musical backdrop that illustrates a characterless continuum, an easy listening "much of a muchness." One might say that it is precisely "not music." Now, of course, electronic music was often also dismissed as "not music" in the 1970s and earlier. There was a persistent assumption that playing synthesizers required no musical ability.[10] It is easy to make an assumption that Carpenter's music is unsophisticated "one-finger" synthesizer playing, but this would be erroneous. During the 1970s, and even more strikingly during the 1980s, keyboard synthesizers became more accessible: both becoming easier to play and program, as well as becoming dramatically cheaper and more available. The proliferation of synth-pop in the late 1970s, such as Gary Numan, The Normal, The Human League, Soft Cell, and Depeche Mode is testament to the paramount importance of technological and production developments of the time. The limitations of musicians are often very evident in this sort of music, although not important.[11] For instance, the Human League's top-selling *Dare* (1981) album was completed with keyboard synthesizers played by people with no training on keyboards. However, the nature of the instruments themselves – which often allowed only one note to be played at a time – precluded the sort of keyboard playing that a trained organist or pianist might perform. The nature of the hardware allied often with untrained and naïve musicians led to a "path of least resistance" approach to synthesizers at this point, and their "presets" of voices dominated over more sophisticated programming of sounds. Yet the instruments nevertheless tended to showcase sound qualities which arguably dominate melodic and harmonic concerns. Now, while the technology to a lesser or greater degree decided how it will be used, as evidenced by the propensity for clear and distinctive timbres and tones, this should not be mistaken for widespread "simplicity" or blanket lack of musical knowledge or ability.

Carpenter's official website fails to note which synthesizers were used for *The Fog*'s soundtrack.[12] However, due to the distinctiveness of the sound, it is most likely that they were Moog synthesizers rather than the

Prophet 5 and ARP synthesizers he used later. Carpenter tends to use regular collaborators on his film soundtracks. Alan Howarth began collaborating with Carpenter on *Escape from New York* (1981), which uses ARP synthesizers, and has a qualitatively different sound from Carpenter's earlier films.[13] For *The Fog*, Dan Wyman was credited as "orchestrator" (as he was on *Halloween* in 1978) and for "electronic realization."[14] The use of Moog synthesizers characterizes this earlier period; the difference is not insignificant. A perusal of progressive rock or electronic "space music" records of the 1970s should illustrate the significance of different synthesizer hardware, which musicians listed precisely as if each brand of synthesizer were a wholly different instrument. Their sounds and "feel" as an instrument are often profoundly different, despite their following a similar basic physiology and sonic logic.

The likely synthesizer was not the Mini Moog but a Moog Series 3. The former was a mass-produced instrument with a simplified programming capability in comparison with the earlier Series 3. This, along with Carpenter's aid from specialist synthesizer players, illustrates that the music is far more than "one finger" simplicity. Upon closer inspection, Carpenter's score for *The Fog* betrays far more sophistication than might be noted upon a shallow engagement. Musical themes are less important than manipulating sound qualities and textures. Indeed, it is interested in exploiting the capabilities of synthesizers rather simply than pumping away at single notes as a basic accompaniment to the image.

The process of analogue synthesis takes place wholly electronically and has its foundation in the manipulation of an electronic speaker often with a keyboard controller (or pre-programmed "sequencer"). The process involves at least one oscillator that provides a basic waveform that often will then be modified by modulating the signal with another signal, and "cleaned up" and adapted by filtering out overtones. In 1970s synthesizers, these operations are all voltage-controlled. This procedure is usually known as subtractive synthesis and leads to highly distinctive timbres.[15] I would like to suggest a high degree of technological determinism in the music of *The Fog*. The current orthodoxy in the humanities persists in human-centred approaches at the expense of all else. Such hyper-humanism finds it difficult to see processes that evacuate human activity as having much validity. It is not terribly fashionable to point to the foundations in human physiology of music (or indeed other culture). Primary sounds include the rhythmic pumping of blood in our veins and the slower rhythm of our breathing, while we are permanently attached to the high-pitched whine of our nervous system. Furthermore, perhaps such sustained sounds might be related to tinnitus, a physical disorder of the ear that gives an impulse of resonance and focuses on often painful noise.[16]

The drones that grace *The Fog* clearly equate with foghorns on a symbolic-representational level. That is the logic of their foundation as music for the film. However, and more importantly, there is an equivalence between the fog in the film and the drones in the incidental music. This is beyond mere representation. It has something of the character of diegetic sound effects rather than non-diegetic music. The equivalence means that the appearance of the drone without the appearance of the fog still indicates that the fog is present.[17] This Pavlovian response is highly reminiscent of John Williams's iconic musical theme for the shark in *Jaws* (1975). Such direct connections between sonic activity and diegetic action provide the music with the function of being a "non-diegetic sound effect," where the conventional function of diegetic sound has been systematically and powerfully adopted by an aspect of the musical score.

In Rod Giblett's discussion of the symbolism of wetlands in literature and wider culture, he notes the "taxonomic anomaly of wetland: mud as mixing earth and water, fog as a mixture of air and water. Water is thus a kind of promiscuous substance that gets around, even sleeps around, too much with earth and air" (Giblett 1996: 14) This characterization suggests something of the mythic resonance that the fog brings with it to the film. Mist and fog are thus an encroachment on air by water, and water commonly signifies the boundary of consciousness (or unconsciousness).[18] Perhaps the musical equivalent would be white noise, a complex of all pitches that sounds like a river or a detuned radio. This sonic "primal soup" might be conceived as a sonic equivalent of the unconscious, from which sounds can emerge. In *The Fog*, the film's stingers (blasts of sound for dramatic shock effect) consist of actual blasts of synthesized white noise, an absolute rarity in the horror genre. There is also an extended passage of music which accompanies the onset of the siege of the church, which consists of a regular pulse of white noise blasts, which have something of the character of explosions or smashed glass. Apart from this, the repetitive pulses are predominantly deep in pitch. According to R.Murray Schafer, "In stressing low-frequency sound popular music seeks blend and diffusion rather than clarity and focus, which had been the aim of previous music" (Schafer 1994: 117) The drones in *The Fog* certainly make something of a sonic continuum for large sections of the film, varying in volume and intensity and at times even remaining on the verge of audibility.

Sustained droning might be conceived as closely related to sonic repetition; indeed, traditional musicology has conceived of the two as closely related in that they use a minimal amount of different musical material (i.e., pitches, durations, and articulations) and might often be notated with the repeat symbol. Such music has often been approached as musically simplistic and not terribly interesting. However, repetition has its own psychology as well as its own aesthetics. In the context of film, particularly horror films, repetitive music functions to induce instant tension as well as having a cumulative effect of disquiet or extreme anxiety. While the techniques of minimalism have been well-established in art music since the 1960s, this is not the same as repetitive approaches in film music. Here, musical processes are never fully autonomous and work with the rest of the film almost as if it were an integral part of the composition. *The Fog*'s final confrontation, the siege at the church and immediately beforehand, illustrates vividly the psychology of repetition, where there is a cumulative effect rather than any specific value in the musical material itself which is being repeated.[19]

The Fog's music is highly distinctive in its approach to repetition, drone, and sonority. It is premised upon playing with resonances and sound intensities, largely through the use of varied volume and frequency filter controls. While this is a regular process in the diegetic music, at times it is also apparent in some of the diegetic music played by DJ Stevie Wayne at the KAB Antonio Bay radio station. Here, from time to time, the songs and musical pieces are treated to sound as if the radio is drifting in and out of tuning, giving a phasing effect and losing higher and lower pitches – in effect becoming as filtered as some of the droning underscore.

The use of fade-ins, as well as raising and lowering volume, supplies a strong intimation of movement in the droning music. Such a clear suggestion of movement, specifically a coming towards the film spectator, conjures a profound threat. It is perhaps surprising that there has been so little written about the sense of movement evident in some music. Robert Morgan noted the sense of distance, and the essential divisions and movement, between musical surface and background (Morgan 1980: 527–538). In *The Philosophy and Aesthetics of Music*, Edward Lippman notes that we perceive high pitch as close by, and that our impression of proximity or distance comes through elements such as high and low pitch, as well as the degree of surface detail and busyness of the music (1999: 27). It is a misnomer to assume that a sense of sonic movement is absent in films before the advent of stereo sound or spatialized sound design. While *The Fog* benefits from stereo sound, rather than relying upon the illusion of spatial placement afforded by different volumes in separate stereo channels, often the general sense of drone volume bringing the sound forwards or backwards in the mix indicates the fog's spatial proximity.

An illustrative moment of the music's processes takes place on the Seagrass trawler when the ghostly sailing ship comes up alongside and attackers come out of the accompanying fog. The fog's appearance is doubled by the appearance of a deep pulsing drone note (at 17:14), soon joined by a higher sustained pitch, which has something of the character of a jet aircraft engine sound. This two-note drone chord is then joined by a distorted pitch in between (which makes one of the most dissonant intervals to one of the existing notes – the tritone). The last tone "tunes in" (at 17:49), and then the intensity of the music lulls, making for a drop-out which leaves the quiet initial single note drone. The development in dynamics matches the on-screen activity, where there is a short period of repose before further action. The initial musical configuration returns with a white noise stinger, which embodies violence in sonic terms. The initial chord then returns with pulsing 4/4 deep notes and some white noise ambience. The middle-pitched tone (which is high) begins a process of "beating" due to its harmonics conflicting with those of the other tones. It then tunes dramatically to a unison note (as the ghost ship pulls aside the Seagrass), which halts the "beating," and then all fades.

The complexity of this piece of synthesizer music demonstrates that it is far from the simple act of a keyboard note being depressed and held down continuously. Upon closer inspection, the sounds are premised upon variations within the same note and with concerns central for density and textural quality of sound. Indeed, the manipulation of the drones with volume and filtering controls (regulating the degree of low and high-pitched harmonics) makes a startling parallel to the general procedure in subtractive synthesis. One of the best illustrations of this takes place at the film's denouement, specifically where the group of people takes shelter in the church from their ghostly assailants contained in the fog. At one point, the music drops out to almost nothing, through a process of filtering out the existing sounds (precisely like synthesizers filtering out defining overtones) and then returns, as before, very dramatically.[20] This is a process of withholding, which suggests that the droning music has less become absent and returned than been consistent and only been obscured from being heard. Such a strategy of withholding is remarkably similar to the general process of "subtractive synthesis," where filters remove overtones from complex waveforms to allow for simpler and less "noisy" tones. (Furthermore, there is also a processual similarity with the sort of withholding strategies evident in horror film narratives.) Perhaps the most obvious similarity is to the so-called "drop-out" sections in popular songs, where most of the instruments stop playing for a short period. This technique proliferates on electronic dance records, where the "drop out" provides a moment of respite but also anticipation, ready for the onset of the music in full effect.

The mixture of manipulating overtones and playing around with tuning (moving pitches upwards and downwards) leads to what is known as "beating," where the extremely close proximity of pitches vibrate against one another and make for interference of their vibrations. This is significant, as such "micro-tunings" (an effect of going "out of tune") form a fundamental dis-harmony and appear only occasionally in horror films as a device, a disturbing effect. It should also be borne in mind that the use of this technique in the form that it appears in *The Fog* might well emanate more from the particular characteristics of the synthesizers. Notoriously difficult to keep in tune, analogue Moog synthesizers had a habit of allowing pitch to "slip," particularly once the solid-state electronic components became hot. Thus, there is the possibility of approaching some of the aesthetics of the music from the point of view of hardware capabilities.

The Fog's utilization of a sonic continuum that embraces and moves between drone and pulse does not derive in any way from the tradition of incidental film music, but emanates from the basics of acoustics, furnishing a *primal* sonic character to the film. This process is far closer to sound design than it is to traditional "music."[21] This can further be underlined with reference to the opening "sound symphony" section of unexplained events providing a succession of distinct diegetic sounds, which takes place shortly after *The Fog*'s prologue, and marks an extended and extremely leisurely title sequence. This sequence ensues immediately after the "ghost story" prologue delivered by John Houseman at the fireside. The following section of the film depicts a number of mysterious incidents transpiring in the town of Antonio Bay, including bottles falling and smashing and untouched diesel pumps spilling their fuel on the ground. This involves an extended part of the film without dialogue or music but premised upon the succession of showcased sounds that is a clear homage to the start of Sergio Leone's *Once Upon a Time in the West* (1968), where the succession of sounds build tension and convey the boredom of the cowboy assassins waiting at the railroad station for their target. Both cases are clear examples of the modernist notion of composing with disparate sounds. It is this logic, more than any tradition of film scoring, which is the principal determinant of Carpenter's music for *The Fog*. Mera and Burnand note a blurring of the distinction between music and sound effects in Carpenter's later film *Escape from New York* (2004: 61). *The Fog*, a year earlier, evinces a similar sonic blurring, with music encroaching upon the traditional domain of diegetic sound for the purposes of terror.

One might ask, "When is Music Not Music?" The answer might be: "When it is film sound design." Of course, this could account for all music in films. Horror films, which tend to retain a visceral focus on brute effect and gain a reaction from the audience, illustrate the modes of film music particularly well, as music's role in film is often of a sensual rather than necessarily of a communicative nature.

In part a story of the sea's perennial mystery, *The Fog* also concerns a return of repressed past events. The repeated piano note that inaugurates the opening theme suggests and then doubles a clock ticking, thereby implying an inevitability or the workings of fate.[22] The fog represents an uncertain state, predating the solidity of the current world. The radio station plays a good amount of antiquated material, with swing and Dixieland jazz prominent. Indeed, it is striking that, apart from the odd piece, KAB seems to play a remarkably old-fashioned roster of music, which manifests an ignored "background," much like the origin of the town itself. So, the radio station's concern with a musical past parallels the centre of the story, about the return of the past for the purposes of revenge on the ancestors of wrongdoers.

There was a related soundtrack album, which later ran to an expanded CD edition with the addition of an interview with Jamie Lee Curtis, who had played Elizabeth in the film. As befits a scholar of film music, I procured a bootleg CD of the film's music that included almost all the music from the film and was twice as long as the official release. The difference between the two CDs is instructive. The official release packages the most traditionally "musical" aspects of the score into a listenable format which, if the listener was unaware of the film, might lead one to believe that the film had a strong set of diverse melodic cues. The bootleg CD, on the other hand, makes no concessions to moulding a listening experience and merely holds together the music that graced the film. As a consequence, it is dominated by droning cues and soporific radio music. The former exemplifies the pressure to develop "music" as a marketable resource, while the latter clearly demonstrates the music's function as film sound and its delineation of a psychological continuum in the film rather than any distinctively "musical" character.

Carpenter's *The Fog* was remade in 2005.[23] The remake "reimagined" the original in the form of a fairly straightforward mainstream teen horror film. One aspect that helped resituate the new film was the fairly "stereotypical" contemporary horror film music by Graeme Revell. His score was fully in accord with the tone of the remake and has some fine atmospheric moments, but it remains strikingly distant from Carpenter's music. Significantly, it lacks the relentless drones that embody the fog and thus loses the fundamental psychology of primal sound that makes Carpenter's film and music so disturbing and so effective. In the original version, music adopts the foreground in the film, constituting a *primary effect* rather than mere "incidental" background. This is exemplified most clearly in the way that the eponymous fog of the film is "sounded" by synthesizers, forming as much a *sonic* as a visual threat. Such an affordance stems from the properties of sound itself, as invisible, enveloping, and potentially disturbing.[24] Like my family's poltergeist with which I started this chapter, disquieting sound can generate a clear and physical embodiment of the threat of the inexplicable in a far more effective manner than mere visuals.

Notes

1 The film is full of cameos, in-jokes, and references. Carpenter appears as Bennett, Jamie Lee Curtis's mother, Janet Leigh, plays Mrs Williams, and characters are named after some of the film's technicians.

2 John Carpenter, sleeve notes to *John Carpenter's The Fog* (new expanded edition, Silva Screen FILMCD 342, 2000).

3 *The Fog* connects directly with the Val Lewton tradition of atmosphere-centred horror films.

4 The mix of timbres has the ethereal synthesizer representing the unknown counterposed with the organic sound of the piano that marks the familiar. These co-ordinate points place us into an "in between" state, emphasizing the "spooky" music as the sonic equivalent of a ghost story.

5 The piece sounds quite distant from the band's song in *Big Trouble in Little China* (1986), starting out sounding a little like Steely Dan and then ending up sounding more like Spyro Gyra. At this time, The Coupe de Villes released an album called *Waiting Out the Eighties*.

6 Indeed, there is a similar mix of diegetic songs and underscore in his later film *Christine* (1983).

7 The radio station also lacks the characteristic advertisements of US radio stations.

8 The radio's music is premised upon band-pass filters that remove high and low frequencies to produce characteristic lo-fi radio sound (also like a telephone), while the synthesizer music is also premised upon the use of a similar frequency filter process.

9 According to Michel Chion, anempathetic music redoubles its effect through its indifference to the action – whilst making apparent the mechanical character of film (1994: 8–9).

10 Indeed, synthesizers regularly were approaches as if they were "machines." This is dramatized by Kraftwerk's song *Pocket Calculator*. "I'm the operator with my pocket calculator," in the German version is rendered as: "Ich bin der Musikant, mit Taschenrechner in der Hand" ("I'm the musician ..."). Apart from merely enabling the rhyme, this suggests that in Germany there was less of a sense of synthesizers being "unmusical" and operated by technicians rather than musicians.

11 Robert Walser notes that trained musicians often fail to register strategies for producing music outside the logic of "trained" musicianship (1995: 198).

12 www.theofficialjohncarpenter.com [accessed 2 May 2008].

13 Howarth worked on special sound effects for the first *Star Trek* films, and also as a sound designer and supervising sound editor on various films.

14 Carpenter and Wyman play the synthesizers although the music credit in the film is to the "Bowling Green Wayne County Chamber Orchestra."

15 They are very good at certain things – indeed, vintage analogue synthesizers are highly prized today for bass sounds. This is in stark contrast to the seventies fear (actually a perennial fear) that analogue synthesizers would simply replace the use of other instruments.

16 John Cage wrote about hearing these two primal sounds upon entering an anechoic chamber at Harvard University (1980: 8).

17 The fog's first appearance cues drone, but this remains in cut-away shots of Stevie Wayne at the lighthouse.

18 Another good example of this is the appearance of amphibious Marshmen at the fogbound "Mistfall" in the *Doctor Who* story "Full Circle" (1980), which also were accompanied by repetitive electronic music.

19 Incidental music in film regularly follows a clear pattern of tension and release which is less straightforward in minimalist art music. Robert Fink notes a focus by analysts on minimalism as non-dialectical and related to Freud's death instinct, a reaction to the compulsion to repeat (2005: 5).
20 Claudia Gorbman notes the "tom tom" rhythm of regular repeated beats with a strong emphasis on the first, which is represents Native Americans and their music in traditional Hollywood film scores. Its clear appearance here might point to the ghosts as a metaphor for those displaced by the "manifest destiny" of the settlement and creation of the United States (2000: 235).
21 In terms of mixing music and sound effects, an argument certainly might be made that horror films have done this regularly, almost as a matter of course.
22 A similar instance of tension and the implication of a ticking clock in the music is detailed in Lerner (2005: 158).
23 Carpenter and Debra Hill were among the film's producers; the film was directed by Rupert Wainwright.
24 See further discussion in Donnelly (2005: 88–110).

Bibliography

Bordwell, David, and Janet Staiger, "Since 1960: The Persistence of a Mode of Film Practice" in David Bordwell, Janet Staiger, and Kristin Thompson, *The Classical Hollywood Cinema: Film Style and Mode of Production to 1960* (London: Routledge, 1985).

Brophy, Philip, *100 Modern Soundtracks* (London: BFI, 2004).

Burnand, David, and Miguel Mera, "Fast and Cheap? The Film Music of John Carpenter" in Ian Conrich, and David Woods, eds., *The Cinema of John Carpenter: The Technique of Terror* (London: Wallflower, 2004).

Cage, John, *Silence: Lectures and Writings* (London: Marion Boyars, 1980).

Chion, Michel, *Audio-Vision: Sound on Screen*, edited and translated by Claudia Gorbman (New York: University of Columbia Press, 1994).

Chion, Michel, *The Voice in Cinema*, edited and translated by Claudia Gorbman (New York: Columbia University Press, 1999).

Donnelly, K.J., *The Spectre of Sound: Film and Television Music* (London: BFI, 2005).

Fink, Robert, *Repeating Ourselves: American Minimal Music as Cultural Practice* (Berkeley, CA: University of California Press, 2005).

Giblett, Rod, *Postmodern Wetlands: Culture, History, Ecology* (Edinburgh: Edinburgh University Press, 1996).

Gorbman, Claudia, "Scoring the Indian: Music in the Liberal Western" in Georgina Born, and David Hesmondhalgh, eds., *Western Music and Its Others: Difference, Representation and Appropriation in Music* (Berkeley, CA: University of California Press, 2000).

Gorbman, Claudia, *Unheard Melodies: Narrative Film Music* (London: BFI, 1987).

Lerner, Neil, "'Look at That Big Hand Move Along': Clocks, Containment, and Music in *High Noon*" in *The South Atlantic Quarterly*, vol. 104, no. 1, Winter 2005.

Lippman, Edward A., *The Philosophy and Aesthetics of Music* (Lincoln, Nebraska: University of Nebraska Press, 1999).

Morgan, Robert, "Musical Time/Musical Space" in *Critical Inquiry*, no. 8, 1980.

Schafer, R. Murray, *Our Sonic Environment and the Soundscape: The Tuning of the World* (Rochester, VT: Destiny, 1994) [f.p. 1977].

Smith, Jeff, *The Sounds of Commerce: Marketing Popular Film Music* (New York: Columbia University Press, 1998).

Walser, Robert, "Rhyme, Rhythm and Rhetoric in the Music of Public Enemy" in *Ethnomusicology*, vol. 39, no. 2, Spring/Summer 1995.

8

ANGEL OF THE AIR

Popol Vuh's Music and Werner Herzog's Films

> Florian was always able to create music I feel helps audiences visualize something hidden in the images on screen, and in our own souls too. In *Aguirre* I wanted a choir that would sound out of this world, like when I would walk at night as a child, thinking that the stars were singing, so Florian used a very strange instrument called a "choir-organ."
>
> *(Werner Herzog, on Florian Fricke, leader of Popol Vuh, 2002: 256)*

The sleevenotes to one of Popol Vuh's film soundtrack albums suggest that "it is through the sensual experience of the music that the audience grasps the intentions of the director for the first time" (Gillig-Degrave 1993). German group Popol Vuh's music found a fitting place in the films of Werner Herzog, one of the leading lights of the "New German Cinema" in the 1960s and 1970s. Indeed, Werner Herzog's films betray an intense interest in music more generally. In *Letzte Worte* (*Last Words*, 1967) there is a lyre-playing leper, while in *Fata Morgana* (1971) we hear an electronically enhanced folk song sung by a young girl in a cave. *Land des Schweigens und des Dunkelheit* (*Land of Silence and Darkness*, 1971) includes the cutting-in of some of Hanns Eisler's score for *Nuit et Brouillard* (*Night and Fog*, 1955), while in *Jeder für sich und Gott gegen alle* (*The Enigma of Kaspar Hauser*, 1974) there is music by Lassus, Mozart, Albinoni, and Pachelbel. *La Soufrière* (1977) couples Wagner and Rachmaninoff to aerial shots of the volcano, while in *Stroszek* (1977) there is American country music and Bruno S's unique musical performances. *Fitzcarraldo*

DOI: 10.4324/9781003299653-8

(1981) opens and closes with opera, while Wo *die grünen Ameisen träumen* (*Where the Green Ants Dream*, 1984) also includes opera and even has a recurring song sung by the Australian Aborigine pilot (Tommy James and the Shondells' *Hanky Panky*) (Badelt 2003: 25). In addition to all these musical moments, Herzog's films have used the highly singular music of German group Popol Vuh to add another dimension to his highly individualized films, and Florian Fricke even appeared on screen in *Lebenszeichen* (*Signs of Life*, 1968) and *Jeder für sich und Gott gegen alle*.

Herzog

During the 1990s, Werner Herzog worked mainly on documentaries although he is still best known for the series of feature films he made during the 1970s and early 1980s. Uniquely, he managed to reach a sizeable public despite making very personal films. These films often focus on an "outsider" figure who makes a remarkable effort to break free from dominant conventions (Elsaesser 1989: 218–222). Herzog's feature films pose profound questions concerning achievement, humanity, human nature, and cultural difference. Some of his feature films are set in exotic locations that are problematic for both on-screen characters and the filmmakers. The use of these locations proves Herzog to be one of the primary film directors to have a deep feeling for landscapes, which are often foregrounded in the documentaries as well as the feature films. These strive for mythic and philosophical resonance. In fact, Herzog's films seem to suggest that we all inhabit private, dream-like worlds connected to our crucial spiritual dimension. This ties his interests to the tradition of German Romanticism. Brigitte Peucker notes that "more than any current writer, and certainly more than any current filmmaker, Werner Herzog is the most profound and most authentic heir of the Romantic tradition at work today" (Peucker 1984: 193).

Herzog was born in 1942 as Werner Stipetic, assuming the more aristocratic *nom de plume* (his professional family name means "duke") when he became a writer and filmmaker. He had something of an exotic life of travel and varied work and study, including doing television work for NASA and working in a steel mill. However, we should be wary of the stories surrounding Herzog's life, just as we should be wary of the stories about the gargantuan problems encountered during filming for, as Thomas Elsaesser notes, Herzog is the consummate self-publicist (Elsaesser 1986: 133).

Herzog's first film was *Fata Morgana* (1968–70), which included a narrator reading from the Popol Vuh (the Guatemalan creation myth), while its soundtrack included an eclectic mix of Handel, Mozart, Leonard Cohen, and rock supergroup Blind Faith. Herzog went on to direct *Auch Zwerge haben klein angefangen (Even Dwarfs Started Small,* 1970) and *Land des Schweigens und der Dunkelheit (Land of Silence and Darkness,* 1971). His first feature film, *Aguirre, der Zorn Gottes (Aguirre, Wrath of God,* 1973), starring Klaus Kinski, and *Der grosse Ekstase des Boldschnitzers Steiner (The Great Ecstasy of Woodcutter Steiner,* 1973–74) both had music by Popol Vuh. The latter was made as a documentary for German television and used Popol Vuh's evocative music to accompany sequences of Steiner ski-jumping in slow motion. After *Jeder für sich und Gott gegen alle (The Enigma of Kaspar Hauser,* 1974) starring the highly singular Bruno S, Herzog again returned to Popol Vuh for the music for *Herz aus Glas (Heart of Glass,* 1976). After making *Stroszek* (1976–77), which again starred Bruno S, and *Woyzeck* (1978), after a Georg Buechner fragment and starring Kinski, Herzog used Popol Vuh to supply the music for his next three feature films: *Nosferatu – Phantom der Nacht (Nosferatu the Vampyre,* 1978), *Fitzcarraldo* (1981), *Wo die grünen Ameisen träumen (Where the Green Ants Dream,* 1984), and *Cobra Verde* (1987). All apart from *Wo die grünen Ameisen träumen* starred Klaus Kinski, with whom Herzog had a fruitful yet fraught relationship, as illustrated by his documentary film *Mein liebster Feind – Klaus Kinski (My Best Fiend,* 1999).

Popol Vuh

Recording artists Popol Vuh were named after the Guatemalan Quiche Mayan Indian holy manuscript. Although it included significant input from other members, Popol Vuh was led and cohered around pianist, singer, composer, and producer Florian Fricke, who was born at Lake Constance in 1944 and died in 2001. He had been through classical training at Freiburg University, and taught by Rudolf Hindemith, brother of the more famous Paul. Fricke trained as a pianist but gave up on such a career and acquired a synthesizer in 1969 after being introduced to electronic music by Eberhard Schoener.[1] Indeed, Fricke was one of the first individual musicians in Europe to have possession of one, a Moog,[2] and it became a central feature of the early Popol Vuh music, played by both Fricke and Frank Fiedler. Early Popol Vuh were informed by late 1960s experimentation and technological developments, and the group's music exhibited a growing influence from diverse music from across the globe, spurred on by Fricke's youthful travels. At this time, German pop and rock music was beginning to carve out a place and identity for itself and began to be known as "Krautrock," first in Britain and then elsewhere.[3]

Krautrock might be seen as the pop/rock music equivalent of the developments in German film that are called the "New German Cinema." It manifested an attempt to create a localized form of the dominant British and American forms of popular music. As in other European countries, Germany had pop groups and rock bands that played music that owed its whole existence to the internationalized format. Krautrock, on the other hand, took inspiration from and attempted to integrate certain aspects of avant garde and experimental music, both in classical music as well as jazz. This included an embracing of new technology by synthesizer groups Tangerine Dream, Kraftwerk, and Klaus Schulze (the producer of Popol Vuh's *Sei Still, wisse ICH BIN*), the eclecticism of Can, the noise experimentalism of Faust, and other, more rock-based groups like Amon Düül II, Neu!, and Ash Ra Tempel. Almost all of these groups had little commercial success, and indeed, few thought in such terms. The groups that assembled under the Krautrock umbrella had little in common apart from the fact that they developed very individual indigenous responses to international rock music.[4]

While Krautrock tended to explore the limits of progressive rock, it had much less of an emphasis on virtuoso musicianship as evinced by British progressive rock groups like Emerson, Lake and Palmer or Yes. They also eschewed the borrowing and allusions to established classical music evident with these groups and instead demonstrated an interest in sound and rhythm inspired partially by electronic music and the avant garde. It is absolutely impossible to disintricate Popol Vuh's film music from their wider *oeuvre*. Their music for films is merely an aspect of the particular developments of their singular musical philosophy. Their overall output includes their film music as an integral aspect, and the following discography lists all their recorded output, noting the soundtrack albums.

Popol Vuh Discography

1970 – *Affenstunde*

1971 – *In den Gärten Pharaos*

1972 – *Hosianna Mantra*

1973 – *Seligpreisung*

1974 – *Einsjäger & Siebenjäger*; *Aguirre* (soundtrack)

1975 – *Das Hohelied Salomos*; Florian Fricke only – *Die Erde Und Ich Sind Eins* (limited edition album)

1976 – *Letze Tage – Letze Nächte*; *Yoga*; *Herz Aus Glas* (soundtrack)

1978 – *On the Way To a Little Way – Nosferatu* (soundtrack on Egg records); *Brüder Des Schattens – Söhne des Lichts* (*Nosferatu*) (soundtrack on Spalax records)

1979 – *Die Nacht Der Seele – Tantric Songs*

1981 – *Sei Still, Wisse ICH BIN*

1982 – *Fitzcarraldo* (soundtrack); *Agape – Agape*

1985 – *Spirit of Peace*

1987 – *Cobra Verde* (soundtrack)
1991 – *For You and Me*
1995 – *City Raga*
1997 – *Shepherd's Symphony*
1998 – *Messa di Orfeo* (live album)

Some notable characteristics of Popol Vuh's music include a concentration on timbre. While it might be argued that some of their sound derives from western classical music, their instrumentation was not orchestral and not the classic pop/rock band line-up either. Fricke played keyboards, often piano, and provided some vocals. At first the group used a synthesizer very prominently on the first two albums, but afterwards tended to use a selection of organic instruments. After the first album, Popol Vuh included a guitarist (at first Conny Veit and then Daniel Fichelscher) as accompaniment for Fricke, sometimes a female singer (Djong Yun, Renate Knaup), sometimes a sitar player (Al[ois] Gromer), and occasionally other instruments such as percussion (although not a drum kit) and oboes. The combination of timbres never sounds like pop music, rarely sounds like rock music, and often sounds more like folk music from some far away, exotic but indistinct place.

As well as using the very distinctive and otherwordly sounds of the Moog synthesizer, Popol Vuh also used another keyboard instrument, the Mellotron (what Herzog referred to in the opening quotation as the "choir-organ"). This had a number of recorded tapes of sounds including strings, choirs, and woodwinds, looped and triggered by a conventional keyboard to produce sustained sounds. The Mellotron had first been produced by small Canadian company Chamberlin in the late 1940s although it was only with the advent of more adventurous pop/rock music in the late 1960s that its haunting and unexpectedly distinct sound became more prominent. It was featured to great effect on recordings such as The Beatles's *Strawberry Fields Forever* from 1967 and King Crimson's *Epitaph* from *In the Court of the Crimson King* (released 1969).[5]

Another notable characteristic of the group's music would be its general lack of drama in favour of more gentle calm serenity. This makes their music highly atmospheric and engages a spiritual dimension. Consequently, their music was particularly suited to films that required an added dimension of feeling but not music that would provide kinesis and dynamics for the screen action. Indeed, the group's pieces usually tend to have regular rhythmic and temporal structures, being based often upon four beats to the bar and strophes of four, eight, or sixteen bars. Again, in terms of form, there is little sense of thematic or material development in the music, which is based more on repetition and gradual unfolding. There is also little sense of alternation of musical material and no evidence of the verse-chorus formats of song form that have dominated popular music. In reality, Popol Vuh did not really produce songs in a manner understood by most popular music at all. Most of their vocal pieces could better be described as chants. This demonstrates how far they were influenced by religious and ritual music and keeps them at a firm distance from any connection with the mainstream of pop and rock music.

During the course of the group's development, they went through a number of changes, in philosophy as well as in personnel. On each occasion, the group pioneered or at least foreshadowed significant later developments in music. At first, they were a group premised upon the use of synthesizers. Upon Fricke's conversion to Christianity, the use of electronics was halted and a significant influence from choral religious music was imported to their style. For example, *Hosianna Mantra* (1972) is religious and acoustic in character. It includes a *Kyrie* and is quietly devotional with Djong Yun's vocals and Fricke's piano to the fore. A number of the 1970s releases were settings of religious texts. Increasingly during the 1970s, Popol Vuh began drawing inspiration from diverse types of folk music, foreshadowing the explosion of interest in "world music" during the 1980s and 1990s. The sense of calm and serenity in their music made them a precursor to the development of "new age" and relaxation music from the mid-1980s onwards, testified to by Fricke becoming a member of the Society for Breathing Therapy in the late 1970s. As the group reached old age they showed an influence from electronic dance music, which was the only occasion where they were not the ground-breaker for a particular musical trend, as evidenced by *City Raga* (1995) including a "Mystic House remix" of the title track.

While it would be wrong to construe Popol Vuh's music as a negative reaction to the Hollywood blueprint of film music, we should see it as an attempt to generate a different type of music for films that have a profoundly different character from mainstream Hollywood feature films. Rather than write music for the rough cut of the film, their film music often consisted of pieces written for the film before and during production, along with remixes and re-recordings of already existing pieces, in both cases cut in concert with the film rather than written to match the exigencies of the film's *decoupage*. Herzog's films exhibit some defining technical aspects. As well as being concerned with dreamy aspects, they also embrace a sense of realism. They are predominantly shot on location and thus privilege a notion of capturing a "real" profilmic event. This Bazinian position[6] leads to a regime of slow cutting and spectacle (that is thus guaranteed as a "real" profilmic event), allied to a "primitive" film style, which matches jagged and at times seemingly "amateurish" edits, with simple and basic camerawork derived from a more *cinéma verité* documentary-style. Herzog notes that *Aguirre, der Zorn Gottes* moves "between what is almost documentary-style filming and these highly stylized frozen stills" (Herzog 2002: 80)

Discussing the same film, Holly Rogers notes that what she calls "musical stills" dominate and that Popol Vuh's music provides "an aural elongation of the terrifying static images" (2004: 77, 85). Through expediency, Herzog's spectacular visual style requires a form of musical accompaniment that will not interfere with the expression of the "real," or become a functional part of a standardized form of narration, like most film music. Popol Vuh's film scoring, while not requiring the discipline and craft of traditional film music is thus more autonomous, more an object in itself than music that (in theory) can only have integrity when combined with the image for which it was constructed. Like songs imported to films, the musical pieces retain a sense of their own organic unity and inner coherence as recordings that are able to exist outside the confines of the film. They are thus more "listening" music than "accompanying" music, which, of course, marks a radical difference from the dominant traditions of music in narrative film established by Hollywood, or indeed, much other cinema. Popol Vuh and Herzog are indifferent to film music traditions. Popol Vuh's music is not functional in the sense of being matched to action, screen dynamics, or providing informational "cues" for the audience, instead, it is wielded precisely for effect, for furnishing thick atmosphere rather than anything else. As such, it is not really structural, and not functional in the sense of developmental film music that retains a consistent presence but is more a momentary object, entering the foreground and then receding, leaving whole swathes of the film free of musical

accompaniment, yet making those sections that contain music into something significant. Thus, the music appears almost like a discrete attraction rather than as an integral part of the film. It infuses significant moments with an added dimension of atmosphere and emotion, lifting Herzog's already striking images onto a higher plane of aesthetic contemplation. Indeed, it is most commonly used for sequences of visual spectacle with no dialogue – converting film atavistically into the sort of poetic visual-musical spectacle of some silent cinema that existed before the advent of synchronized recorded sound, particularly the acclaimed film works of directors such as Sergei Eisenstein and Abel Gance.

The Feature Films

Popol Vuh's music for *Aguirre, der Zorn Gottes* consists simply of the same few pieces cut into the film. Three principal themes dominate: the first is the opening of the track *Lacrimae di re*, which is known simply as *Aguirre* on some recordings; another is the second section of the same piece, while the third is a quiet guitar-dominated piece. The opening of *Lacrimae di re* accompanies the celebrated opening of the film, where a long line of *conquistadores*, Peruvian Indians, and llamas snake slowly across a misty mountain. This is shown in a single take with the camera moving to embrace the whole convoy in both long shot and close up. This spectacular scene is accompanied by highly ethereal music. It consists of a Mellotron choral sound playing high-pitched chords, punctuated by an echo-repeat on electric guitar that marks out the second and third beats of each bar of 4/4. There is a *rubato* feeling to the rhythm, where strict time and coordination between the instruments is not enforced. The length of the opening sequence is about three and a half minutes with almost no dialogue (only a short voice-over where the music is turned down and then up again) allowing full rein to the combined audiovisual spectacle of the remarkable images and music. This discrete sequence, marked by music finishes with a sudden explosion as a canon falls into the river and explodes. This same piece is simply cut in again later for the sequence where Guzman (who has been dubbed "King of El Dorado") weeps, literalizing the Latin title of the piece of music.

The second theme appears on recordings as the second section of *Lacrimae di re*, where there is a *segue*, a rather rough transition, between two pieces of music of distinct character. This consists of deep Mellotron choral chords with aimless and modest guitar improvisations over the top of them and is about three minutes in length. This piece appears as an accompaniment for the entourage's movement through the jungle. Near the start of the film, there is a sustained and startling shot of rough waters that is highly static and takes on something of an abstract appearance.

This is accompanied by another theme by Popol Vuh, which consists of a lone electric guitar playing a slow improvisatory succession of two- and three-note chords while using a volume pedal/control to remove the attack (and thus the defining quality of the timbre) to each note and chord. This same theme also appears as accompaniment for a scene of the entourage's women at a camp by the river, a sequence where a former aristocrat now a slave talks to Aguirre's daughter, and for scenes with the raft on the river. The ethnic and ethnographic concerns of the film are apparent during a brief long-take sequence that simply "captures" an Indian playing the pan pipes on screen as Aguirre listens. Popol Vuh's music in *Aguirre* marks the film as very different from mainstream feature films. The opening sequence is stylistically as well as sensually remarkable, premised as it is upon dramatic long takes (including one of over a minute and a half) in long shot and handheld close-up shots of the entourage walking past the camera. This is moved onto the transcendent plane by Popol Vuh's music, which has a distinctly religious character through sounding like an uncannily defamiliarized church choir.

Herzog and Popol Vuh also worked together on *Die Große Ekstase des Bildschnitzers Steiner* (*The Great Ecstasy of Woodcarver Steiner*, 1974), with their music accompanying the ski-jumping shots, interrupting their silence. William van Wert noted that "The Popol Vuh score for *Steiner* ... seems to shadowbox with the visuals; it drops off when the jumpers soar, it rises in crescendo when they fall" (van Wert 1986: 70). This suggests something of the individual way that Herzog uses Popol Vuh's music – not to heighten tension in the mainstream sense of film music but essentially to cut across the image and add a sense of emotional and spiritual depth.

For *Herz aus Glas* (*Heart of Glass*, 1976), Herzog famously insisted that the whole cast were hypnotized before shooting (Peucker 1984: 184). *Herz aus Glas* alternates Popol Vuh music with historically accurate songs performed by the Studio der Frühen Musik (early music specialists). This alternation is evident in the film's memorable opening (and title) sequence, which runs for seven and a half minutes before any real engagement with the film's narrative. The Studio der Frühen Musik provide an unaccompanied choral song, which includes some short odd yodelling vocalizations. While it is wordless, it has something of the character of a *Sanctus*, based around tonic and dominant harmony. This accompanies a shot of a visionary called Hias. As he sits, we see shots of cows, mountains, mist, and clouds (some in fast motion). The music then fades out for a voice-over monologue about "seeing." This is just after four minutes of this opening sequence. Then there are shots of a waterfall, quite static, also through muslin/gauze across the camera lens, which furnishes an effect of making the image look like an oil painting on canvas. This visual abstraction is reminiscent of the succession of shots of turbulent waters to Popol

Vuh's music near the start of *Aguirre*. The waterfall shot is accompanied by Popol Vuh music comprising a sheen of electric guitars that set up a rhythmic and timbral density that is monochordal, without modulation. This is music as texture rather than the more traditional sense of music as melody and harmony. After over a minute of this, the music's volume is turned down for another, shorter monologue voice-over on top of the music. Once this finishes, the music volume is resumed as it accompanies more mountains and clouds shots and about 30 seconds after the start of the voice-over a guitar solo over repeated electric guitar backing ensues. However, this is a long way from the sort of melodic, screaming, blues-based electric guitar solo beloved by progressive rock bands at this time.[7] It appears more aimless and refuses to build a melody upon which to provide variations or to show off instrumental virtuosity. This is less an indication of a musical strategy for use in film than it confirms Popol Vuh's conscious lack of engagement with popular music tradition more generally. The music's rhythm becomes a much more insistent and swinging 12/8 beat during the guitar solo, while harmony of the repetitious chiming guitar backing alternates between the notes of two chords. This piece is available on disc in a different version as *Die Umkehr* on the *Nosferatu* soundtrack album *Brüder des Schattens – Söhne des Lichts*. The film's opening minutes are an unambiguous instance of Popol Vuh's music being used to express visionary aspects, engaging beyond standard sound and vision, which is precisely how Herzog has exploited Popol Vuh's music in most of his films. The music is not structurally integrated with *Herz aus Glas* as a whole and merely proves to be a momentary diversion, helping to elevate this sequence onto a poetic level before the film's engagement with dialogue and narrative.

Nosferatu – Phantom der Nacht* was Herzog's first big-budget feature film, co-produced by Gaumont (France) and distributed by 20th Century Fox. The film recontextualizes some existing pieces, such as Gounod's *Sanctus* from *Messe Solennelle* as Jonathan Harker rides into the distance, and Wagner's *Rheingold* overture as Harker passes through spectacular scenery on the way to the castle and Nosferatu first arrives in Bremen. In terms of Popol Vuh music, the film uses a number of pieces, some especially written and others developed from earlier pieces of music already released on disc.

The opening of the film showcases two principal Popol Vuh pieces, both of which appear on *Tantric Songs* (1979) as well as on soundtrack albums. *Nosferatu* opens with shots of a mausoleum. This is accompanied by the opening of *Brüder des Schattens – Söhne des Lichts* (*Brothers of Shadow – Sons of Light*), which is medieval chanting based on two notes a tone apart, increasingly supported and overridden by other instruments, most notably oboes and cymbals. There is a notable resonance and emphasis of

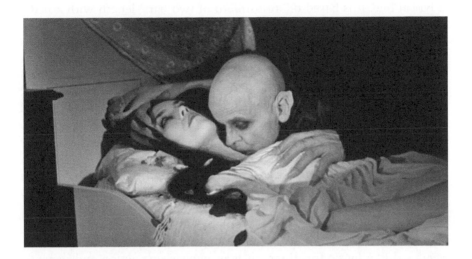

overtones on the sustained second note. This repetitive opening leads to a more orchestral-sounding interlude, led by a melancholy duet of oboes (and sounding medieval, Germanic, and vaguely Wagnerian), along with some punctuating by short Mellotron chords and percussion. This is not typical of Popol Vuh in that there is a clear sense of harmonic movement, particularly helped by the deep bottom line of bass notes played by Fricke on the piano. This insistent choral section reappears in the film as Jonathan Harker reaches the Borgo pass, when coffins are put on a river raft, when the ship is on the sea, and then for a memorable slow montage sequence which includes slow motion shot of a bat, Nosferatu on the ship, Harker riding, Lucy in the window, and the crewless ship arriving in Bremen harbour. This has the effect of seemingly starting the film again, signifying the onset of the next act of the story in northern Europe. On a more mechanical level, the music unifies a montage sequence of disparate images and different spaces.

Brüder Des Schattens – Söhne des Lichts moves from the Gothic choir of the opening to the persistent woodwind section and then bursts into an extended, repetitive, and bright acoustic guitar and piano piece, bolstered with an increasing amount of droning sitar. This section accompanied images of Wismar (actually Delft in Holland), Jonathan with Lucy on the beach, and Jonathan riding away on a horse. This is a lengthy piece of music, which is highly repetitive and fairly hypnotic, making little in the way of any notable development. The piano and clean electric guitar make something of a "groove," a sheen of sound, and the guitar then plays short melodic cells that almost make a melody but certainly never cohere into a lyrical one. It is based on an *ostinato* of two bars' length with a pedal point where the bass hangs a tone below the tonic of the single chord and after a while the melody is joined and supported by oboe. A section then ensues of alternating stasis and movement (where the instruments play a phrase and then leave a corresponding gap for the sound to sustain and ebb away), with piano, guitar, and sitar playing a slow melody in unison, before returning to the previous music. This whole structure is repeated again. This is hardly typical of Popol Vuh in that their music tends to develop in itself, organically, rather than being based on a structure of presentation and repetition. Indeed, Popol Vuh's music tends to be more organic than much in the way of popular music in that the group often do not follow strict song-based time formats and many pieces seem to develop in an almost improvisatory manner (despite their actually being written pieces rather than improvisations). With music that is thus conceived, it is easy to see how difficult it might be to twist it into more conventional film music functions, such as emphasizing action and thematic repeats paralleling action and making for musical coherence across a film.

One notable repeated theme in *Nosferatu* is a synthesizer monody. As Lucy sleepwalks, there is a succession of very resonant single synthesizer notes (played on the monophonic Moog synthesizer). This same piece appears as Lucy enters the warehouse and later as Nosferatu looks from the warehouse window. The piece is a development from an earlier piece by the group, the title track of *In den Gärten Pharaos* (*In the Gardens of Pharoah*), particularly its opening section. Similarly, as Lucy walks on the beach, we hear the Popol Vuh piece *Höre der Du Wagst* (*Listen, He Who Ventures*), as it is named on *On the Way to a Little Way – Nosferatu*. This very calm piece with slow solo downward piano runs was a development of some of Florian Fricke's solo piano work that was recorded as *Spirit of Peace (part two)*.[8]

Typically for Herzog and Popol Vuh's collaborations, the music was not written to fit action or screen dynamics, and hence it appears only once or twice under dialogue. The music tends to be used for spectacular sequences that lack dialogue or loud sound effects. This is common in cases where music has not been written for the momentary exigencies of a film but has been written more as mood pieces to accompany more generic scenarios in films. This is perhaps inevitable in that Herzog's process of filmmaking eschews the use of storyboards and tight planning in favour of catching the moment, improvising, and fitting the film together later from existing shots. Consequently, music is badly edited in and especially badly edited out, and this is highly evident in *Nosferatu*. On some occasions the music is just cut dead, while on some others it is quickly, and rather unceremoniously, faded out. This is not "bad technique," but rather an instance of Herzog's insistently "primitive" film style. There is some confusion surrounding the music for the film in that the film had two different soundtrack albums on different record labels: *Brüder des Schattens – Söhne des Lichts* on Spalax records and *On the Way to a Little Way – Nosferatu* on Egg records, both released in 1978. None of the songs from *Brüder des Schattens* are duplicated on *On the Way to a Little Way*, although some appear in different versions. Yet much of the *Brüder des Schattens – Söhne des Lichts* album fails to appear in the film, most notably the abundance of sitar-led pieces on the album. The contents of the two albums suggest a significant amount of music was presented to and then rejected or unused by Herzog in the final cuts of the film.[9]

Fitzcarraldo (1981) tells the story of an Amazon rubber tapper (played by Klaus Kinski) who wishes to build an opera house in the jungle. With the help of a tribe of Indians, he manages to drag a large boat over a hill separating one river from another. The film starts and finishes with opera, the first being Verdi's *Ernani* at the Manaus opera house and the end where Bellini's *I Puritani* is performed on the river by a company of singers and musicians.

The film uses pre-existing pieces by Popol Vuh, three from *Sei still, wisse ICH BIN* (1981) and *Engel der Luft*, sometimes called *Engel der Luft, part 1 (Angel of the Air)* from *Die Nacht der Seele – Tantric Songs* (1979). The opening sequence depicts the jungle and Klaus Kinski with Claudia Cardinale, intercut with opera in Manaus. For the jungle shots we hear the second section of *Wehe Khorazin (Woe to Khorazin)*. The first part of *Wehe Khorazin* appears when Kinski is sitting on some wood, and then the camera completes a long shot pan across the misty forest. *Wehe Khorazin* is a choral piece with bass drum punctuation, based on a repeated vocal structure. This leads to a guitar chord sustaining and the vocals changing to encompass wordless vocal chanting over clean electric guitar power chords with piano with bass drum punctuation and a little metallic percussion, that almost but never quite becomes a beat. *Engel der Luft, part I* has an essentially different character, comprising solo oboe which is then joined by another, playing a plaintive melody with some punctuation from bass notes on the piano.

Engel der Luft later appears prominently after the boat has crossed the mountain and enters the river listing and smoking in long shot. A piece called *Im Garten der Gemeinschaft (In the Garden of the Community)* appears as Kinski and Cardinale look over the boat and when they work on the boat. It accompanies a spectacular long take as the mist hangs over the boat as it rests on the slope and then we are shown the Indians working the capstan. It is also used when the boat re-enters the water after its trek across the mountain. *Im Garten der Gemeinschaft* consists of bass drum and piano with a solo wordless vocal, guitar joins as part of the rhythmic mesh in a major mode, creating a looped strophe of four bars of 4/4.

Chanting then begins over the top of this after a while, in minor mode. This modal character is also reminiscent of the way that blues gains effect through the tension of mixing and playing off major and minor scales. This is not the sort of tension that supplies a sense of forward movement in the manner of dissonance in traditional tonal music but marks more of a static dialectic, which might be interpreted as a homology of the film's backdrop of interaction between the Indians and the *conquistadores*.

Another piece, ...*Als lebten die Engel auf Erden* (*As If the Angels Lived on Earth*), accompanies the boat on river, then it fades out and subsequently fades back in over images of the town of Iquito. Its harmony is rooted on one chord throughout and it consists of a chorus-effect electric guitar picking short arpeggios, with overdubbed melodic guitar playing. The melody is banal in rhythmic terms and has something of an "oriental" character. This is borne out by the guitar playing without much sustain and thus sounding something like plucked eastern stringed instruments, such as the Japanese koto or Chinese pipa. This adds a sense of more general exoticism to sections of the film. Rather than allowing the music to depict a specific location, this paints a wash of global rootless, yet transcendent spirituality to the film. Generally speaking, *Fitzcarraldo* tends to use operatic pieces as indications of dreaming and the cultural incongruities of "civilization," while the Popol Vuh pieces tend to exemplify the grand scale of endeavours and the sublime of the jungle, river, and nature more generally.

Cobra Verde (1987) received rather less acclaim than Herzog's previous feature films. Again, it starred Klaus Kinski, this time as a white Brazilian who rises from abject poverty to be the Viceroy of Dahomey during the time of the slave trade. The film uses pieces written specially for the film by Popol Vuh and does not raid their back catalogue. It has its own soundtrack album. The opening piece has similarities with previous pieces by Popol Vuh, like *Engel der Luft, part II* on *Tantric Songs* (1981) – it has a similar harmonic progression based around a plodding, regular extended diatonic melody. The piece is based on an extended melody which is articulated in a basic rhythmic manner with each note falling on dominant beats of the bar. This gives it something of the character of plainchant and devotional music where rhythm is a matter of the expression of unity, rather than something for variation. On the soundtrack album, *The Death of Cobra Verde* is a different version of this piece, consisting of more prominent (*Requiem*-like) deep male choral vocals over a swinging guitar rhythm. Like Herzog's other features, music is still important in this film, as witnessed by the extraordinary diegetic performance by the singing girls of the Zigi Cultural Troupe, which appears less like part of a feature film and more like an ethnomusicological document on film. Here in these two pieces of music, two of Herzog's principal concerns are apparent: one with the convincing depiction of a level of reality in a film fantasy, and a persistent interest in the transcendent or religious, and cinema's ability to engage it. It should come as no surprise that these two concerns often are both manifested through music in his films, as both of these tendencies can be identified in cinema more widely, although in a less evident manner.

Conclusion

In the wake of his run of feature films with music by Popol Vuh, Herzog went on to direct operas in the 1980s, including Wagner's *Lohengrin* at Bayreuth in 1987. He also went on to make a short film called *Pilgrimage* in 2001, an 18-minute film about the feverish devotion of pilgrims at the Basilica of the Virgin in Guadeloupe, Mexico. It was part of the BBC2 "Sound on Film" series, which had been premised upon a close collaboration between a film director and composer, in this case pairing Herzog with British composer John Tavener, an artist similarly interested in transcendence. Herzog has commented,

> An image does not change *per se* when you place music behind it, but ... certain qualities and atmospheres in the images ... could be seen more clearly when there was certain music playing. The music changes the perspective of the audience; they see things and experience emotions that were not there before.
>
> *(2002: 256)*

Herzog's quotation suggests that the music clarified elements of his vision that were already there, yet the sublime and atmospheric music plays an absolutely central role in the definition of key moments in Herzog's films. The character of Popol Vuh's music never really changed to fit the film, it was rather the reverse: the film had to *accommodate* their music, which provided something of an essential character for the films in which it appeared. Popol Vuh's music has had a central role in Werner Herzog's films, even when it makes only occasional appearances. Music is integrated with the film in a profoundly different manner from mainstream Hollywood films. Rather than being written to complement a film that is perceived in production terms as a virtually finished object, Herzog's films integrate Popol Vuh's music as part of the artistic vision of the film, either through existing music-inspiring film activity or through exploiting the music as an object to which the visuals can be cut, almost as if they were an accompaniment to the music. The transcendental character of Popol Vuh's music also provides a crucial experiential dimension to the films as well, marking out the very singular status of Herzog's films as exceptional objects concerned both with philosophy and feeling. This is a "sensual" cinema – concerned with the materiality of visual and audio aspects – more than simply relating a story.

It is striking how opening sequences in Herzog's films showcase music and spectacle, most notably in *Aguirre, Herz aus Glas*, and *Cobra Verde*. These constitute an "overblown" version of the mainstream film title/opening sequences, which also allow some increased scope for film music. Yet in Herzog and Popol Vuh's case these sequences are precise set-pieces that can be seen to emblematize the entire film to follow. Music is not matched or written to fit the action on screen and tends only rarely to be used under dialogue, whereas it comes into its own for spectacle sequences, often showcasing majestic landscapes. Herzog's technical primitivism, most notably in terms of editing, is also highly evident in the way that the music is edited and faded in and out in a most unsophisticated manner.

Popol Vuh were a unique group, setting and inspiring a number of musical trends. They certainly stretched the rubric of "pop/rock" and were among a number of other German experimental rock groups who are looking more influential as time goes on. Indeed, some of the Krautrock groups, spearheaded by Popol Vuh, took their experimentation out of the recording studio and into films, which proved most receptive to individualistic music.[10] A concurrent trend in the cinema, the New German Cinema marked a rebirth of German national cinema (Elsaesser 1989: 2). Promoting a very particular character for film, including the rejection of commercial cinema and cohering around a number of film directors, including Herzog, Rainer-Werner Fassbinder, Alexander Kluge, Hans-Jürgen Syberberg, and Volker Schlöndorff. There are distinct parallels between the New German cinema and Krautrock, and perhaps the most important point of convergence between the two was the collaboration of Werner Herzog with Popol Vuh.

Notes

1 Composer Schoener received a degree of acclaim in art music circles, producing eclectic music that derived inspiration from the far East, spirituality and the capabilities of electronic instruments.
2 These were an early modular synthesizer, based on voltage-controlled oscillators and filters, were monophonic keyboard-controlled (a significant innovation) and produced startling sounds. Robert Moog developed these and made them available commercially from 1968–69 onwards. These instruments, in the form of Mini Moog, Micro Moog and Polymoog, became a staple of electronic and rock music in the 1970s.
3 Neu! produced a parodic piece of music called *Krautrock*, which meant to embody the stereotypical aspects expected of Krautrock groups.
4 Indeed, Daniel Fichelscher, Alois Gromer and Renate Knaup had been in Amon Düül II before Popol Vuh.

5 A notable Krautrock example of Mellotron usage was Tangerine Dream's *Mysterious Semblance at the Strand of Nightmares* from *Phaedra* (1973).
6 Influential French film theorist André Bazin declared that the essence of cinema was its "realism," that it has able to catch something of the reality it photographed. Consequently, cinema that was "cinematic" should be premised upon long takes without edits and a building of the film world through on-screen aspects (*mise-en scène*) rather than through editing.
7 It is vaguely reminiscent of the sound and articulation achieved sometimes by Mike Oldfield, notably on David Bedford's *Instructions for Angels* (1977).
8 This piano solo appears on the Celestial Harmonies release of *In the Garden of Pharao/Aguirre* (released 1983, 13008-2).
9 *Both* final cuts, as *Nosferatu* was shot back-to-back in an English language version and a German language version of the film.
10 It is notable that films had a hold on some Krautrock groups: Can's first two albums were called *Monster Movie* (1969) and *Soundtracks* (1970), while in the late 1990s Faust provided music for F.W. Murnau's silent film *Nosferatu: eine Symphonie des Grauens* (1922), which was released as the album *Faust Wakes Nosferatu* (1998), and included a subsequent screening with a live musical performance at the Royal Festival Hall, London, on 25 October 2000.

Bibliography

Badelt, Klaus, interviewed in "Shiver Me Timbres" in *Film Score Monthly*, vol. 8, no. 6, 2003.

Elsaesser, Thomas, "An Anthropologist's Eye: *Where the Green Ants Dream*" in Timothy Corrigan, ed., *The Films of Werner Herzog: Between Mirage and History* (New York: Methuen, 1986).

Elsaesser, Thomas, *New German Cinema* (Brunswick, NJ: Rutgers University Press, 1989).

Gillig-Degrave, Manfred, sleevenotes from *Popol Vuh, the Best Soundtracks from Werner Herzog Films* (CD, Bell Records, BLR 84 705, 1993). Translated by Diana Loos.

Herzog, Werner, in Paul Cronin, eds., *Herzog on Herzog* (London: Faber and Faber, 2002).

Peucker, Brigitte, "Werner Herzog: In Quest of the Sublime" in Klaus Philips, ed., *New German Filmmakers: From Oberhausen Through the 1970s* (New York: Frederick Ungar, 1984).

Rogers, Holly, "Fitzcarraldo's Search for Aguirre: Music and Text in the Amazonian Films of Werner Herzog" in *Journal of the Royal Musicological Association*, vol. 129, no. 1, 2004.

van Wert, William, "Last Words: Observations on a New Language" in Timothy Corrigan, ed., *The Films of Werner Herzog: Between Mirage and History* (New York: Methuen, 1986).

9

RAVENOUS AND THE EUROPEAN TAKE ON AMERICAN HISTORY AND THE WESTERN

The Canadian documentary *Beaver People* (1928) is not only of anthropological and historical value, it also featured the only notable footage of North American Indian luminary Grey Owl, who toured Britain in the 1930s giving lectures about the Canadian wilderness and First Nation culture. He became something of a celebrity and his talks were as popular as his best-selling books *The Last Men of the Frontier* (1931) and *Tales of an Empty Cabin* (1936). One of his principal attractions was his authentic exoticism as a classic noble savage bedecked in Native American costume. However, he was in fact born in Hastings in England, as Archibald Belaney, and had come to Canada nearly 30 years before his return to England. Although now fêted as a champion of early naturalism and conservation, his life had been full of fabrications and deceptions.[1]

There is also a cinematic tradition of fabricating America and Americans, through making westerns in Europe and with predominantly European casts. As Grey Owl's life and success visiting Europe as an ambassador for the First Nation illustrates, there has been a fascination in Europe with the American West and perhaps more with its representation on film. Westerns are the most characteristic of America's film genres, yet there was a thriving European industry producing westerns in the 1960s and 1970s, most of which are often commonly referred to as spaghetti westerns.[2] European film industries, when not subsidized heavily by their state, regularly have aimed at popular success in the substantial American market as much if not more so than the home. The flip side to the dominance of US films abroad is that Europe knows American culture only too

DOI: 10.4324/9781003299653-9

well, and feels able unproblematically to fabricate as quintessentially an American film genre as the western.

The British western *Ravenous* (1999) was partially produced by a Hollywood studio yet was a British production and registered as an international co-production between the USA, UK, Czechia, Slovakia and Mexico. It was produced by an English producer (David Heyman), written by an American screenwriter (Ted Griffin), and directed by an English director (Antonia Bird). *Ravenous* was largely shot in the Czech and Slovak Republics (some in Poland and Mexico) and starred an Australian (Guy Pearce) and a Scotsman (Robert Carlyle).

Two weeks into the production, Yugoslavian/Macedonian director Milcho Manchevski was replaced by Bird. It had music written by English musicians Damon Albarn (best known as the singer in pop group Blur) and Michael Nyman, an experienced film composer who is also known for writing art music. Pop star Albarn and scholar turned film music composer Nyman created music of a highly singular character and supplied the film with some credentials. Albarn's music at times is pop-influenced but also embraces an influence from American folk music and Native American music, thus drawing upon the authenticity of ethnic North American music. Similarly, Nyman's music also appeals to realism through an evocation of the time and space the film represents, a historical and scholarly approach which includes attempts to reproduce the performance limitations of amateur musicians. These "world music" and "avant garde" approaches mark responses to the universality of the classical Hollywood film score and have a strong tradition in revisionist

westerns. Yet, despite the surface of Americana, there remains something stoically and determinedly European. While *Ravenous* is highly singular, its music is also extremely characteristic and furnishes a large part of the film's distinctive identity. The film at least partly endeavours to negotiate the minefield of film and cultural tradition through its music.

Ravenous is a black comedy about cannibalism rejuvenating individuals through their being possessed by a spirit the Native Americans call the "Weendigo."[3] Captain Boyd (Guy Pearce) has discovered the life-giving powers of human meat in the Mexican-American War and has been sent to the isolated Fort Spencer in the western Sierra Nevadas in California. The appearance of a mysterious figure calling himself Colquhoun (Robert Carlyle) leads to a party from the fort making an expedition to a cave where he claims cannibalism has been taking place. It turns out that Colquhoun is the cannibal and he attacks and kills the whole party apart from Boyd who dives off a cliff and remains in a hole in the ground until he rejuvenates himself through partaking of the flesh of one of his dead colleagues. Upon his return to Fort Spencer, he finds that Colquhoun, now calling himself Colonel Ives, has taken up residence at the fort. Boyd and Colquhoun have a final and lengthy confrontation which culminates in both being caught in a bear trap and seemingly expiring. It is an unusual story with a strong cast, including Jeffrey Jones as Colonel Hart and David Arquette as Cleaves. The exteriors for *Ravenous* were shot at Tatranska National Park in Slovakia, with its evergreen forests and snow-capped mountains making a fairly convincing replacement for the Sierra Nevadas. Hollywood majors still dominate international film distribution and *Ravenous* was released by 20th Century Fox, although the soundtrack album was released by British corporation EMI.

Westerns and Musicians

Writers such as Jim Kitses in *Horizons West* have ennobled the western, deeming it amongst other things the epitome of Americana (Kitses 1969: 8–11), and consequently many film scores have drawn upon self-consciously American orchestral music, particularly that by Aaron Copland, Virgil Thompson, and Roy Harris. The distinctiveness of musical Americana has been held within Hollywood's industrial structure, which led to scores sounding fairly standard, being orchestral, by and large functional, and with often stereotypical music for chases or Indians (Gorbman 2000: 235). Hollywood western scores broadly conformed to Kathryn Kalinak's formulation of the industrial and aesthetic pattern of the classical film score (1992), although they often contained some distinctive elements. One of these was the regular use of expansive melody, particularly in the opening titles or for sequences of open landscape. A good example is Jerome Moross's main theme for *The Big Country* (1958), which also included another characteristic: a repetitive kinetic rhythm (with the suggestion of horses running quickly), which opens the film.[4] Scores can often exploit what has become accepted as characteristic western timbres: harmonicas, tom-toms, Spanish guitars, banjos, and jaw harp. There is a degree of historical veracity for the use of these instruments, as they were popular during the frontier period, and they were woven into orchestral film scores increasingly from the 1930s onwards. The revisionist western made some significant changes to the film music model established by the Classical Hollywood cinema. *A Man Called Horse* (1970) had a score by Leonard Rosenman that included Native American music alongside dissonant music inspired by Modernist art music, and Arthur Penn's *Little Big Man* (1970) had a soundtrack of Delta blues by John Hammond. Delta blues had no clear relationship to the western and works as something of a commentary in a film that might easily be construed as a commentary on the western and its version of American history.

However, the European western arguably had more impact on the aural repertoire of the western.[5] Ennio Morricone's music for Leone's trilogy and other spaghetti westerns became highly celebrated and emphasized a Mexican aspect with use of the shrill mariachi trumpet, although Morricone used many disparate but characteristic elements, such as whistling and other vocal effects, whip cracks, organ, and electric guitars.[6] For instance, *For a Few Dollars More* (*Per qualche dollaro in più*, 1965) had a main theme that mixes the sound of a chiming music box melody with twangy electric guitar and Gothic organ perhaps inspired by Bach's *Toccata and Fugue in D Minor*. Morricone's influence cannot be underestimated, yet much in the way of music for westerns sounds traditional, the way we might expect music for westerns to sound – i.e. a customary Hollywood film score but with specific western aspects featured in it. There is an Italian tradition of bold film music, mixed loud in post-production. Christopher Wagstaff notes that "(t)he music of the spaghetti western was important in signaling to inattentive viewers the moments when they should pay attention" (Wagstaff 1992: 254). Leone and Morricone went on to a larger budget western, shot in the US, *Once Upon a Time in the West* (*C'era una volta il West*, 1968). Uniquely, this had different themes representing the film's three principal characters, each with a distinctive timbre: high soaring wordless female vocal, banjo, and harmonica with some artificial reverb. The music was written before shooting began and was played constantly on set, and then the images were cut to the music. *Once Upon a Time in the West*'s music has proven influential, and whilst retaining Morricone's signature the music arguably included a degree of return to elements of traditional western scores.

Generally speaking, the Hollywood tradition for incidental music in westerns involved the use of broad, sweeping melodies, with bold uncomplicated harmonies. Many of the melodies were either derived from or inspired by Presbyterian hymns or Appalachian folk songs often of Anglo-Scots-Irish origin, while occasional instrumental timbres were the sort of thing that might have been found on the prairie (jaw harps, harmonicas, banjos, or acoustic guitars). However, *Ravenous* has some musical aspects alien to the broad tradition, both of the Hollywood mainstream and the spaghetti western. These comprise playing out of tune – a taboo in almost all recorded music – and electronic music, which traditionally has been corralled into modern or futuristic films rather than those set in the middle of the 19th century in the American West.[7] The choice of two distinctive musicians as composers indicates that the producers were aiming at a non-standard product rather than an unremarkable invisible Hollywood-style score. Indeed, the two musicians were an inspired choice as composers for the film. Albarn was engaged initially but was thought to need aid from a more seasoned film composer.[8] Nyman had worked with Albarn recently and the score for *Ravenous* was a partnership, although it seems that each cue was written by one or the other rather than the project being a full collaboration. Albarn began working on the film before Nyman, choosing his scenes and writing music, leaving Nyman to write the remaining cues.[9] There was separate writing but collaborative rehearsal and recording. Nyman conducted the Michael Nyman Orchestra, which provided a sense of sonic unity to the film's music. Even when the band of session musicians playing country instruments is used, the appearance of orchestral instruments manages to impart a sound reminiscent of Nyman's other musical recordings.[10]

At the time of *Ravenous*, Michael Nyman was an established film composer, albeit one with a reputation for producing highly distinctive music. Initially at least, he had an art music reputation.[11] As a film composer, he has, as Ap Sion notes, a "belief that film music is central rather than incidental" (Ap Sion 2007: 185) and thus has not generally been commissioned to write a traditional film score. Instead, filmmakers who hired him desired music in Nyman's own highly idiosyncratic style, which was based on the repetitive character of minimalism allied to modifying elements derived from elsewhere, (or at least using them as a basis for his musical variations).[12] His reputation was established by two scores for Peter Greenaway films, *The Draughtsman's Contract* (1982) which reworked many motifs from Restoration Baroque composer Henry Purcell,[13] and *Drowning By Numbers* (1988), which made variations upon elements derived from the slow movement of Mozart's *Sinfonia Concertante* for violin and viola. His score for Jane Campion's *The Piano* (1993) was massively successful and added a piece of film music to the concert hall repertoire, as well as establishing Nyman as a top-rung film composer. Despite success Nyman retained his strong views on film music and has not significantly altered his style to fit mainstream films. For instance, Nyman has stated his distaste for "indulging in the pointless activity of musical pastiche usually found in the soundtracks of films located in the 'historical past'" (Nyman 1989) He also appears to have had little interest in genre music. Both of these aspects feed directly into his music for *Ravenous*, which avoids generic conventions as well as film music traditions for representing the past.

Ravenous includes some music that aims to set a sense of time and place strongly, namely some brass band music, although his approach is unusual. The first is *O Columbia* which plays as Boyd is given his award, and then Stephen Foster's *Old Folks at Home* (aka *Way Down Upon the Swanee River*), which appears quietly under dialogue between Boyd and Colonel Hart. Nyman is responsible for these pieces, which are played in a shoddy, amateurish manner. The second is performed by Foster's Social Orchestra, Nyman's own ensemble who were characterized by self-consciously "amateurish" playing of rough and ready versions of Stephen Foster tunes. On the one hand, this gives a strong sense of the sort of music that might well have been played at that time and in that place. On the other, it engages with Nyman's connections with out-of-tune-sounding experimental music ensembles in Britain in the 1970s, such as the Portsmouth Sinfonia and the Scratch Orchestra, both of which were premised upon musicians playing instruments to which they were not accustomed. The Michael Nyman Band also affected a degree of shoddiness, that gave their music a rough and ready character inspired by rock and folk music and in stark contrast to what some might characterize as the arid polished performances endemic in art music circles. Nyman manages to deal with what in most films would have been a fairly functional requirement for diegetic music by infusing his interest in non-professional musicianship into music that works as a historical signifier.

Damon Albarn initially came to prominence as the singer in flagship Britpop group Blur in the 1990s, which was eclipsed internationally by his success as part of the group Gorillaz in the 2000s. As is often the case with ageing pop stars, there is a tendency to want to diversify into other activities. Albarn acted in the gangster film *Face* (1997) which was directed by *Ravenous* director Antonia Bird and became involved in other musical activities, including music for films. He contributed a song (*Closet Romantic*) as well as Blur's evocative *Sing* to *Trainspotting* (1996) and after *Ravenous* provided some music for the film *Ordinary Decent Criminal* (2000) and shared the score for *101 Reykjavik* (2002) with Einar Örn Benediktsson (once of the Sugarcubes). Albarn had already worked with Nyman on a version of Noel Coward's *London Pride* for the album *Twentieth Century*

Blues: The Songs of Noel Coward (1998) a project that reworked Coward's songs using contemporary pop stars.[14] Although some might imagine Albarn was a naïve musical *ingénue* on a project such as *Ravenous,* his work with Blur was often subtle and complex, and apparently as a youth he had won a regional competition for young composers (Higgins 2010).

A film set in America in the middle of the 19th century might be approached through having a seemingly neutral score that merely becomes an unobtrusive aspect of the film's narration. On the other hand, the time and the place are potentially fertile ground for an anthropological impetus to a film's music. Albarn has exhibited an interest in world music, releasing an album of musical field recordings *Mali Music* (2002), and collaborating on the Chinese opera *Monkey: Journey to the West* (2007). Elements of the music for *Ravenous* betray an interest in ethnic music, which had already translated to a few westerns. Claudia Gorbman discusses Ry Cooder's music for *Geronimo: An American Legend* (1993) noting:

> In the 1980s, as exotic ethnic musics became raw materials to pass through the mills of global media commodification and consumption by western markets, a world music soundtrack began to stand for a style in itself, defining the film audience as much as the film.
>
> *(Gorbman 2000: 250)*

While on the one hand there had been an increasing interest in consuming ethnic music, particularly in Europe and North America, on the other, there was a desire for anthropological documentation of a reality of what was being represented. For *Ravenous,* Albarn completed research into Appalachian folk music, listening to recordings at the Smithsonian Institution in Washington DC. Following the typical musical division in westerns, he divided the film's music into music inspired by white folk music and Native American Indian music. For the latter, he enlisted Milton "Quiltman" Sahmi, with help from his wife, both of whom he recorded on a reservation performing traditional singing.[15] This appears in *Ravenous* when Native American Martha (Sheila Tousey) is looking for the arriving men. The chant is traditional, and a similar one is also used when Boyd is wandering around the fort in the snow supporting himself with a stick. Indeed, Albarn says that he felt like a custodian of culture after anthropological dealings with Quiltman and the reality of Native American culture (Albarn 1999).

Ravenous *Music*

The incidental music for *Ravenous* was performed by the Michael Nyman Orchestra, conducted by Nyman alongside a small band of musicians playing country or folk instruments, including violin, guitar, jaw harp, banjo, percussion, accordion, and dulcimer. In addition to this, there are some contributions from a female singer and the London Voices ensemble, as well as a couple of cues of Native American singing by Quiltman.

The score for the film includes a wealth of traditional western instrumentation, which imparts a strong ethnic and historical flavour to the film. However, Albarn pointed out that the dulcimer, which features prominently, was not an instrument used to any degree in the American West of the time, but was used in the score because of Morricone's use of it in his spaghetti western scores (Albarn 1999). The use of the Michael Nyman Orchestra means that the sound of the incidental music is often orchestral. However, the score for the film also includes instrumental sounds that are extremely uncharacteristic of westerns, namely electronic sounds and looped digital sound samples. Some of the most obvious samples, such as the strange, repeated phrase as the party enters the cannibal cave, have a distinctly inorganic quality. Albarn created the sound through manipulating a sample of an oboe with pitch shifting software to give an almost vocal tone. On this and other occasions, digital samples, when not treated with electronic reverb or echo, have a strikingly rapid release time; they die immediately, which is a key characteristic of the sharp cutting points in digital audio editing.

The film's use of the electric keyboard is also a far cry from tradition in the western film. However, it is an instrument that Albarn has given some prominence to in his previous music, particularly in its most synthetic manifestation. For instance, Blur's best-selling album *Parklife* (1994) has pieces such as instrumental *The Debt Collector*, a fairground waltz with a cheap organ sound (and session saxophonists, flautist, and trombonist); the organ start of subsequent track *Far Out*; and the opening of the album's closing track *Lot 105*. The tendency is to use organs as sustained chords, exploiting their particular static timbre over their melodic and harmonic capabilities.

The film's principal theme exploits electronic keyboards as well as more traditional instruments,[16] although in its initial appearance it is played by acoustic instruments. This piece provides the main aural character of the film, appearing at the start, the finish, and at a significant point in the middle of *Ravenous*. It is a striking piece of music. As the pre-title sequence concludes with Boyd vomiting when faced with eating bloody-rare meat, regular, almost mechanical plucks of the banjo on E and D sharp, a Major 7th higher alternate with the first note a bar of 6/8 and the second a bar of 7/8. This is ambiguous and an unusual musical foundation for the principal theme of a film, which often will have something defining for the character of the film and an indication of what audiences might expect.

This bed of banjo is joined by an accordion playing a pentatonic melody. However, the structures of the music are uneven and work across each other. This piece is in E Major but the banjo suggests more a modal rather than tonal usage.[17] After a time, a solo high trumpet enters playing the melody of *O Columbia,* the music we have already heard played diegetically by the brass band in dubious tune and timing at Boyd's presentation and dinner. The melody has a rustic character but its structure is not even, indicating a jagged eccentricity in the film.

This theme returns spectacularly later in the film when Boyd emerges reborn from the hole in the ground having become rejuvenated through eating human flesh. This later arrangement is slightly different. Its regular drumbeat is more easily related to popular music beats. The mechanical plucking is now played by the dulcimer and the melody played by an electric organ rather than the acoustic accordion. Thus, it is less folksy and more ebullient alternative (perhaps extremely alternative) rock-inspired.

With this piece, we expect regularity but the structure is not straightforward. The whole is 12 and a half bars long and breaks down into four-bar, three-bar, and five-bar phrases. In contradistinction, some of the music in *Ravenous* is utterly regular in structure. For instance, the most obvious example of digital looping in the film is the striking music that accompanies Colquhoun's narration (an extended flashback sequence with voiceover) about the misadventures of a wagon train and the onset of cannibalism as they shelter starving in a cave. This music was produced by Albarn making a loop of one bar of an Appalachian-style jig, and then adding a dulcimer melody with some flute accompaniment entering later.[18] Despite the digital loop being in A♭ Major, the two instruments occupy themselves between the major and minor key of A♭: the dulcimer melody is in minor, while the flute moves between major and minor.[19] After the flute additions, monotone strings enter and build in density, sounding very characteristic of Nyman's work.

There are broad dynamic changes in the music matched directly through film editing to events in the story being narrated and changes in the image track. At the point where the visuals change from the face of the narrating Colquhoun to the images of the flashback, the dulcimer enters with its slow deliberate melody and the point where Colquhoun notes that "things got out of hand" as human flesh was eaten, the orchestra enters dramatically, and the music ceases precisely at the point where he stops narrating the story. Despite the successive musical additions, the music is very static, and a strong sense of movement is added by the orchestra providing some loud and strident syncopated chords behind the accumulation of sounds. Nevertheless, the piece remains a repeated loop, of eight bars of 4/4, its regularity expressing some of the inevitability of disaster in the events being narrated. The piece has a formal character, with something emotionally cold about the music's indifference to the events depicted and its regular unfurling irrespective of the shocking events that Colquhoun is illuminating. This indifference is a musical characteristic across the film, and although the piece is by Albarn, such criticism has been levelled at some of Nyman's film music, which seems to have a coldness not evident in most emotionally manipulative Hollywood film music.

A notable moment where the music's indifference meets the film's uncertain black comedy takes place at the cave when Colquhoun has attacked the soldiers from Fort Spencer and then chases one of them, Toffler (Jeremy Davies), through the woods. This is accompanied by a fiddle-led country jig with yodelling. This is a striking instance, as a grave situation is accompanied by ironic and happy music, inviting the audience to be involved with the energy of the chase but remaining "anempathetic," as Claudia Gorbman (1987: 159) and Michel Chion (1994: 123) put it, to the plight of the soldier who is about to die. This dislocation of emotional tenor between the event and the music can often rouse an enhanced emotional effect. Yet here it does not. In dynamic terms, this marks a release of the pent-up energy that has been built up by the extremely dramatic previous sequence of finding bodies in the cave and the revelation of the

real and protean nature of Colquhoun. The music plays a valuable role in this process and while it arguably has the character of a disposable piece of music in the context of the film, it is also an almost anthropological showcase for the authentic style and timbre of American folk music in the middle of the 19th century.

The charge of emotional disconnection or anempathy might also be levelled at the music during the film's climactic sequence. This is a repeated loop of eight bars in 3/4 time and runs for over nine minutes – for the whole concluding action/denouement of the film, the confrontation between Boyd and Colquhoun/Ives whereupon at the conclusion they both die. The music is an additive waltz, inserting successive layers of electronic keyboards, electronic drums, synthesizer drones, and sustained deep bass notes. The onset of the confrontation is startling in that the music repeats with absolutely no development for nearly two minutes. The sound of electronic keyboards with a distinctive wobbly pitch begins at 1.19:43 in the film's running time, during dialogue between Boyd and Hart. At the point where the latter asks the former, "Can you be trusted?" to which Boyd replies "Of course not," the regular pulse of three notes of the waltz foundation commences but continues without development as Boyd cuts Colonel Hart's throat and then goes looking for Colquhoun/Ives.[20] It is almost two minutes before the first change to the musical *ostinato* when some echoed percussion and dulcimer enter. The piece again follows an additive logic, with each new layer of music accumulating density for the repetitive piece. In succession, there is a deep synthesizer drone (on E*b*) with a very modern sounding filter sweep (sounding like a wah-wah pedal) which accompanies the sword fight between the two characters, a descending high synthesizer line,[21] dulcimer, and finally vocal chorus. The entry of the dulcimer matches the dramatic appearance in close-up of Colquhoun/Ives with a red cross painted on his forehead, with the image track again exploiting the structure of the music. Indeed, this procedure has been evident throughout *Ravenous*, where dramatic events are underscored by the entry of a particular instrument in a repetitive (and usually additive) piece of music. The building of drama in the music is through an additive process that also exploits the cumulative effect of extreme repetition. The conclusion of the duel occurs at 1.28:56, when a large bear trap shuts loudly trapping both of the characters in a deadly embrace. The music that has been building stops precisely at this moment but a deep synthesizer drone remains and continues through the ensuing sequence, joined by a solo deep Native American wail, as the arriving general eats the stew containing human meat and presumably the Weendigo spirit enters him.

During this sequence the music develops very slowly. Each successive addition is a musical loop that builds the density of the music. The image track is interesting, including close-ups, moving camera, and point of view shots. However, as the list below indicates, developments are keyed to progress in the additive piece of music.

Concluding Confrontation between Boyd and Colquhoun/Ives

Running time	Narrative events	Music
1.19:43	Dialogue between Boyd and Hart.	Three notes rising in pitch and in waltz time begin as Boyd says, "Of course not." The texture is sparing at this point. Dialogue continues.
1.21:40		Echoed percussion hits and dulcimer tremolos are added.
1.22:45	Boyd cuts Hart's throat and a sword fight ensues between Boyd and Colquhoun.	A deep droning synthesizer tone enters and the continuous pitch is elaborated through filter sweeping which accompanies the sword fight.
1.23:34	Boyd goes out into the Fort's yard looking for Colquhoun.	A sustained high note enters and then develops into a loop of high synthesizer notes sounding like female voice playing a descending melody.
1.25:08	Cutting to a dramatic close-up shot of Colquhoun turning to reveal he has a cross daubed in blood on his forehead.	Loud dulcimer is added at the precise point of cutting.
1.25:39	The pair re-engage.	The music becomes louder, and rhythmic triplets in the voices are added.
1.27:45		Voices clearly enounce the words "Save Our Souls Lissa."
1.28:56	The bear trap shuts loudly, trapping the two fighting men.	The music stops at precisely the same moment but the deep synthesizer drone remains.

The table illustrates how closely the structure of the action and the music are interlocked. The music also has a highly logical structure, developing almost automatically with regular and mechanical additions of successive layers to the existing piece.[22] Narrative developments parallel musical developments. Changes in music match changes in activity, rather than the situation in most mainstream films where points of impact and important words are underscored and emphasized musically. This sequence of confrontation has some moments of distinct inspiration from Sergio Leone's spaghetti westerns, with the dramatic facial close-ups and slow build-up to a duel being reminiscent of the denouements of *The Good, the Bad and the Ugly* (1967) and *Once Upon a Time in the West* (1968). The piece from *Ravenous*, like some of the rest of the music in the film, includes a number of elements that betray Albarn's origins as a pop musician, yet the music nevertheless remains highly effective within the context of the film.

Ravenous contains some extremely long sequences of images and loud music with no dialogue. For example, there is a sequence of over eight and a half minutes from where Boyd jumps off the cliff, is prostrate in the hole in the ground, and, after agonizing, eats some of his dead comrade and then emerges rejuvenated to re-enter Fort Spencer. Music dominates the soundtrack, with few incidences of diegetic sound, with just a couple of spoken lines from characters. In one of the most impressive sequences in the film, Boyd leaps from the cliff to escape Colquhoun and falls down a slope and into a hole in the ground. Colquhoun then gazes off the cliff and a waltz begins, which is an additive piece with harp and eerie strings and short motifs, and described by Albarn as highly romantic (Albarn 1999). It accompanies a slow montage of the passing of time with Boyd setting his broken leg, Colquhoun looking for Boyd, and his final surrender to the urge to survive by eating his dead comrade. At 49:55, the music changes as Boyd emerges from the hole and wanders back to Fort Spencer. The waltz recedes and the principal theme begins with the mechanical plucking on dulcimer rather than banjo, while percussion creates a beat emphasizing the third beat of the measure. An electric organ plays the main melody and strings join in punctuating the piece, which fades out as Cleaves exclaims, "Boyd?" While the waltz does indeed have something of a romantic character, it is also rather dislocated and, through its relentlessness and inward-looking character, anempathetic in its relation to the action. The return of the principal theme, despite its mechanical character, appears much more emotional, particularly allied with the images of the film's protagonist triumphally leaving the hole and returning in a dramatic resurrection from the dead. The waltz suggests inevitable fate, and like the overwhelming majority of the film's music, retains a repetitive stasis rather than movement towards a satisfying closure.

Overall, the film's music is premised upon repetition, sometimes with a mechanical character and in terms of structure is usually additive and modular. There is a tendency to use uneven time structures. Rather than introducing a human element, this suggests a cold mathematical logic. The principal theme has banjo playing in alternating bars of 6/8 and 7/8 and has an uneven structure of phrases. The cue that accompanies the first appearance of Colquhoun at the window has an additive time structure, starting with a bar of 4/4 followed by a bar of 5/4 then an alternation of two bars of 6/4 followed by two bars of 5/4. It settles into the last alternation and is a bass monody of E and then an octave higher followed by descending notes, and embodies the strategy of musical indifference that is evident in *Ravenous*.

However, on the other hand, some pieces use very strict regular structures based on unerring pulses (such as the two prominent waltzes). There is a tendency towards heavy pulses and beats. Nyman's music is often heavily rhythmic and based on thumping beats, while Albarn's pop background has meant that he is accustomed to music that is based on dance beats. The music is based upon dynamic progression rather than musical development as such. It lacks cadences and closure and usually builds in intensity through addition rather than changes and development of musical material. The clear structures owe something to minimalism and seem to suggest a music and drama that is going nowhere.[23] This is a rarity in film scores, where the Hollywood model is based on less rigid structures and more unobtrusive forms of expansion. Nyman would not Mickeymouse or match music to action and is partial to music which retains its own integrity. This, of course, can be a problem in film, where music has to fit the film's requirements rather than its own. Albarn was not accustomed to writing to the image and tended to stay with an approach that had proven successful for him in popular music. Both Nyman and Albarn's tendencies lead to music that retains its own integrity. However, while this situation may not have been evident in many Hollywood westerns, in spaghetti westerns music often consists of distinct pieces, at times appearing almost unrelated to image dynamics, rather than being unobtrusive cues written precisely to aid and fit with on-screen developments.[24] Indeed, most musical cues occupy the foreground, giving the film a strong sense of musical depth. Loud music usually works to aestheticize images, rendering them more acceptable and the audience more impressionable. On a couple of occasions in *Ravenous*, there is striking music mixed low to allow dialogue and sound effects to dominate. Most clearly in the case of Colquhoun's story, the fact that the music is forced into the background is, as Albarn admits, due to his lack of experience scoring films (Albran 1999). Indeed, this would be one of the only moments where *Ravenous* would have benefited from a DVD score-only option, where dialogue and sound effects can be removed on some DVDs to allow merely musical accompaniment to image.

Conclusion – European America

The mix of scholarly and historical through the prism of modern technology, looking at the "real" past, makes for a curious mix. The dominant character of the film score, embracing repetitive structures, additive and modular development, allied to regular pulses but uneven temporal structures, is exceptional in any film let alone in a western. The music tends to be quite sustained pieces with their own integrity rather than music responding momentarily to film activity. Indeed, there is little clear evidence of a substantial influence on the music in *Ravenous* from Hollywood genre traditions, although there is definitely some from European westerns, particularly spaghetti westerns. However, across the score, there are a number of tunes that are either historical or pastiches of melodies that might almost be recognized as music from the American West. When Colquhoun/Ives cuts onions for the stew there is a quiet non-diegetic accordion and banjo country-style waltz that sounds very similar to *There's No Place Like Home* (aka *Home Sweet Home*, a song dating from the 1820s). Earlier, when the party make ready to leave the fort to find the cave, the incidental music consists of a banjo and violin playing a melody country-style that sounds similar to Stephen Foster's *Oh! Susanna*. Foster has been known as "the Father of American Music," writing such classic songs as *Old Folks at Home* (aka *Way Down Upon the Swanee River*), *Camptown Races, Jeanie with the Light Brown Hair, Old Black Joe*, and *Beautiful Dreamer*. He was writing in the middle of the 19th century – slightly after the film's historical setting.[25] Also, perhaps signalled by the seemingly assumed name of one of the film's protagonists, a partial shadow is cast upon the film's music by American composer Charles Ives. His orchestral music used folk songs and hymn tunes to establish a musical Americana, a similar raw material that regularly formed the basis of later film scores for westerns. His music not only included substantial quotations from song melodies but also utilized Stephen Foster's songs.[26]

The film begins with an epigram, which cuts to a fluttering US flag accompanied by *O Columbia*, which was an effective national anthem for America. This very patriotic inauguration of the film informs the audience that the action takes place in 1847 during the Mexican War. The film's very clear metaphor is of the US as cannibalistic, promoting the "eating" of rather than loving and respecting your fellow man. Cannibalism is presented as something Native Americans understand as an ancient evil they have avoided, while whites find it more difficult to resist temptation. The corrupting spirit added to the notion of Manifest Destiny suggests something evil and contagious about America. The logic of the film, though, is that it manifests Boyd's fantasy, although it might equally be approached as a European fantasy of America.[27]

As a film, *Ravenous* is very much a mixture of European and American impulses, while the music is more European in inspiration rather than following the traditions of Hollywood westerns. Damon Albarn thought that director Antonia Bird "brought a real European sensibility to it" (Albarn 1999). Bird herself said that many of the people in America during this period would have been Europeans and that the US was a "country made out of a lot of lost Europeans" and that Americans fail to see their past as being "European" (Albarn 1999). *Ravenous* depicts North America as an amalgam of European and Native American as well as containing elements more recognizable as contemporary America. This melting pot of culture is represented as an ideal by the music – not simply the inclusion of authentic music but mixing genres/types of music (art music, pop style, folk, traditional instruments, ethnic world music, and electronics).

Notes

1 He was not a total sham and had lived with Ojibwa and Mohawk Iroquois and cared deeply about the land, its people, and its animals, working for the Dominion Parks Service. Grey Owl was married three times without legal annulments and joined the Canadian Army during World War One but supplied them with false information (including informing them that he had been a "Mexican scout" for the US Army and was also part Native American). He is depicted in Richard Attenborough's film *Grey Owl* (2000) by Pierce Brosnan.

2 Initially, Karl May's western novels were adapted by German-dominated international productions but these increasingly were outnumbered by Italian productions of western films as the 1960s progressed (Bergfelder 2005: 67).

3 In *The Six-Gun Mystique*, John Cawelti suggests the western is limited to seven archetypal plots: the Union Pacific story, the ranch story, the revenge story, the empire story, the cavalry and Indians story, the outlaw story, and the marshal story. While *Ravenous* has some aspects of the "Union Pacific story" with its implications that cannibalism is a component of expansion westwards, it probably has more in common with the "cavalry and Indians" western. The military in this case are not opposed directly to the Indians but to an Indian spirit that possesses their number (one might say that some whites "go native") (Cawelti 1971: 19).

4 There was also, from time to time, the use of relaxed lolloping "horse" rhythm, which approximated the mood and leisurely pace of the cowboy in the saddle.

5 Although Frayling notes that Italian westerns did not aim explicitly to "revise" the Hollywood western tradition (1998: xxiii).

6 An example of Morricone's influence would be a recent Hollywood western, *The Quick and the Dead* (1995), which contained a score by Alan Silvestri that doubles the film's references to Leone's westerns with music that references Morricone in terms of instrumentation as well as melodic and harmonic inflection.

7 There are no notable electronic scores for American westerns as far as I am aware, although *Breakheart Pass* (1975) includes a short burst of electronic music. Musical anachronisms in the genre are often played as such, with rock group ZZ Top appearing in *Back to the Future, Part III* (1990) and Neil Young's electric guitar score for the exceptional western *Dead Man* (1995), directed by Jim Jarmusch.

8 Albarn (1999) notes this and the fact that some of the music had to be turned down to allow dialogue to be heard.

9 "Interview – Michael Nyman" at *Soundtracknet*, www.soundtrack.net/features/article/?id=53 [accessed 28/04/2010].

10 While Albarn used a digital sequencer, some of his music survives in a similar form in the film while other cues were orchestrated by Gary Carpenter who Nyman introduced to Albarn. Interview – Michael Nyman" at *Soundtracknet*, www.soundtrack.net/features/article/?id=53 [accessed 28/04/2010].

11 In the 1970s, Nyman wrote the influential book *Experimental Music* (1974), the first book to chart developments in the wake of John Cage in the sort of music that regularly failed to be accepted in art music circles as it was often confrontational or conceptual in nature. Nyman's own musical activities included playing and conducting on EG Records, which showcased many marginal and experimental musical pieces.

12 Ap Sion points to Nyman's *In Re Don Giovanni* as the origin of his mature musical style, noting compositional practices relating to musicological analysis and stylistic inspiration from pop and rock music (Ap Sion 2007: 10–12).

13 This derived from scholarly research done by Nyman with Thurston Dart at King's College, London in the 1960s (Ap Sion 2007: 22–23).

14 *Twentieth Century Blues: The Songs of Noel Coward* (1998, EMI7243 49463127).

15 According to Timothy Brennan, world music "remains a flight from the Euroself at the very moment of that self's suffocating hegemony" (Brennan 2001: 46). It is telling that Quiltman's singing is associated negatively, with the cannibalistic Weendigo spirit to the point where it might be conceived as an embodiment of that native spirit.

16 The main theme has a sense of irony about it that is slightly reminiscent of Nyman's music for *The Draughtsman's Contract* (1982) and *Drowning by Numbers* (1988).

17 The chords are primary (I, IV, V, and VI [relative minor]). This is more like folk or popular music without notable directional harmonic development.

18 The dulcimer tune appears later unaccompanied when Boyd and Ives/Colquhoun talk before they fight.

19 The play is upon the defining third note of the scale. Such attention to mixing major and minor thirds is a notable characteristic of the blues, like its parent black culture, an important American tradition absent from the film.

20 E♭ followed by B♭ a fifth higher and then E♭ a fourth higher than that, with each on the downbeat of the looped bar of 3/4.

21 It sounds a little like a female voice and runs down a minor scale, including a chromatic sixth, from E♭ to B♭ (E♭ D♭ C C♭ B♭). This melodic motif (in different rhythmic formation) appeared earlier in the film for the first appearance of Colquhoun, who puts his face to the window.

22 Musical pieces across the film tend to be structured in this way. Whilst pop music and Nyman's particular form of orchestral music often have structures like this, electronic "softstudios" or DAWs (Digital Audio Workstations) also encourage the construction of music in this way, as witnessed by much electronic dance music.

23 Repetition in culture is thought to negate teleological desire, be non-dialectical, antithetical to Eros, and goal-directed patterns of release that define the Ego-creating "life instinct" (Fink 2005: 5).

24 Indeed, the tradition in Italian genre films is that music can be bold and mixed loudly, often aiming to sound distinctive rather than aim towards the model

sound of high quality but similar-sounding film scores like in Hollywood films.
25 One piece by the Foster's Social Orchestra appears on the soundtrack CD but not in the film. This suggests that it originally was to be used but was removed in the latter stages of post-production. Interestingly, this piece is the only piece from the film discussed in Ap Sion's study of Nyman's work (Ap Sion 2007: 51).
26 For example, the melody from Foster's *Camptown Races* appears in his Symphony No. 2, Symphony No. 4, and *Washington's Birthday*. Ives's Symphony No. 4 not only includes Foster's *Camptown Races* but also his *Massa's in de Cold Ground* and *Old Black Joe*. Ives' Symphony No. 2 also includes a rousing version of *Columbia, the Gem of the Ocean*, and the hymn *Bringing in the Sheaves*.
27 Or perhaps even an American fantasy of immigrants being corrupted by something ancient that "turns them native."

Bibliography

Albarn, Damon, "DVD Commentary, Ravenous, Twentieth Century Fox Home Entertainment, F1-SGB 00323DVD" 1999.

Ap Sion, Pwyll, *The Music of Michael Nyman: Texts, Contexts and Intertexts* (Aldershot: Ashgate, 2007).

Bergfelder, Tim, *International Adventures: German Popular Cinema and European Co-Productions in the 1960s* (Oxford: Berghahn, 2005).

Brennan, Timothy, "World Music Does Not Exist" *Discourse*, vol. 23, no. 1, 2001.

Cawelti, John, *The Six-Gun Mystique* (Bowling Green, OH: Bowling Green State University Press, 1971).

Chion, Michel, *Audio-Vision: Sound on Screen*, edited and translated by Claudia Gorbman (New York: Columbia University Press, 1994).

Fink, Robert, *Repeating Ourselves: American Minimal Music as Cultural Practice* (Berkeley, CA: University of California Press, 2005).

Frayling, Christopher, *Spaghetti Westerns: Cowboys and Europeans from Karl May to Sergio Leone* (London: I.B.Tauris, 1998).

Gorbman, Claudia, "Scoring the Indian: Music in the Liberal Western" in David Hesmondhalgh, and Georgina Born, eds., *Western Music and Its Others: Difference, Representations, and Appropriations in Music* (Berkeley, CA: University of California Press, 2000).

Gorbman, Claudia, *Unheard Melodies: Narrative Film Music* (London: BFI, 1987).

Higgins, Ria, "Relative Values: Damon's Albarn and His Sister Jessica" in *The Sunday Times*, 30 May 2010. http://women.timesonline.co.uk/tol/life_and _style/women/families/article7133293.ece [accessed 09/28/2010].

Kalinak, Kathryn, *Settling The Score: Music in the Classical Hollywood Film* (Madison, WI: University of Wisconsin Press, 1992).

Kitses, Jim, *Horizons West: Anthony Mann, Budd Boetticher, Sam Peckinpah, Studies of Authorship Within the Western* (London: BFI/Thames and Hudson, 1969).

Nyman, Michael, sleeve notes to *The Draughtsman's Contract CD* (Virgin CASCD1158, 1989).

Nyman, Michael, *Experimental Music* (Cambridge: Cambridge University Press, 1974).

Wagstaff, Christopher, "A Forkful of Westerns – Industry, Audiences and the Italian Western" in Richard Dyer, and Ginette Vincendeau, eds., *Popular European Cinema* (London: Routledge, 1992).

10

WHITE LABELS AND BLACK IMPORTS

Music, Assimilation, and Commerce in *Absolute Beginners* (1985)

As a form, film musicals perhaps should be approached from the point of view where the images and the narrative are seen as emanations from the music, rather than the other way round. While music and the stylized language of "the spectacular" are able to discuss complex ideas, what is said often is not taken seriously, and this is further compounded by the regular association of the spectacular with commercialism. *Absolute Beginners* (1985) seems interested in ebullient and uplifting songs and dances, yet it is also concerned with American and Caribbean imports to Britain while pursuing a format of making "history" along commercial lines.

Absolute Beginners was arguably the most glossy and glamorous musical the British film industry has ever produced. It was also one of the biggest risks of British cinema of this period: British musicals largely had not been popular and its budget was substantial. It was an unprecedented large-scale musical, a bold film, co-produced by the diversifying record company Virgin. Yet it was not the success its producers had hoped for, despite having one of the most expensively hyped openings in British cinema history (Yule 1988: 292). It was a culturally ambivalent film, being audacious in the sense that it was a brave departure to make a big pop music-based musical film, but a cultural retreat in that nostalgia culture and its concomitant desire to resell back catalogues clearly was one of its central motivations. So, while it may have been courageous in filmic terms, it was largely conservative in musical terms.

DOI: 10.4324/9781003299653-10

Cinematic History

History has been at the forefront of some recent debates concerning film and television. Robert Rosenstone's monograph *Visions of the Past: The Challenge of Film to Our Idea of History* (1995) and his edited anthology *Revisioning History* (1994) have elicited further research and discussion about film and television as a form of writing history. Hayden White, in an earlier response to Rosenstone, referred to "historiophoty" (history as audiovisual object) to distinguish it from historiography (writing history).[1] Historian Alan Munslow in his book *Deconstructing History* (1997) distinguishes between three types of historians working today. The first he calls "reconstructionists," who believe the past can be apprehended as an ideology-free "truth" (a fully empiricist and realist position). The second he calls "constructionists" (or "social theory school"), who believe that history is a construct, but the process of history is explicable through the imposition of a large-scale explanation that is outside history (such as Marxism). The third he calls "deconstructionists." These historians see history in terms of process and textuality and centrally are concerned with the manipulation of knowledge as a discourse (Munslow 1997: 18–19). While the ascendant "new film history" is often reconstructionist, *Absolute Beginners* could be understood as constituting a "deconstructionist" history (or a "historiophoty").

Before production, the film's director Julien Temple said "*Absolute Beginners* won't be a movie set archaeologically in 1958, it's going to be a film about now as well ... And that's important because that's when Teenage began and now it's over" (Matheson 1985: 8). Two central tenets of postmodern or deconstructionist history are that firstly, aesthetic objects constitute history as much as scholarly empirical writings, and secondly that in the absence of a guaranteed "real" and measurable standard, all histories have a distinct cast and can never be simply neutral. *Absolute Beginners* is a rejoinder to a 1985 agenda that had tabled anti-Afro-Caribbean racism and momentous economic change. It dramatizes and writes "as history" a significant historical moment – the arrival and assimilation of American culture (including consumerism and rock 'n' roll) as well as significant numbers of black immigrants from the Caribbean. Music is one of the main ways the film inscribes these.

Absolute Beginners provided a competing history of 1958 with others in circulation in 1985. However, the language of its history mitigates against its potency. First, it uses the language of the audiovisual spectacular ("frivolous" music, stylization, and colourful design), and second, it has a plainly commercial motivation. In tandem, these determinants tend to delegitimize what the film is saying by eschewing a "serious" mode of discourse about the subject at hand. Furthermore, *Absolute Beginners* provides a historical perspective from the point of view of popular culture. It is a demotic history. It speaks the argot of "light entertainment," popular culture of the time of its setting and this prestige-free level of British culture since that time. It is not only a musical carnival of different styles and artists but also a rich tapestry of popular culture references. Indeed, the film has a strongly developed esoteric discourse; it is run through with historicity, yet its points of reference pertain more to traditional light entertainment than the vast majority of films which espouse pop music culture.[2] The film featured celebrities such as Mandy Rice-Davies, one of the protagonists in the Profumo Affair of the early 1960s, which was later depicted in the British film *Scandal* (1988). There were also reports that Keith Richard from the Rolling Stones was going to appear as a "music hall cheeky chappie" (Matheson 1985: 8), although this evidently came to nothing. As well as pop stars like David Bowie, Sade, Ray Davies from the Kinks, and Tenpole Tudor, the film culled actors from light entertainment and who readily were known to British audiences. *Absolute Beginners* features television personality and dancer Lionel Blair, who had appeared briefly in The Beatles' *A Hard Day's Night* (1964) and disc jockey Alan Freeman, who had appeared in *It's Trad, Dad!* (1962). Blair's part echoed the figure of pop music Svengali Larry Parnes. In an interview, Blair declared that his role, Harold Charms, was clearly based on Parnes (Cosgrove 1986: 24), who had also been the likely inspiration for the Johnny Jackson character of *Expresso Bongo* (1959). The film's design certainly owed a great deal to *Expresso Bongo*'s vision of Soho and was strikingly set in the same period. Thus, *Absolute Beginners* pointedly refers back to one of the founding moments of the pop musical in Britain, the point where coffee bars were a cultural centre and a new Britain was opening, fuelled by the new popular culture based on rock 'n' roll.[3]

The Rebuilt Pop Musical

Absolute Beginners seems unique, yet it self-consciously follows – and self-consciously plays around with – the relatively young traditions of the British pop musical, an indigenous rendering of an imported American film form. In the mid-1980s, it certainly was a bold move to make a large-scale big-budget musical. Apart from one or two small-scale films like *Billy the Kid and the Green Baize Vampire* (1985), *Absolute Beginners* was the first big-scale adult musical attempted in a decade since *Tommy* (1975). Its screenwriter Don MacPherson commented:

> the very word "musical" would make a sane person reach for their gun after sustained assault by the Bee-Gees-Evita-MTV-Paul McCartney, multi-headed monsters of a couple of decades … It didn't make sense

to do it any other way than by breaking all the rules: mix it up, go pell-mell, swop vanilla for tutti-frutti with a cherry on top. After all, playing safe was bound to get you nowhere. By 1985 all the rules for making "musicals about the glamour-studded 1950s" had changed. All the traditions were up for grabs, with Prince, Brecht and Weill, Giuseppe Verdi and Gene Kelly all claiming credit where credit was due.

(MacPherson 1986: 23)

Despite the rhetoric, *Absolute Beginners* was a very traditional musical in many ways. It espoused the tradition of film musicals, specifically those of the glossy 1950s Vincente Minnelli and Joshua Logan variety. Director Julien Temple declared before the film's production: "*Absolute Beginners* will be a musical first and foremost and you've got to have dynamic performers. We need entertainers with … charisma. We need Gene Kellys, Fred Astaires and David Bowies. And we've got David Bowie" (Matheson 1985: 8). This statement underlines the continuity between musical performers, firmly connecting *Absolute Beginners* with the film musical tradition. A further example is where Ray Davies (of The Kinks) as Colin's father sings his musical contribution to the film, *Quiet Life*, in the Busby Berkeley-referencing cut away family house set, interspersed with dialogue from other characters and domestic activity such as vacuuming the floor. In an article about the film before it was shot, the *New Musical Express* noted the way that songs were going to be used in the film:

Working closely with Temple, the songs are designed both to advance the plot and reinforce the characters and ideas of the film: they're for a proper musical … An anachronism in the age of formulaic, anodyne dance movies such as *Flashdance*, *Absolute Beginners* will be looking back to such magical '50s musicals as *Guys and Dolls*, *An American in Paris* and *Singing in the Rain* [sic] for its inspiration.

(Matheson 1986: 8)

The pastiching of these musical classics is highly apparent in the film; the look of the film duplicates the glossily colourful musicals of the 1950s while adding the pace of action that had been commonplace for pop music and images since the proliferation of pop promos on music television. Director Julien Temple had started his career with the punk film *The Great Rock 'n' Roll Swindle* (1980), then made promos for Culture Club, ABC, and The Rolling Stones, and was convinced of the merits of involvement in music video ("pop promos") for filmmakers (Jenkins 1984: 231). MTV started broadcasting in the United States in August 1981,[4] and fairly quickly British bands of the "new pop" ilk, such as Duran Duran and Culture Club, enacted a British music video invasion of the American market. This gave a great fillip to British pop music culture, and the concept of *Absolute Beginners* as a British blockbuster musical film clearly was inspired by the success and proliferation of British acts in pop videos.

Pop musicals are premised upon assimilating the new and showcasing the modern. Thus, it is possible to trace some of the concerns of *Absolute Beginners* in a direct line of descent through British pop musicals since the late 1950s. Certain notions of ethnicity and sexuality have been tied to rock 'n' roll. While rock 'n' roll was seen simply as reductively "black" – both by conservative forces and even by some scholarly writers on the subject, *Absolute Beginners* similarly homogenizes black people. Rock 'n' roll in British culture has only rarely been tied to black immigrants from the West Indies, although it often occupies the same cultural zone as notions of imperial degeneration and postcolonialism. Pop musicals have figured British Empire decline and decolonization, in varying terms. *Expresso Bongo* (1959) is fairly direct in its depiction of "jungle music" while displacing any black performers. *Performance* (1970) – which might well qualify as the first British postcolonial film – thematically deals with English decadence and the influx of the "foreign." *The Great Rock 'n' Roll Swindle* (1980) shows off punk as a very English form of "degeneration." Finally, *Absolute Beginners* attempts to represent multiculturalism,[5] although selling musical back catalogues sets the terms of its historical representations.

US Imports

In 1958 Britain, there was a fear of American cultural "swamping." Not only popular music, but also American films dominated cinemas and American shows graced television sets. Landmark book *The Uses of Literacy* by Richard Hoggart was published in 1957 and contained a section called "The Jukebox Boys" which denigrates British teenagers who adopt American culture. This imported "Americanism" is represented explicitly in *Absolute Beginners*. Vendice Partners (David Bowie) sports a gloriously bogus American accent, and his agency represents the new commerce imported from the United States. This is embodied by the song *That's Motivation*, although the lyrics exhibit precisely the sort of jargon of sales culture that was infused into Britain in the 1980s.

The film seems explicitly pro-American. Colin says in voice-over as he enters Harold Charms' office: "Mustn't throw stones, especially not at Americans ... 'England for the English' and all that, but being anti-Yank is a sure sign of defeat."[6]

However, there is a fundamental confusion here: the teddy boys that represent conservative anti-American England sing "American" rock 'n'

roll! This contradiction is the centre of a faultline in the film's logic. Rock 'n' roll, the music that was revolutionizing youth culture and causing social approbation in the late 1950s, to some degree is denigrated by the film. *Absolute Beginners* has a whole section that trivializes rock 'n' roll by depicting the construction of a child pop star, "Baby Boom," by the manipulative middle-aged businessman Harold Charms. Perhaps rock 'n' roll has been displaced from a central position in the film for an ulterior motive, perhaps for commercial purposes?

The music in the film consists of a series of old "relics" and modern music that adds a veneer of jazz style to pop songs. Furthermore, the portrayal of "jazz culture" also serves to encourage sales. In the 1970s, there was an LP of Pink Floyd music called *Relics*, which sold for a far cheaper price than regular records. This is because it was seemingly an album of old and unwanted material; it was detritus, much of it recorded before the group was internationally successful. *Absolute Beginners* is part of the "relic" culture that was developing in the 1980s, where old recordings and styles were dug out from the attic, dusted down and then sold as commodities. The film mixes music of the late 1950s with contemporary artists commissioned to write new music for the film, the latter conjoining the two periods.

While the paralleling of 1958 and 1985 bridged social concerns of Britain between the two periods, the film was perhaps more interested in paralleling music of the two periods. Music and musical styles from the late 1950s and the mid-1980s are coexistent and intermingled. The appearance of some 1950s jazz and the rock 'n' roll song *Rocking at the 2Is* in the film work as periodizing devices in the film but its pop songs all tend to function as contemporary frames to the representation of the past. Pop music in the film constantly displays its contemporary (1980s) status while retaining aspects of historical musical forms. For instance, Tenpole Tudor (as Ed the Ted) performs his own song *Ted Ain't Dead* which, although it seems to correspond with the styles of rockabilly that were prominent in the late 1950s, owes more to the revival of the form that came out of the punk movement in the late 1970s.[7] Similarly, David Bowie's title song for the film, also the scout single and a hit, provided an entry to the 1950s from the 1980s, first in terms of its status as a contemporary hit by a contemporary pop singer and secondly in terms of its formal make-up. The song uses some jazz chord changes while opening with and reprising a doo-wop vocal section that is self-consciously modelled on the vocal style that was prevalent in some 1950s American popular music. Other artists, like Sade, perform music that was in no way at odds with her smooth style that comprised part of the 1980s jazz revival, while Ray Davies from the Kinks sings his song cameo in the mock-1930s style that is evident on some of the Kinks' recordings such as their hit record *Sunny Afternoon* from the late 1960s. Many of the songs in *Absolute Beginners* demonstrate a concern with historicism, with rearticulating the past and integrating it with the musical present. Original Sound Entertainment, an American licensing company based in Hollywood that had dealt with old records since 1959 and worked on American films such as *Stand by Me* (1986) and *Hairspray* (1988), had acquired old songs and musical pieces for use in the film.

Absolute Beginners guaranteed a certain musical pedigree for itself. Gil Evans, once Miles Davis's arranger and sometimes credited with inventing so-called "cool jazz" in the 1940s, was secured as musical director for the film. In addition, several contemporary British pop artists were commissioned to write songs for inclusion in the film. A succession of tied-in hits thus publicized the film, including David Bowie's title song and the Style Council's *Have You Ever Had It Blue*,[8] which arises non-diegetically, accompanying a montage sequence of images of London in the early morning as the film's protagonist Colin wanders home. *Absolute Beginners* constituted the culmination of the jazz revival that occurred in the 1980s. This is not to say that jazz needed reviving – it had always been thriving in its own quarters that were usually specialist circles beyond the immediate view of mainstream culture. The difference was that a number of jazz-styled groups appeared that were aiming at a pop music market rather than the traditional market for jazz.[9] As early as 1981, the *New Musical Express* was starting to deem jazz *à la mode* by incorporating an unprecedented double-page spread about historical jazz musicians.[10] By 1983, the *New Musical Express* had its own weekly jazz section, while groups directly embracing jazz such as Blue Rondo à la Turk and Working Week emerged and Joe Jackson had converted from being a new wave singer into a jazz singer and band leader with his *Jumpin' Jive* LP. By the middle of the decade, artists were having a degree of success in the pop mainstream using this style, perhaps summed up by the smooth and auspiciously "sophisticated" jazz singer Sade, who appears in *Absolute Beginners*, yet who had currency purely in pop rather than jazz circles.

While one aspect of the jazz revival stressed contemporary material publicized as pop music, the "revival" itself brought with it the "redis-covery" of historical jazz recordings. While the whole tendency was argu-ably conservative, especially in terms of reviving moribund fashions, the opportunities afforded to the record industry by the postmodern recy-cling of jazz back catalogues proved to be symptomatic of the decade that would end with mass back catalogue recycling on CD.[11] As a saturated commodity, *Absolute Beginners* had a selection of directly tied-in prod-ucts. Notably, it had two soundtrack albums released, one of which was a double LP. There was also MacPherson's book, *The Beginners' Guide to Absolute Beginners* (1986), a glossy poster magazine and recordings such as the unconnected RCA Victor compilation of old jazz recordings *The Absolute Beginner's Guide to Jazz* and its inevitable sequel, *Son of Absolute Beginner's Guide to Jazz*.

This process matches the recycling that was endemic across culture in the mid-1980s. Record companies were milking musical catalogues and rosters, and a new form became prominent, where old songs – often ones that fitted the industry's reconception of jazz songs – were revived in a different context, simultaneously having a nostalgic effect while being invested with a new contextual meaning. In the same year as *Absolute Beginners* was released, there were two examples of this: the television serial *The Singing Detective* (1986), written by Dennis Potter, contained regular occurrences of the 1930s and 1940s songs in unexpected song sequences, and Neil Jordan's film *Mona Lisa* (1986) used Nat King Cole's song as a flavour for the film as well as a thematic key to its narrative. *Absolute Beginners* demonstrates not only the period's emergent (post-modern) nostalgia for the popular culture of the past but also the new intersection of commodities, with records, pop videos, and other mer-chandise being sold at the nexus point of the film itself. In the same year, an advertisement for Levi's jeans summed up the power of the new form of cultural consumerism. Set in a launderette, the advertisement elevated to fame the non-speaking model who appeared, Nick Kamen, as well as causing the rerelease and hit status of its soundtrack of Marvin Gaye's 1968 song *I Heard It Through the Grapevine*. This process matches the recycling that was endemic across culture in the mid-1980s. Record com-panies milking back catalogues for the screen was highly evident. Denisoff and Plasketes described the industrial strategy called synergy, involving the coordination of record releases from a film soundtrack as mutual pub-licity (Denisoff and Plasketes 1990: 257), while Jean Rosenbluth pointed to the accommodation where "Studios and record companies began to work together regularly to maximize their products' financial potential" (Rosenbluth 1988: S-4).

Absolute Beginners is most interesting in relation to its choice of music. As I have noted, rock 'n' roll, the new and vibrant force of the late 1950s, is derided and trivialized. Skiffle, an intriguing and wholly British phenomenon, is ignored.[12] Instead, jazz is elevated as the characteristic music of the film's version of 1958. Why jazz? Is it simply because it is more directly associated with black people? While an interest in jazz may be evident in the original story, this is certainly no literary adaptation. The sourcebook by Colin MacInnes is almost irrelevant in the face of the film as a multilayered palimpsest, which is led by the music, the film musical tradition and the artists, some of whom were already tied to the project before the script was written.[13]

Jazz is now seen as something of a "black high art" and *Absolute Beginners* exploits jazz's relatively high cultural status. While the film welds this "high art" association with black characters on screen, and it associates white characters more with rock 'n' roll, this seems to be part of the film's multiculturalist agenda. Yet the status of jazz as "legit" and its valorization in the film are likely symptoms of industrial developments at the time, specifically the reorientation of the music industry towards adult consumers.

The late 1970s and early 1980s was a period of crisis for the music industry. As one journalist in *Sounds* put it in 1982, "With the British record industry now in the depths of the severest decline it has ever known, there are real fears that rock music will never regain the lion's share of the entertainment market it held in the mid-seventies" (1982: 2). The mood of the record industry was demonstrated vividly by their central overbearing concern in the early and mid-1980s, that of piracy. The industry's campaign which united behind the slogan "Home taping is killing music" put pressure on the British government with an aim of levying a charge on blank recording tapes to "compensate" record companies for the revenue lost by illegal but endemic home taping of records. One corollary of this industrial contraction was that pop music's past glories became the basis for future sales, which is why the conservatism of the July 1985 Live Aid roster was so striking: Eric Clapton, Status Quo, even Led Zeppelin reformed in order to appear. This meant that the focus of the music was more in the 1970s than in the 1980s, more looking to the past than to the future, and reflecting marketing rather than aesthetic developments.

The atmosphere of seemingly lost revenues, heaped upon dwindling profits led to a retrenchment of the international music and recording industry, which towards the end of the decade was boosted by the CD "revolution" (Eckstein 1993: 45). This was the conclusion of a strategy that allowed record companies to reanimate and resell all their back cat-alogues as much as, if not more than, they sold contemporary artists. Record companies could thus concentrate on adult-oriented rock (AOR), aiming at adult audiences rather than the poorer youth audience. These currents are evident in the version of jazz promoted by the film. It is not the more challenging versions of jazz, nor is it the sort of "trad jazz" that had a strong following in Britain in the late 1950s. *Absolute Beginners* showcases a more vague form that in many cases simply involved pop musicians playing what they thought was jazz (or perhaps vice versa). *Absolute Beginners* hedged its bets by including existing jazz recordings, along with new recordings by jazz artists, and adding a large amount of jazz-inflected pop music to the soundtrack which was made available by co-producer Virgin Records.

In musical terms, there is a resounding question that hangs over *Absolute Beginners*: where is the West Indian music? There is a little ambient reggae in the Napoli street scenes and in one of the club scenes the band play jazz with a soca beat. Yet both of these musical forms came to prominence later. In 1958, there was a thriving calypso scene, which was internationally successful. Indeed, one of the leading exponents of calypso, the intriguingly named Lord Kitchener, was already residing in Britain. The likely reason for calypso's non-appearance in *Absolute Beginners* is that it was not a marketable commodity in 1985, as the so-called "world music" market was only in an embryonic state. Since that time, calypso has remained obscure, missing out on a revival, except in the form of soca.[14] *Absolute Beginners* represents Americanism (rock 'n' roll, consumerism) but is also concerned with the legacy of the British Empire, particularly immigration from the West Indies. Yet the film's musical con-trivance betrays that *Absolute Beginners* is less about Caribbeans and their culture than about selling old records and generic "blacks" appear-ing as the origin of that music.

Multiculturalism

The arrival of the ship Empire Windrush at Tilbury, London in 1948 is seen as the starting point of immigration to Britain from the Caribbean.[15] A decade later, there were in the region of 125,000 West Indians in Britain, and their hostile reception was embodied by the Notting Hill "riot" of the same year, which is represented as the denouement of *Absolute Beginners*. The film explicitly references and parallels the riots of 1985, which took place in areas with predominantly Afro-Caribbean popula-tions (Handsworth in Birmingham, Toxteth in Liverpool, and Broadwater Farm, Tottenham in London). These were at least partly a result of Prime Minister Margaret Thatcher's domestic politics of confrontation, added to institutionalized racism, both of which indirectly provided an agenda for *Absolute Beginners*. In the film, the malignant forces are manifested by shady business interests manipulating the racist teddy boys.[16] This very British subculture, represented by Ed the Ted and Flicker, appears as "ethnic whites" – like American redneck hillbillies – which embody the repressed aspects of the film's other white characters.

According to Walter Benjamin in his "Fifth Thesis on the Philosophy of History," history should "seize hold of a memory as it flashes up at a moment of danger" (1992: 247). However, there is an arresting ambiguity in Benjamin's statement, allowing possibly for history to constitute a reactionary positioning against the danger of change. The riots of the 1980s certainly manifested moments of danger and the film explicitly represents rioting, which is shocking in the context of the film's previous light-hearted images. Yet these violent images proceed to transmogrify into a harmless dance representation of a riot. Arguably, the amelioration of the striking imagery undermines any political or representational potential.

The film endeavours to show a fantasy of a postcolonial multicultural utopia (under the auspices of a creative cultural explosion). Colin says, in voice-over as he introduces the audience to "Napoli" (Notting Hill), "The thing I love most about these streets was the thing that made some people positively hate them. Because here nobody cared where you came from, or what colour, what you did or who you did it with." Napoli is shown as a periphery, a liminal space of London, while the other film space, Soho is made into a central Foucauldian heterotopia, where everything and all conventions are up for grabs and redevelopment (Foucault 1986: 24). However, within these "progressive" spaces there is also racial, and gender, segregation. For example, when Suzette is at Henley's show, four flunkeys are black men. She dances and they join in, shedding their clothes. Their status as support dancers to Suzette, and obviously signalled as black and masculine in contradistinction to Suzette's white femininity, keeps them subordinate to a white. Here, the ethnic divide is doubled by a gender divide. Black men appear as stereotypical sex symbols, whereas black women simply do not figure. In fact, there are only a handful of black women in the film and, apart from Sade's appearance on stage, they are firmly at the film's margins. In another sequence, Sade goes to sing *Killer Blow* in the Soho club. All the dancers on the floor are black men, while the seated audience are white. Indeed, Afro-Caribbeans are represented in stereotypical manner throughout, appearing almost exclusively as musicians and dancers. The principal black character, "Cool," first appears playing a trumpet in the street and constantly wears sunglasses both onstage and off, while there are copious amounts of black male dancers, who seem to embody a white notion of black masculinity as symbol of sexual prowess.

In attitude, *Absolute Beginners* is pre-multiculturalism, the concept having only started to take hold in Britain in the 1980s. The film is essentialist in its race relations, seeing a strict and simple divide between white and black, irrespective of culture or origin. This is not the carefully discussed unified heritage and culture described by Paul Gilroy's notion of the "Black Atlantic" (1993), where blacks in America, Africa, and Europe are seen as a single entity. Instead, this is an imposed unity from elsewhere: a conflation by white culture that sees blacks as "the same." So, the film's multiculturalism is more what Thomas Fitzgerald describes as "romantic racialism" (1992: 131). *Absolute Beginners* is less a "multiculturalist history" than simply a history from a white paternalist (and integrative) point of view. This is underlined by the fact that the film shows only one Asian (a Sikh) even though there were approximately 55,000 Asians in Britain at the time (nearly half the number of West Indians). The likely reason for this parsimonious portrayal is that Asians were generally considered "unhip" in the mid-1980s.[17] This is the opposite of the film's blacks, who are all undifferentiated and Americanized, stereotyped and overbearingly "hip."

Conclusion

The "white labels" of this chapter's title refers not only to records with white labels sent out to promote music but also to the propensity for black culture to be packaged for white consumption. In the film, Ed the Ted shouts at Colin: "Go home, Yank, and take Sambo with you!" This moment conflates the two (in derogatory terms) and underlines *Absolute Beginners*' attempts to depict US culture as West Indian. This has an immediate effect of homogenizing black cultures, converting both American and Caribbean cultures into a single item unified by an implicit white (and oddly "English") point of view.

Absolute Beginners was an astonishing attempt to reinvent British pop music culture by bypassing the dominant popular cultural heritage of the protean 1960s and The Beatles. This denial of the 1960s' effect pointedly parallels Margaret Thatcher's attempt at a renewal of Britain and desire to erase the effects of the 1960s, or at least her desire to blame the decade for the problems faced in the 1980s. Yet Colin and Suzette's rise to fame (and the film's emphasis on photography) matches the rise to stardom in the Swinging London musical *Smashing Time* (1967). There are similarities between the two films but with a significant difference: in *Smashing Time* the present is depicted as exciting, whereas in *Absolute Beginners* the present is considered dull and we escape to an exciting past. The film was a watershed for popular music being used by the heritage industry, speeding up a train of heritage films about pop music running into *Hours and the Times* (1991), *Back Beat* (1993), *Still Crazy* (1998), and *Velvet Goldmine* (1998). *Absolute Beginners* is a peculiarly historical film. The film is "historiographic" – it is less concerned with what "really happened" than it is concerned with history as a living entity in the present, reimagining the point of entry of American and Caribbean culture to Britain. The film's attempts to represent this multiculturalism effect a format through which musical back catalogues can be sold. Hence the specific form of representation in the film is, to a lesser or greater degree, the product of a history emanating from commercial interests. The key is to think of the film less in relation to cinematic traditions, than in relation to the music industry and pop traditions. From this perspective, *Absolute Beginners* demonstrates the new configuration of intersecting commodities at the time, with records, pop videos, style, and other merchandise being sold at the nexus point of the film itself.

Notes

1 Hayden White (1988: 1193) coins the term "historiophoty." However, the term is notably ocularcentric, failing to express the audiovisual character of film.

2 In terms of the density of its references and allusions, *Absolute Beginners* is almost like a popular culture version of T.S. Eliot's poem *The Waste Land*, although its character is perhaps closer to Andrew Lloyd-Webber's adaptation of Eliot's *Old Possum's Book of Practical Cats*.

3 Despite Temple's quotation earlier, the strange fact that coffee bars are marginal to *Absolute Beginners* suggests that the film is not particularly interested in teens and "youth" culture of the late 1950s. For the development of the British pop musical, see Donnelly (2001).

4 Euro-MTV started six years later, although terrestrial television shows were already showing pop videos and exhibiting the "MTV style."

5 In Britain, as distinct from the United States, rock 'n' roll and music in its wake arguably invoked fearless for its association with blacks than to its threat to the class system. While there was general xenophobia against blacks, and to a lesser degree other Americans, rock 'n' roll as an uncontrolled influence threatened the rigid class structure and people "knowing their place" in it. Class appears as a discourse in *Absolute Beginners*, crassly depicting Henley as an upper-class gay stereotype, whose world is threatened by youth's vigour and innovations.

6 This figures the renewal of the "special relationship" between Britain and the United States, which was much touted at the time by Prime Minister Margaret Thatcher.

7 Tenpole Tudor (also known as Edward Tudor-Pole), apart from appearing in *The Great Rock 'n' Roll Swindle* (1980), had two big UK hits in the early 1980s with rockabilly-influenced records *Swords of a Thousand Men* and *Wunderbar*, and later presented television game show *The Crystal Maze* on Channel Four from 1993 to 1995.

8 Bowie's *Absolute Beginners* single was sandwiched between the two relatively unsuccessful film song projects for him, *When the Wind Blows* and *Labyrinth*, where he appeared as the King of the Fairies. It reached Number

Two in the charts and remained on the chart for nine weeks after entering on 15 March 1986.

9 Karen Lury (2000: 104) rightly notes that in the film 1950s jazz is marginalized by manufactured and contemporary pop.

10 Carr (1981: 29–30). The same music newspaper had another large feature over a year later (Carr and Dellar 1982: 19-19), which demonstrates that it was no short-lived concern.

11 Later there was a successful charity LP of Cole Porter's songs recorded by a number of contemporary artists, called *Red Hot and Blue*, released in 1990.

12 Skiffle has had a striking lack of attention from scholars and popular writers alike, apart from Dewe (1998).

13 The source book may be about jazz aficionados, but the film is more interested in jazz that can be sold as pop music.

14 Soca is the pop music version, "Soul-Calypso," also associated mainly with Trinidad.

15 The BBC instituted a television season in 1998 to celebrate 50 years of West Indians in Britain, called *Windrush*.

16 These could well be related to the beleaguered "Little Englanders" discussed in Darcus Howe's television series *White Tribe* (1999, Channel Four), in which he went in search of "Englishness."

17 It is not until the 1990s that "Finally, it appears that the 'coolie' has become cool" (Sharma, Hutnyk and Sharma 1996: 1).

Bibliography

Anon, *The Beginners' Guide to Absolute Beginners* (London: Corgi, 1986).

Anon, news article in *Sounds*, 17 July 1982.

Benjamin, Walter, "Theses on the Philosophy of History" in *Illuminations* (London: Fontana, 1992).

Carr, Roy, "Hi-De-Hi: A Lighthearted Look at the Era of Jump Jive and Jitterbug, the Honking Hornmen, Screamers and Shouters" in *New Musical Express*, 18 July 1981.

Carr, Roy, and Fred Dellar, "In the Land of Oo-Bla-Dee" in *New Musical Express*, 14 August 1982.

Cosgrove, Stuart, "The Creeping Czars of the Coffee Bars" in *New Musical Express*, 22 March 1986.

Denisoff, R. Serge, and George Plasketes, "Synergy in 1980s Film and Music: Formula for Success or Industry Mythology?" in *Film History*, vol. 4, no. 3, 1990.

Dewe, Mike, *The Skiffle Craze* (Aberystwyth: Planet, 1998).

Donnelly, K.J., *Pop Music in British Cinema: A Chronicle* (London: BFI, 2001).

Eckstein, Jeremy, ed., *Cultural Trends 19*, vol.3, no.3 (London: Policy Studies Institute, 1993).

Fitzgerald Thomas, K., "Media, Ethnicity and Identity" in Paddy Scannel, Philip Schlesinger, and Colin Sparks, eds, *Culture and Power: A Media, Culture and Society Reader* (London: Sage, 1992).

Foucault, Michel, "Of Other Spaces" *Diacritics*, vol. 16, no. 1, 1986.

Gilroy, Paul, *The Black Atlantic: Modernity and Double Consciousness* (London: Verso, 1993).

Hoggart, Richard, *The Uses of Literacy* (London: Chatto & Windus, 1957).

Jenkins, Steve, "Absolute Beginnings" (interview with Julien Temple) in *Monthly Film Bulletin*, vol. 51, 1984.

Lury, Karen, "Here and Then: Space, Place and Nostalgia in British Youth Cinema of the 1990s" in Robert Murphy, ed., *British Cinema of the 90s* (London: BFI, 2000).

MacPherson, Don, "Next Stop Napoli" in *New Musical Express*, 22 March 1986.

Matheson, Nigel, "Inside the Temple of Teen" (interview with Julien Temple) in *New Musical Express*, 27 April 1985.

Munslow, Alan, *Deconstructing History* (London: Routledge, 1997).

Rosenbluth, Jean "Soundtrack Specialists: Maximizing Cross-Market Connections" in *Billboard*, 16 July 1988.

Rosenstone, Robert, ed., *Revisioning History* (Princeton, NJ: Princeton University Press, 1994).

Rosenstone, Robert, *Visions of the Past: The Challenge of Film to Our Idea of History* (London: Harvard University Press, 1995).

Sharma, Sanjay, John Hutnyk, and Ashwani Sharma, "Introduction" in Sanjay Sharma, John Hutnyk, and Ashwani Sharma, eds, *Dis-Orienting Rhythms: The Politics of the New Asian Dance Music* (London: Zed, 1996).

White, Hayden, "Historiography and Historiophoty" in *American History Review*, vol. 93, no. 5, 1988.

Yule, Andrew Yule, and David Puttnam, *The Story So Far* (London: Sphere, 1988).

11

VISUALIZING LIVE ALBUMS

Progressive Rock and the British Concert Film in the 1970s

Although rarely registered, other film formats derive directly from music apart from only the film musical. A whole zone of British cinema of the 1970s makes more sense when approached from the perspective of the music industry rather than the film industry. Music formats of the time were translated onto celluloid: concept albums led to rock operas and live albums became concert documentaries or "rockumentaries." While from a film perspective, British cinema of the 1970s might have been fairly weak and unsuccessful, from a music point of view, British popular music of the decade was unproblematically outstanding. Live concert films emerged at a specific moment in British cinema in the late 1960s and early 1970s due to film and music events. Whilst the success and acclaim heaped upon American rock documentaries had doubtless been the inspiration, the buoyant status of British rock music and the shortcomings of the film industry in Britain produced something quite specific. At the turn of the seventies, the term "crisis" was used in relation to the British film industry.[1] The evacuation of US funding which had bankrolled British films for a few bumper years led to a more frugal industry in the UK. However, the production of feature films starring pop music and musicians remained something of a constant into the seventies, culminating in Ken Russell's *Tommy* (1975), an extremely expensive adaptation of The Who's rock opera album. Rockumentaries or "rock documentaries" had emerged in the previous decade. The first was the Canadian production *Lonely Boy* (1962) about Paul Anka (Grant 1986: 201). It seems that in its first years, the rock documentary was essentially North American, with such notable films as D.A. Pennebaker's British-shot but American-registered

DOI: 10.4324/9781003299653-11

Don't Look Back about Bob Dylan (1967), and *Monterey Pop* (1968), *Woodstock* (1970), and the Maysles brothers and Charlotte Zwerin's *Gimme Shelter* (1970). These were event-based films and included much besides the on-stage performance.

At the turn of the 1970s, the British film industry had a significant downturn in production and budgets; concurrently, there was a massive boom in worldwide record sales. It was therefore no surprise that the 1970s saw a large-scale move to use pop and rock music in films, where it offered new aesthetic possibilities for filmmaking as much as accessed to youth audiences. It should perhaps have come as no surprise that British cinema should exploit British musical success. In terms of popular music, Britain had been the centre of attention since the mid-60s and the massive international success of The Beatles. Dramatic developments had befallen British music in less than a decade: from the "beat boom" of the mid-1960s, through late 60s psychedelia and the counterculture, to the "glam rock" and progressive rock of the early 1970s. In contrast with the film industry, there was a lot of money around. There was a boom in world record sales in the 1970s (Harker 1994: 249). For example, Elton John earned more than The Beatles at their peak (Harker 1994: 244). The proliferation of live albums as a phenomenon ran for about a decade, from a heyday at the end of the 1960s to a virtual disappearance by the early 1980s. Rock concert films quite closely correspond to the same period. Against a backdrop of rising recording costs, live albums clearly made good business. The most basic were cheap to record, with outputs being taken from the concert's mixing desk, and the package having a character similar to a "greatest hits" album. Also, they exhibit important characteristics of progressive rock of the time, those of musicianship and authenticity, both of which are particularly evident in a live setting. Such music was also particularly suited to film, as it projected the showmanship and ambition of these musicians, leading to a close relationship between the two forms.

Progressive Rock

Progressive rock defies simple definition and perhaps was more a tendency or a vague marketing category for music than anything more solid. It was also a banner of aspiration, for musicians and consumers who wanted to aim beyond the simplicities of pop and rock. Initially it was a *British* (in fact, overwhelmingly English) phenomenon, and remained dominated by British groups.[2] It emerged from late 1960s psychedelia and was influenced by jazz-rock fusion and art music experimentation (including electronic music). Its general characteristics are that musical compositions are longer and much more ambitious and sophisticated than in pop, with elaborate arrangements (rather than simple alternating verse-chorus structures). There were extended instrumental sections (allowing musicians to show off their virtuosity) and often complex, conceptual, or fantasy-inspired lyrics. It was album-oriented (sometimes ambitious "concept" albums) rather than singles, was geared towards career longevity, was interested in technological innovation, and was "serious" (some might say self-important).

Progressive rock groups include perhaps most notably Pink Floyd, King Crimson, Genesis, Emerson, Lake and Palmer, Yes, Gentle Giant, Van der Graaf Generator, Camel, Soft Machine, and many more who might cross categories. All that I have listed are British. Their work has tended to be described as "sophisticated," "self-indulgent," and even "pretentious." From the late 1970s, progressive rock regularly was demonized,[3] until the late 1990s when it came in for something of a reappraisal. Notable books on the subject include Edward Macan, *Rocking the Classics: English Progressive Rock and the Counterculture* (1997) and Kevin Holm-Hudson's edited collection *Progressive Rock Reconsidered* (2002), as well as John Covach's article about Yes's *Close to the Edge* (1997). In July of 2007, *Classic Rock* magazine published a progressive rock special issue with a DVD of interviews with Yes attached to the cover. Current musicians such as Porcupine Tree have openly espoused progressive rock, while the King Crimson song *Moonchild* was covered by the Doves and also appeared in the film *Buffalo 66* (1998).[4]

While music historians and analysts might have written about progressive rock in recent years, there has been little written about rock documentaries, and even less written about live concert films.[5] An isolated article by Adrian Wootton discusses key aspects of rock documentary (such as backstage and "setting up" components). Led Zeppelin produced one of the most prominent British rock concert films, *The Song Remains the Same* (1976), and Wootton cites this as a "classic example" of films "being produced by the so-called dinosaur groups [which] were often pretentious, uninteresting and uncinematic" (Wootton 1988: 356). Yet these films were for fans rather than general film audiences (or indeed film critics), and directly reflected their interests in the music involved. *The Song Remains the Same* is first and foremost a recording of a live concert, although it also includes fantasy sections which function as inserts while retaining the continuity of the live soundtrack recording. Such criticism misses the point. Wootton's comment – once we strip away the disdain – confirms that these films fail to "make sense" as "cinema."[6] These films make more sense as live albums with added images. Many of them are compounded by the simultaneous release of the soundtrack album, which arguably is the primary product. In terms of distribution, the discs far outweigh the films: that is where the real money is being made. Consequently, it is no surprise that the overwhelming majority of these films were produced by record labels rather than film companies. In fact, live films could be characterized simply as counterparts to live albums. However, we might make a working distinction between the more fulsome rock documentary and the more direct concert film.

Sliding scale	
Concert film <----------------------------> Rock documentary	
"Recording" (cf. TV promo tradition)	Documentary film tradition
Made by technicians	Made by filmmakers
Concert only	Interest in periphery (interviews, other activities)
Fan product	Wider audience interest
Visualized live LP	Similar to the backstage musical

While this may not be a solid distinction, we might note that there are broad tendencies within this format. Rock documentaries/rockumentaries often appear like DVDs of concerts but with optional DVD extras cut into the film from time to time. An interesting example of this is *Born to Boogie* (1972), which includes a selection of outtakes integrated in the film, most notably perhaps the "Some Like to Rock" section. However, the film is essentially a live concert recorded for posterity despite its inserts and bizarre paddings. *Born to Boogie* was an exception, focusing on Marc Bolan and his glam rock group T. Rex, whose audience were dominated by young teenagers. The concert films appeared particularly suited to progressive rock groups and often were less concerned with cinematic variation than with "authentic" duplication of the exciting reality of performance and the veracity of high-level musicianship and serious endeavour.

Although there were many British-made short films and television programmes,[7] significantly there were an astonishing number of feature films, most of which had a fitful cinematic release for short runs (and sometimes only single screenings). However, they also had a shelf-life that ran for a few years, sometimes appearing as late-night attractions. Below is a list of all British concert and rock documentary films released in the 1970s:[8]

Let It Be (1970 Michael Lindsay-Hogg) [The Beatles]
Reggae (1970 Horace Ove) [a festival]
Supershow (1970 John Crome) [concert including Led Zeppelin]
Mad Dogs and Englishmen (1971 Pierre Adidge) [Joe Cocker]
Bird on a Wire (1972 Tony Palmer) [Leonard Cohen]
Born to Boogie (1972 Ringo Starr) [T. Rex]

Pictures at an Exhibition (1972 Nicholas Ferguson) [Emerson, Lake and Palmer]
Glastonbury Fayre (1973 Peter Neal) [a festival]
The London Rock 'n' Roll Show (1973 Peter Clifton) [concert including Chuck Berry]
Yessongs (1973 Peter Neal) [Yes]
The Butterfly Ball (1976 Tony Klinger) [a stage show mixed with animations]
Pleasure at Her Majesties (1976 Roger Graef) [a concert event]
Genesis: On Stage (1976 Tony Maylam) [Genesis]
The Song Remains the Same (1976 Peter Clifton, Joe Massot) [Led Zeppelin]
Bob Marley and the Wailers Live (1978 Keef [Keith Macmillan]) [Bob Marley]
The Punk Rock Movie (1978 Don Letts) [various groups]
The Secret Policeman's Ball (1979 Roger Graef) [a concert event]

Many of these films are obscure and not held in official film archives. Most remain in the more popular/commercial "archive" of television screenings in slots far away from prime time and on obscure stations. Many had limited video and DVD releases, and for years historians and collectors had to scour second-hand sources although more recently, such films are often available as small-run DVDs from "microbreweries" (both legal and illegal), through internet filesharing, or perhaps even on YouTube. If the artist remains bankable, then the film will retain a higher distribution profile. Consequently, some films have disappeared without a trace. A few isolated examples apart,[9] the British concert film had disappeared by the 1980s. Progressive rock went out of fashion and fewer live albums were released, while at the turn of the decade, the music industry went into a sustained crisis (Harker 1994: 253). There were fewer groups who wanted their onstage exploits expensively preserved for posterity and the advent of home video shifted live music films away from cinema release.

Concert Films

Emerson, Lake and Palmer were a "supergroup" formed by members of The Nice, King Crimson, and Atomic Rooster. They released *Emerson, Lake and Palmer* (December 1970), *Tarkus* (June 1971), and then *Pictures at an Exhibition* (November 1971). The last had been recorded live in March of 1971 and was a dramatic rearrangement of Mussorgsky's *Pictures at an Exhibition*, a late 19th-century concert hall piece originally for solo piano, but better known in its orchestral arrangement by Maurice Ravel. This was a loose "concept album" rather than a collection of unrelated songs. Mussorgsky's piece had been used in rehearsals at the time of their debut LP's release and was recorded live at Newcastle City Hall. Distinct from the album, the corresponding film had been released in February of 1971, before the recording of the LP. It had been shot in December of 1970 at the Lyceum Theatre in London, at the time when their debut LP was on release. It was 95 minutes long although some versions are in existence are as short as 40 minutes (the VHS video is short; the Japanese Laserdisc is long).

Pictures at an Exhibition contains some startling visual effects, which are reminiscent of psychedelic light shows. These swirling patterns which on occasion overlay the images of the group on stage are an example of video feedback effects. Indeed, the film was shot wholly on video, and two cumbersome television cameras on dollies are fitfully visible in shot to "catch the action" of the live event, much like in televised sport. According to a *Melody Maker* article, their use of video was due to the future arrival of video as a medium as well as its technological possibilities (1972: 34). This is a production that has little to do with filmmaking in Britain and more connections to the television industry. It was filmed by the band's friend producer Lindsey Clennell, for Visual and Musical Entertainments. The visual recording equipment was television standard and it was directed by television director Nicholas Ferguson. Drummer Carl Palmer commented on the film:

> There are lots of basic shots of the band ... we had a lot of ideas about modern filming techniques which we wanted to see done, but instead ... it was done as a straight film, like the early Beatles films ... Because a friend of ours is doing it is the only reason we let him release it.
>
> *(Forrester, Hanson and Askew 2001: 70)*

So, it seems that "progressive" music embraced a "regressive" film style. There was an air of uncertainty about the whole endeavour. According to Palmer, the group did not intend to release the live LP, as it was not their original material (Forrester, Hanson and Askew 2001: 69). More significantly, perhaps, their normal engineer Eddie Offord was absent and the sound recording quality of the film was poor and hardly acceptable to the increasingly "hi-fi" demands of progressive rock audiences. The demand for a soundtrack album stimulated by the film led to a plan to record a coming live show, with the aim of achieving excellent sound, and indeed the LP apparently was used as a demonstration disc in some hi-fi shops (Forrester, Hanson and Askew 2001: 70–71). *Pictures at an Exhibition*'s corresponding soundtrack LP, rather than existing as a supplement and advertisement for the film, was in fact the principal commodity itself.[10]

For British progressive rock groups, *Pictures at an Exhibition* set something of a precedent. Musicians wanted films to showcase their abilities and imaginations, but also there appears to have been an extra tier added to rock's product chain: the repeated normality of album and associated tour could include a feature-length film as part of rock groups' intermittent bursts of product. *Yessongs* was released at a time when Yes had become suitably successful. They had been featured on the front cover of *Melody Maker* for the first time in early 1972, had their first sell-out tour and had two albums go gold in terms of sales. The second of those, *Fragile* (released in January 1972) was the first with the "classic" line-up of Jon Anderson, Bill Bruford, Rick Wakeman, Steve Howe, and Chris Squire. It was also the first with a futuristic cover by artist Roger Dean, an aspect of the group's albums that became a continuous characteristic. This LP was followed by the more highly acclaimed *Close to the Edge*, released in September 1972.

The *Yessongs* album was a triple-album with a sumptuous Roger Dean gatefold sleeve and must have been a risk for Atlantic Records. Indeed, triple albums have remained a rarity.[11]

It was recorded mostly in late 1972 at a selection of concerts and released on 18th May 1973, reaching Number Seven in the UK album chart and Number 12 in the USA. However, the film is not the same as the album. It was recorded at one event, the London Rainbow Theatre Christmas night concert in 1972. In fact, there is only one section of a song shared with the album and some songs appear that are absent from the triple LP. The film is a single event, while the album is a composite of

different events, despite having the feeling of being a coherent single event. Technological expediency means that it is easier to record sound at events (through the mixing desk), while film footage is much more difficult to secure. Sound also can be "sweetened" more easily through equalization and filtering, remixing, and in some cases even re-recording passages in the studio afterwards. The structure of the film, as in the case of most concert films, follows the structure of a concert. In this case the dynamic order of song presentation remains, while each member of the group is allowed an extended solo section.

According to the *Monthly Film Bulletin* review, there were no shots of the audience (1976: 111). This is not true. There are few, however, with two appearing during the encore. This structural "reverse shot" to the fetishistic focus on the stage is often an important, although sometimes not regular characteristic of the concert film. *Monthly Film Bulletin*'s statement shows that there was an *expectation* to see the audience. Indeed, *Pictures at the Exhibition* shows the audience a few times. They are sitting down, thoughtfully and do not add any sense of dynamism to the proceedings.[12] These moments when the camera turns onto the audience are something like a supplementary rockumentary "DVD extra" but function more clearly as a guarantee of the veracity of the concert as an event.

Yessongs includes some visual distortion effects like *Pictures at an Exhibition* but contains more sustained passages of animation, retaining a sense of desire for visual variation despite the likelihood that film audiences would prefer to see the group. The aim perhaps is to make it seem more of a "film" than simply a "recording" of the group in action. Significantly, *Yessongs* was released in a quadraphonic version. Much has been made of Ken Russell's *Tommy* (1975) as the first film released in a quad version but despite being recorded two years earlier, *Yessongs* was released at about the same time. Such impressive stereo would have done justice to the group's intricate progressive rock, and a *Melody Maker* article just before the film was shot noted that musicians were less interested in quadraphonic than were hi-fi companies.[13] Indeed, quadraphonic's development into multi-speaker systems for cinemas has been a lasting bequithement of the music industry to the film industry.

Similarly, Led Zeppelin's *The Song Remains the Same* (1976) had a release in four-track stereo, in this case with the music on the magnetic strip of the film print rather than synching up a magnetic tape recording to a silent print. The album was billed as the "original soundtrack" and the record and film are closely related, although some parts of the double LP are different from the film. Footage was taken from a few nights at Madison Square Garden, New York, at the conclusion of Led Zeppelin's 1973 tour.[14] *The Song Remains the Same* is first and foremost a recording of a live concert, although, significantly, it contains fantasy sections which embellish the primacy of the performed music. These are bold and remove the focus from the productive origins of the music. For instance, Jimmy Page's sequence in *Dazed and Confused*, during an extended solo where he plays the guitar with a violin bow, has images of the group on stage replaced by a short film depicting a shrouded figure climbing to the top of a mountain and swinging a sword that looks remarkably like the light sabres that appeared in *Star Wars* the following year. For just over four minutes the music has remained constant while the images have become in effect non-diegetic, like an accompaniment to the soundtrack emanating from elsewhere.

Despite rock music's appeal to authenticity and the self-proclaimed "honesty" of many bands during this period, *The Song Remains the Same* was dramatically "sweetened." The album is a composite of not only songs from different days mixed together with audience noises to sound like a continuous event but individual tracks are comprised of edited together sections of different performances.[15] Similarly, the images are an amalgam of shots from different performances. Furthermore, some shots are from a restaging of Led Zeppelin's show at Shepperton Studios in London, where a facsimile of the Madison Square Garden stage was recreated to allow for more in the way of close-up shots. Bass and keyboard player John Paul Jones had cut his hair short after the original concerts and was forced to wear a wig at Shepperton to aid the illusion of continuity.

Genesis: In Concert (1976) has no corresponding live album, although a year after its release a double live album, *Seconds Out*, was released. The film was shot during the 1976 tour at two concerts (Glasgow 9 July and Stafford 10 July), while the group's album *Wind and Wuthering* was residing at Number One in the album charts. The live album was recorded a year later during the 1977 tour (apart from one song recorded earlier with a different drummer), during a five-night stint at the Palais des sports in Paris (11–14 June). The film was on release at the same time that the live album was being recorded. *Genesis: In Concert* had its gala premiere in July 1977 with royalty (Princess Anne) present (Smith and Hewitt 2000: 49), but it had no "official release" and distribution. It toured the country selectively on a double bill with another film directed by Tony Maylam, *White Rock*. This was a documentary about the Winter Olympics presented by James Coburn but sold through its musical soundtrack by Rick Wakeman, previously the keyboard player in Yes. Apart from being a straightforward record of the group on stage, *Genesis: In Concert* includes some non-diegetic inserts where the soundtrack remains the same (continues diegetically), while images "move" to somewhere else (thus becoming non-diegetic). For *I Know What I Like* the soundtrack is of the group performing live, while the images following roadies constructing the stage sometime earlier, subsequently changing to showing the group performing towards the end of the song. Along similar lines, *The Cinema Show* includes an excerpt of an old silent comedy film about a rolling globe. Whilst the album was sweetened in studio it is clear that the film was not to any noticeable degree.

While these films tend to include little or nothing in the way of interviews and backstage insights into the musicians, they often include some form of visual interlude from the concert. Perhaps the most famous is *The Song Remains the Same*'s, where each Led Zeppelin group member has a visual "solo" cut across the continuing soundtrack of the band's concert. Although not a British production, *Pink Floyd: Live at Pompeii* (1972) has interlude sequences showcasing the ruins of Pompeii and Mount Vesuvius. Similarly, the image effects of *Pictures at an Exhibition* and *Yessongs* also amount to non-diegetic interventions. These facets make proceedings visually more varied and interesting, and appear to be a concession to a perceived need to compensate for the lack of "liveness" and the excitement of the actual concert event. This "interference" with the image track underlines the centrality and sense of integrity assigned to the concert sound recording, and the malleability of the "accompanying" images (reversing the commonly conceived relationship of film image and sound). When it came to film, progressive rock groups certainly lived up to their name in that they used innovative visual technology (videotape, quantel) and cinema sound (quadraphonic). Only now can we see the impact that this musical impetus has had on more recent cinema, while the influence on music television might also convincingly be traced.

Conclusion

In terms of aesthetics, live concert films are seemingly more "music" than they are "film." They remain firmly minority interest films, often not pandering to a wider audience and lacking the aspiration to be mainstream films with a general release. Distribution could often be through "roadshowing" – making a succession of appearances at different locations rather like a rock band on tour. Exploiting late-night bills, double-bills, and special showings, these were more an event than part of any regular visit to the cinema. As an example, in January of 1972 the celebrated Jimi Hendrix film *Jimi Plays Berkeley* (1971) was screened in the UK as a touring event, accompanied by two American groups that had some connection with him (Anon, *Melody Maker* 1972: 1). Whilst special films might be roadshown, this is far more like a musical group tour than conventional film distribution.

Distribution aside, who financed and produced these films? In the majority of cases, it was not established film production companies. Britain did not have many and the audiovisual industry was changing, fuelled by companies conglomerating.[16] The 1970s saw the dramatic convergence of British film and music industries, most obviously in the music company EMI, who diversified into film production. This continued into the 1980s, where the further diversification of audiovisual companies was embodied by Richard Branson's Virgin, which had started as a record distributor, then producer, and later moved into film production, an airline, and beyond. In a number of cases, film became used as a vehicle for the music. The most obvious case is the expensively made musical *Absolute Beginners* (1985), as discussed in a previous chapter, which was part of the increasing move towards films having simultaneous release with "synergetic" soundtracks.[17] Over a decade earlier things were already moving solidly in this direction: *Reggae* was produced by Bamboo Records, *Mad Dogs and Englishmen* was produced by A&M Records, and *Let It Be* and *Born to Boogie* were produced by Apple (the label owned and run by The Beatles). So, in terms of both aesthetics and production consumption, these films might be seen as more closely related to musical formats than to traditional film forms. Indeed, these films emanate directly from musical concerns of the time: while the "concept album" might be seen to have an equivalent in the rock opera, the live album is almost directly translated into the concert film. Their essential function is as a vehicle for the prime commodity: the music. The films are incidental, more like a tie-in, adjunct, or secondary product (like video games of films). Indeed, from an industrial point of view, it is highly surprising that the British film industry did not exploit British music more than it has, seeing as since the early 1960s Britain has been a world leader in popular music, punching well above its international weight. These films are more fruitfully approached from the point of view of music history than of film history, although their disappearance in the 1980s can be accounted for by both film and music determinants. Cinema has had a not inconsiderable influence on rock music, and perhaps live films have had a more tangible influence. It seems ironic that over the past 20 years, large concerts in stadia almost always involve large-screen live projection.[18] So contemporary audiences in effect end up watching a concert film at live events.

Notes

1 "A major crisis is undoubtedly developing in the industry, says Film Production Association president Clifford Barclay in a report on his recent visit to America ... [He] says the main purpose of his visit was to strengthen communications with the world's richest film market, [and] the main source of finance for British films" (Anon, *Kinematograph Weekly*, 1970: 3).

2 A significant determinant in the rise of British progressive rock was the outlet enabled by the new development of a universities circuit of concert venues in the wake of the proliferation of universities in the 1960s. This is clearly evident with reference to Genesis tour date lists in the early 1970s in Smith and Hewitt (2000).

3 John Street sums up the "problems" of progressive rock: "In trying to transform popular music into electronic classical music, progressive music was, in fact, 'regressive'; it sought to establish aesthetic criteria and patterns of consumption which were both elitist and traditionalist" (Street 1986: 101).

4 Despite being demonized, progressive rock was also misconstrued: in the early 2000s British soap opera *EastEnders*'s story about a noisy neighbour had him playing King Crimson's *Red* as a form of exuberant noise that might have stood for punk rock or similar.

5 There are a handful of general reviews, such as Simon Reynolds', where he declares that rock documentaries are "Rarely inspired and often less than enthralling, they nevertheless have a curious quality of watchability. Low key verging on the ambient, they seem made for TV" (2007: 32). This misses the significant fact that those of the 1970s were made for the big screen and indeed, are highly impressive in a cinema rather than idly consumed on a TV in a home living room.

6 Jonathan Demme's concert film of Talking Heads, *Stop Making Sense* (1984) – which Wootton lauds – ironically adds other layers of structure to the concert format (props, progressive development), precisely so that it "makes sense" as a film.

7 There were plenty of short films produced, for instance Van der Graaf Generator's *Godbluff Live in Charleroi* (1975), and Derek Jarman's film of Throbbing Gristle: *TG: Psychic Rally in Heaven* (1981). There were also contemporaneous television equivalents in the BBC's *In Concert* and *Rock Goes to College* programmes.

8 Included in this list are feature-length film that were registered in the UK and secured a vaguely systematic cinema release.

9 There was the diverse compilation *Urgh! A Music War* (1981), D.A. Pennebaker's late rock documentary about David Bowie's final Ziggy Stardust concert from 1973 in *Ziggy Stardust and the Spiders from Mars* (1982), *Culture Club – A Kiss Across the Ocean* (1984) and *The Cure in Orange* (1987).

10 *Pictures at an Exhibition* reached Number Three, remaining on the chart for five weeks after entering on 4 December 1971.

11 Double and even triple-albums were something of a characteristic of progressive rock and had certainly been a rarity before the 1970s. They allowed a space for longer songs and musical pieces and more elaborate and developed narrative concepts.

12 This contrasts with the exuberant audience in other concert films of the time such as *Born to Boogie*.

13 Leo Lyons (producer and ex-member of Ten Years After), studio manager at Wessex Studios, noted that rather than musicians, "The main pressure for [quad] is coming from the domestic hi-fi manufacturers" (Jones 1975: 37).

14 Peter Clifton constructed and directed most of the film. Some had been shot by Joe Massot, and Led Zeppelin manager Peter Grant went to extreme and intimidatory efforts to secure this footage (Davis 1985: 269–270).

15 An extraordinarily detailed analysis of album and film is provided by "The Garden Tapes" (Edwards 2011).

16 Similarly, PolyGram had formed from the merger of Polydor Records and Phonogram Records in 1972 and was jointly owned by Phillips and Siemens. It ate up many more companies and moved rapidly into film production.

17 A process emblematized by successful record and film collaborations such as *Flashdance* (1983) and *Footloose* (1984).

18 Of course, this might mean that if the relay is recorded footage can be released later in some form.

Bibliography

Anon, "Barclay Warns: A Major Crisis Developing" in *Kinematograph Weekly*, vol. 629, no. 3241, 1970.

Anon, "Hendrix Film Tour" in *Melody Maker*, 8 January 1972.

Anon, "A Quad View of Quadraphonic Sound" in *Melody Maker*, 23 January 1972.

Anon, "Yessongs" (review) in *Monthly Film Bulletin*, vol. 43, no. 508, May 1976.

Covach, John, "Progressive Rock, *Close to the Edge* and the Boundaries of Style" in John Covach and Graham M. Boone, eds., *Understanding Rock: Essays in Music Analysis* (Oxford: Oxford University Press, 1997).

Davis, Stephen, *Hammer of the Gods: Led Zeppelin Unauthorized* (London: Pan, 1985).

Edwards, Eddie, "The Garden Tapes" www.thegardentapes.co.uk/ [accessed 08/05/2011].

Forrester, George, Martyn Hanson, and Frank Askew, *Emerson, Lake and Palmer: The Show That Never Ends* (London: Helter Skelter, 2001).

Grant, Barry Keith, "The Classic Hollywood Musical and the 'Problem' of Rock 'n' Roll" in *Journal of Popular Film and Television*, vol. 13, no. 4, Winter 1986.

Harker, Dave, "Blood on the Tracks: Popular Music in the 1970s" in Bart Moore Gilbert, ed., *The Arts in the Seventies: Cultural Closure?* (London: Routledge, 1994).

Holm-Hudson, Kevin, ed., *Progressive Rock Reconsidered* (London: Routledge, 2002).

Jones, Edward, "Studio Session: Why Rock is Fighting Quad" in *Melody Maker*, 24 May 1975.

Macan, Edward, *Rocking the Classics: English Progressive Rock and the Counterculture* (Oxford: Oxford University Press, 1997).

Reynolds, Simon, "Tombstone Blues: The Music Documentary Boom" in *Sight and Sound*, May 2007.

Smith, Sid, and Alan Hewitt, *Opening the Musical Box: A Genesis Chronicle* (London: Firefly, 2000).

Street, John, *Rebel Rock: The Politics of Popular Music* (Oxford: Blackwell, 1986).

Wootton, Adrian, "Looking Back, Dropping Out, Making Sense: A History of the Rock-Concert Movie" in *Monthly Film Bulletin*, vol. 55, no. 659, 1988.

12

TELEVISION'S MUSICAL IMAGINATION

Space: 1999

Space: 1999 was a dramatic science fiction (SF) series which proceeded from the premise that nuclear waste explodes on the moon, sending it careering out of Earth's orbit. The crew of its moon base ("Alpha") thus embark on an extended adventure through space, encountering the weird and the wonderful. The programme is very much in the wake of the six Apollo moon landing missions (1969–72), and whilst this short and pro-tean period ended abruptly, space exploration continued on television with *Space 1999* marking something of a space programme for impoverished Britain. This British TV series came from Gerry Anderson's stable. The British producer had by this point already produced a remarkable body of work, mostly aimed squarely at children. His programmes started with *The Adventures of Twizzle* (1957–59) and went on to include *Supercar* (1961–62), *Fireball XL5* (1962–63), *Stingray* (1964–65), *Thunderbirds* (1965–66), *Captain Scarlet and the Mysterons* (1967–68), *Joe 90* (1968–69), *The Secret Service* (1969) and *UFO* (1970–71, his first with full live action and with less child orientation). Anderson has been the most successful marionette animator in British television history, with programmes very much based on a distinctive brand or house style (based on what he called "Supermarionation"). A crucial but critically underestimated element in this was incidental music, provided by Barry Gray in all programmes up to and including *Space 1999*.

While Anderson was *Space: 1999*'s overseeing ("executive") producer, the hands-on producer was his wife Sylvia Anderson for the first year and Fred Freiberger for the second.[1] It was an expensive production. Some of the episodes were directed by highly respected film directors, including

DOI: 10.4324/9781003299653-12

Charles Crichton, Val Guest, and Peter Medak. Special effects director Brian Johnson had already worked with Anderson on *Thunderbirds* and then went on to *2001: A Space Odyssey* (1968), while after *Space: 1999* he worked on *Alien* (1979). Costumes were a feature of the show. The first year's were designed by Rudi Gernreich, an acclaimed fashion designer, and the second by Emma Porteous, who later designed clothes for James Bond films.

Shooting began in December of 1973 and the first broadcasts were in September of 1975 but events did not go to plan. *Space: 1999* was extremely expensive by British standards and demanded overseas (read: US) success to be viable. A clear statement of intent in this direction was the casting of American couple Martin Landau and Barbara Bain in the leads.[2] However, Abe Mandell, the head of Anderson's production's New York office, failed to get the show picked up by a US network and so sold the series into a less lucrative first-run syndication.[3] *Space: 1999* was completed as a whole series and then taken to market, which is less attractive to US networks, who often are fond of forcing changes on shows. Indeed, the customary way in US television was to shoot a pilot and then wait for a contract before shooting the rest of the series.

Fred Freiberger and Year Two

They very nearly never made a second year of *Space: 1999*. Experienced American producer Fred Freiberger was brought in to allow the series to proceed to a second year but through remodelling it as something more attractive to the US TV networks. Freiberger – probably undeservedly – has gained the nickname of "The Series Killer" among SF fans due to his involvement in the final (concluding) years of *Star Trek* (1966–69), *Space: 1999*, and *The Six Million Dollar Man* (1974–78).

Freiberger made significant changes to characters, script and programme tone, and aesthetics. New characters were introduced, including Maya, an attractive female shape-shifting alien (Catherine Schell), and Tony Verdeschi, a young heroic action figure (Tony Anholt). Others were removed, most notably Professor Bergman, an elderly thoughtful scientist (played by Barry Morse), along with Paul Morrow (played by Prentis Hancock) and Kano (Clifton Jones). Allied with this was an attempt at stronger and more immediate characterizations (including giving Barbara Bain's character a much stronger sense of humour). Indeed, the scripts for the second year as a whole accentuated humour far more, as well as achieving a faster pace, with less lengthy dialogue scenes than in the first year.

There was also less in the way of continuity, as *Space 1999* became more of a chain of self-contained episodes, and lost many of the continuous drama elements and long story concerns of its first year. In terms of aesthetics and props, the sets became smaller and with a different geography, the highly distinctive costumes were changed, with colours transferring from buff to grey, and the distinctive character of the music was replaced.

The modifications were not fully welcomed by some of those involved. Star Martin Landau said, "I liked the first year better. They changed it because a bunch of American minds got into the act and decided to do many things they felt were commercial" (Hirsch 1986) According to Freiberger, the first year was "too English" (Clark and Cotter 1980). He removed two (seemingly) English characters, but also a fairly prominent black character (one of only two in the cast). Irish principal writer Johnny Byrne said that the cast became

> some kind of ghastly alternative Star Trekkers: they were Space Men; there was nothing they couldn't handle; they could deal with anything that was thrown at them by aliens – who are inevitably malevolent. Their attitude was, "Get the bastards before they get us. Kick arse quick or they'll kick us." I told Freddie that he was going to lose the sense of wonder that we had had in the first series, and he told me not to worry because he was going to bring wonder into it, so we got a story called "The Bringers of Wonder" ... He completely changed the scripts that I had written, primarily to make it more like *Star Trek*.
>
> *(Byrne no date)*

Something similar might be said of the music. Indeed, the change in music for *Space 1999* might be understood as an attempt to "normalize" the series for US TV. Gray was not asked back. The second year could easily have been "tracked," fitted out with the existing music recorded for the first. Indeed, this would have been a cheap option but there was a clear desire for something different and new music was at the heart of the remodelling of the show. Freiberger stated that he wanted a palpable change to *Space 1999*'s music, to music more energetic and aggressive as befitting an action-adventure series (Wadsworth no date). Matt Hills convincingly argues that the regenerated *Doctor Who* (from 2005) aimed at "mainstreaming" the programme by replacing the tradition of electronic and often dissonant "science fiction music" with music associated with more mainstream (and perhaps more commonplace) TV drama (Hills 2010: 179). In the case of *Space: 1999*, a similar procedure was followed, with music functioning as one of the principal elements that reimagined the series, shifting its character away from that of its first year.

Year One: Barry Gray

The music for year one was written by Barry Gray (1908–84), who received classical training in music, studying at the Royal Manchester College of Music and musical composition with Hungarian-born serialist composer Matyas Seiber. He went on to compose for music publishers, radio, commercials, and film and in the 1950s he was musical arranger for Vera Lynn. In 1956, became musical director for AP Films (later known as Century 21), Gerry Anderson's company. He also set up his own electronic music studio in 1950 and played the specialist electronic instrument the Ondes Martenot for films such as *Doctor Who and the Daleks* (1965) and for Herrmann's score for Truffaut's *Fahrenheit 451* (1966).[4] Gray noted that:

> In the very early days of the Anderson shows it was Gerry's idea not to write kiddie music for the puppet shows and I should not let the fact that the show's stars were puppets affect the music at all. I should write as one would for a film, in the normal way, and this is what I always did.
>
> *(Gray no date)*

Indeed, *Thunderbirds* had a big-sounding orchestral score, like one might expect in a dramatic film. I would argue that the music *misdirects* the audience away from the puppets. Furthermore, high-quality music can misdirect away from other shortcomings of television programmes and films. Gray's scores also served as conspicuous production values, and in a crowded international television marketplace, Anderson knew the importance of the immediate impact of a show's surface. Music can be one of the most palpable signifiers of superior production values in audiovisual culture, and Gray's music always added a sense of quality to television programmes. It was always highly characteristic and he will be remembered as Gerry Anderson's regular musical collaborator, providing a symphonic style of music sometimes with an electronic edge. His music for *Space: 1999* remains highly regarded.[5] There were 24 episodes in the first year:

1) Breakaway
2) Matter of Life and Death
3) Black Sun
4) Ring Around the Moon
5) Earthbound
6) Another Time, Another Place
7) Missing Link

8) Guardian of Piri
9) Force of Life
10) Alpha Child
11) The Last Sunset
12) Voyager's Return
13) Collision Course
14) Death's Other Dominion
15) The Full Circle
16) End of Eternity
17) War Games
18) The Last Enemy
19) The Troubled Spirit
20) Space Brain
21) The Infernal Machine
22) Mission of the Darians
23) Dragon's Domain
24) The Testament of Arkadia

The early episodes "Breakaway," "Matter of Life and Death," "Black Sun," and "Another Time, Another Place" were the only ones to be scored fully by Gray.[6] Episodes such as "War Games" and "Death's Other Dominion" were constructed for the large part from tracked cues, derived not only from Gray's scores and his own back catalogue of compositions for Anderson productions, but also using the Chappell, EMI, and Delyse Envoy music libraries (Hirsch 2000: 18). The incidental music comprises predominantly traditional orchestral forces, with moments of atonal atmosphere music along with some sparse-textured electronic music.

There are some notable determinants upon *Space 1999*'s music. According to British Musicians Union regulations, only 20 minutes of music was allowed to be recorded per three-hour television session (Wadsworth no date). While this made recording large amounts of music prohibitively expensive, it led to higher-quality music in terms of performance and recording; reuse was unproblematic.[7] In fact, this regulation actively *encouraged* the reuse of musical recordings. So, industrial imperatives, including both budget and regulations, dictated that a minimal amount of recorded music provided a cohesive character through its repetition across the series. Whilst on the surface the music for each episode seemed coherent, as if written for the episode, it was either written by Gray to fit specific action or tracked, and picked in later episodes not by Gray but by the programme's music editor Alan Willis. Music editor Willis fashioned coherent musical soundtracks from disparate elements, and thus might be considered a "composer" in his own right. Whilst Gray's scores for *Space: 1999* were recut to make "new" scores, many of Gray's cues from other

Anderson shows were also folded into the mix. This redoubled Anderson's "house sound" with Gray's distinctive style providing textural continuity with those shows, notably *Thunderbirds* and *Stingray* (particularly "The Ghost of the Sea" episode, the music from which was reused consistently) and *Joe 90*.[8]

In episode 9, "Force of Life," there is a score collaged overwhelmingly from the Chappell Recorded Music Library. It shows the range of library music: the extremely banal muzak of Giampiero Boneschi's "The Latest Fashion" appears dietetically as the crew relax in the solarium, yet far more challenging music appears for the alien undertakings in the rest of the episode. It was dominated by Cecil Leuter's "Videotronics no. 3," and Georges Teperino's "Cosmic Sounds no. 1" and "Cosmic Sounds no. 3," which are almost avant garde in character, consisting of electronics and tape manipulation with isolated instrumental sounds processed with copious echo. *Space 1999*'s second year used much less music and less library music. Across the whole series, music is utilized in "blocks" (Donnelly 2006: 119–124). These are not merely "cues" but often cutdown recordings reused (sometimes constantly). They can be substantial and are always the same. The effect of this can be quite crude. While their use is expedient, dramatically, they proceed from the assumption that – broadly – dramatic situations are the same, or have the same emotional and dynamic tone – and thus we can think of television drama as successive repetition with minor, perhaps even inconsequent, variation.[9] Sometimes there is a degree of disjunction. "The Last Sunset" (episode 11) uses a cue from *Joe 90* for a sequence where is crew member is mentally disturbed after eating an alien plant. This cue includes a stereotypical "Arabic" melodic motif (using a scale with a flattened second degree), although there is nothing remotely "Arabic" about events on screen. The reason for this is that the cue is derived from the *Joe 90* episode "King for a Day" (Tx. Nov 10 1968) which takes place in the Arabic state of "Ardaji"! However, in passing it is easy to miss this, even when the same recorded passage appears again in "Mission of the Darians" (episode 22).

There has been a tradition of "integrated sound design" in some British television science fiction. This is best illustrated by *Doctor Who* from the 1960s to the 1980s, where strange, "otherworldly," electronic, or concrete sounds appeared – rather than more traditional musical "tunes." In unfamiliar situations, there can be an ambiguity as to what we hear: is it music or is it extraordinary ambient sounds? Often there might be an ambience of "space sounds" (echoes, wind), which might be taken as ambient sound until we remember that there is no sound in space! There is an industrial expediency for this merging of traditionally separate channels: sources for sounds and music habitually derive from the same technology. Often sources are electronic instruments (hardware or software), treated field recordings and electronic effects. Indeed, console and control room sounds, such as the Tardis in *Doctor Who* or the sounds from the bridge in *Star Trek*, perhaps ought to be construed more directly as a form of "music" in themselves.[10] In the "Force of Life" episode of *Space 1999* discussed earlier, there are sounds with a massive-sounding electronic echo, synthesizer tones and magnetic tape recordings played backwards.

Year 2: Derek Wadsworth

The second year's music was provided by Derek Wadsworth (1939–2008), who scored five episodes with that music subsequently being tracked across the remaining 19. Unlike Gray, Wadsworth was a self-taught composer, who had followed a correspondence course. He had played with the Brighouse and Rastrick brass band, been arranger for Dusty Springfield from 1963 onwards, and played as a prominent session trombonist on records including the Rolling Stones' *Their Satanic Majesties Request* (1967). He had been musical director on the London run of *Hair* (from 1968 to 1973) and had done orchestral arrangements for George Harrison's *All Things Must Pass* (1970), as well as for Rod Stewart, Colloseum, and Manfred Mann. He had a modicum of scoring experience, having arranged and orchestrated Alan Price's music for the films *Alfie Darling* (1975) and later *Britannia Hospital* (1982).

Wadsworth had a good musical pedigree but clearly was from a different *milieu* from Barry Gray. While Gray had a good career in what was then called "light music" as well as providing dramatic scores for film and television, Wadsworth had minimal film and television experience but copious experience as a top session player and arranger for pop and jazz. Anderson and Freiberger's desire was for something sounding very different from Gray's music-sound world. Apparently, they had asked for "something like *Hawaii Five-O*" (especially in terms of rhythm) (Wadsworth 1998). Year two also had 24 episodes:

1) The Metamorph
2) The Exiles
3) One Moment of Humanity
4) All that Glisters
5) Journey to Where
6) The Taybor
7) The Rules of Luton
8) The Mark of Archanon
9) Brian the Brain
10) New Adam, New Eve
11) Catacombs of the Moon

12) The AB Chrysalis
13) Seed of Destruction
14) The Beta Cloud
15) Space Warp
16) A Matter of Balance
17) The Bringers of Wonder, part 1
18) The Bringers of Wonder, part 2
19) The Lambda Factor
20) The Séance Spectre
21) Dorzak
22) Devil's Planet
23) The Immunity Syndrome
24) The Dorcons

Like Gray, Wadsworth scored only five episodes: "The Metamorph," "The Exiles," "One Moment of Humanity," "The Taybor," and "Space Warp." Due to the vagaries of production, most of the score written and recorded for "Space Warp" was reused in "The Beta Cloud," the episode shown immediately prior to it.

Wadsworth's musical style is distinctive, if not as immediately identifiable as Gray's. It showcases a wide range and variation of sounds and instrumental mixture, but often "on top" of a big band sound founded upon a solid jazz-rock rhythm section (using the television staple of the Jack Parnell Orchestra). There is a tendency toward brass domination, a common strategy in television music, facilitating the music "cutting through" and sounding "bigger." Broadly speaking, the music is "jazz-rock." For instance, "Space Warp" (episode 15), contains characteristic sounds of electric piano, saxophone solos, jazz-rock organ, prominent (sometimes fretless) bass guitar alongside "space rock" synthesizer. At times, some of Wadsworth's music sounds patently close to "easy listening music." It is less orchestral than Gray's, with a small string section which was used only occasionally. Instead, Wadsworth's music is much more rhythmic, with jazz-rock beats and some disco grooves. Throughout his music for the programme there is a certain consistency of the rhythm section of bass guitar and drum kit, while the band sometimes play exciting offbeat "stabs"/"punches" across the beat. A characteristic sound is the prominent use of synthesizer; in this case a Polymoog, a new polyphonic keyboard instrument that afforded both programming and ready access to sounds through preset buttons. It also allowed the playing of chords like a piano or organ, unlike most synthesizers of this period which only afforded the playing of a single note at a time. Wadsworth had the idea he was "pioneering" the use of synthesizer in television music: "In some parts, I felt that the effects I achieved sounded unlike anything else on air at the time" (Wadsworth 1998). Indeed, the sounds are more like the sort of synthesizer sounds evident during the following decade, where these instruments were exploited primarily for melodic and textural purposes rather than as they had been: as a novel sound source. Whilst often sounding like 1970s jazz-rock, Wadsworth's score includes some overwhelmingly jazzy passages.[11] For instance, episode 3, "One Moment of Humanity," has an electric guitar solo that begins by bending the strings – blues-rock style – but then moves rapidly to isolated staccato notes and legato runs – in characteristic jazz style. One notable aspect of Wadsworth's music was his use for *Space: 1999* of well-respected individual session musicians, which has been more customary in the jazz world than in film and television scoring.[12]

Contrasting Traditions

As an unequivocal statement of the difference between the two years of *Space 1999*, new title music accompanied a new and vastly different title sequence. Changing and updating theme tunes has not been uncommon, with shows like *Starsky and Hutch* (1975–79) changing its title music for each of its four years. When ATV's *Thriller* (1973–76, ATV) was syndicated in the USA new title sequences were shot with new music, in order to make the programme seem more like its surrounding American TV shows.[13] This is perhaps comparable to *Space 1999*'s fate, with the second year's appearing more "contemporary" with the style of other shows.

The title theme for the first year of *Space 1999* was a collaboration between Gray and Vic Elmes, who is credited as "Music Associate" on the series.[14] It begins with a stately fanfare and then progresses into a more energetic section with a principal melody. It has something of a contrasting and contradictory character, mixing orchestral and disco elements.[15] For the middle section, the music moves to an orchestral interlude, making variations on the theme before returning to the main music. Gray's title music varies tempo and energy, alternating a traditional orchestral music sound (most apparent in the slow fanfare start and interlude) with modern pop (muscular disco and the electric guitar melody line).[16] In contrast, Wadsworth's title music is fast and kinetic with a rock backbeat, and led by a synthesizer melody with brass and electronic blasts and "spangles." It has a clear antecedent-consequent melodic structure. It has a syncopated melody with a "pushed" final note of each line anticipating the main beat.[17] There is a surprise in the middle of the piece's energetic foot-tapping beat. The regularity of the beat falters as it enters 7/4 time, making something of a "drop out," after which the return to the original fast backbeat makes the kinetic 4/4 beat all the more compelling. While both have their merits, the first is a more traditional "theme and variations" with a play of musical dynamics to the fore. The second is structured more clearly like a popular song (with "verse" and "chorus" sections) and has more of the character of an exciting "full throttle" musical thrash.

I am not interested in identifying a direct sense of "national character" in British and American television. Yet there are traces of differences in TV and music industries and cultural traditions – with the union regulations perhaps being the most tangible determinant. These are direct assumptions about differences in audience *taste* as well as broadcasting tradition. We might identify two different traditions in music for television science fiction: the British and the American. The British would include the *Quatermass* trilogy (1953, 1955, 1958–59) with its occasional bursts of library music, the first run of *Doctor Who* (1963–89), with its electronic and strange, sometimes avant garde library music (particularly in the 1960s and early 1980s) (Donnelly 2007), *The Tomorrow People* (1973–79) (which often used electronic library music)]and Gerry Anderson's productions. Examples of the American model would include Irwin Allen's *Lost in Space* (1965–68) and *Land of the Giants* (1968–70), *Star Trek* (1966–69), *Planet of the Apes* (1974) and *Buck Rogers in the 25th Century* (1979–81). In these serials, a handful of orchestral scores were tracked repeatedly into successive episodes. Broadly speaking, this division might be schematized as the difference between the music as "set" or part of the location, or as "camera" and part of the narration, although strict demarcation is not tenable. Whilst there might be different national and traditional sensibilities, there are also some significantly different industrial and practical determinants, such as budget and resources available, frequency of commercial breaks, target audience, and union regulations, to name a few.[18]

Space 1999's first year mixed the two traditions: the "British" *Doctor Who* and *The Tomorrow People* model, with their use of electronic and exotic library music; and the "American" *The Twilight Zone*, *Lost in Space* and *Star Trek* model, where a few orchestral scores were tracked. Significantly, *Space 1999*'s second year removed the "British" side of the equation, leaving a more solid "American" model of tracked dramatic cues. Gray's music attempted to retain a sense of the tradition of "quality," sounding like the musical gold standard of a symphony orchestra in expensive films. Yet it also included the exoticism of electronics, as part of a sense of integrated sound design, mixing music and sound effects to make an unfamiliar space world. The characteristic sounds, I would argue, are vibraphone allied with electronic echo, which marks many atmospheric sections of the series. The first year contains much incidental music and exhibits Gray's distinctive sound, a form of "branding" that makes these shows instantly recognizable as Gerry Anderson productions.

Wadsworth's music often maintains a big band sound, with a strong jazz-pop character that at times drifts into the "easy listening" category. Its key timbres are more traditionally "American" sounds for British audiences: particularly the electric piano (a Fender Rhodes piano) and synthesizer.[19] There is less incidental music than in the first year, and unlike Gray's music, it is more clearly "music" and less drifting into the integrated sound design evident in the first year. Like American shows such as Star Trek, the music is more obviously "music" and less exotic tonalities. Indeed, it is less distinctive, and makes *Space: 1999* sound more like other television programmes of the time.

Conclusion

In the wake of *Space 1999*, Gray pretty much retired, while Wadsworth scored no more TV shows. He ended up appearing as an orchestral conductor in a TV advertisement for diarrhoea pills.[20]

What are the effects of the changes between the two series of *Space 1999*? In terms of narrative and tone, the second year appears more immediate and contains more action rather than the slow unfolding and philosophizing of the first year. As for music, the self-consciously "modern" replaces the more traditional, along with its sense of quality and complementary edge of experimentation. I mean "modernity" in the sense of the brand of "pop" modernism that was prevalent in the 1970s. A far cry from traditions of "aesthetic modernism," it emanates more precisely from developments in consumerism, where being "modern" is constantly to consume a new, "up-to-date" product with its own built-in obsolescence. The irony of this last point is that Gray's seemingly "old-fashioned" music now sounds less dated than Wadsworth's "modern" sound.

The developments in music from year one to year two proceed from concrete assumptions about a difference in audience taste, with a solid aim at an American audience taken in the second year. Sound and music can set the limits of the imagination in fantasy TV (or film for that matter). Sonic aspects often expand the vistas and imagination of the shows, making up for poor sets or cheap CGI effects through sonic misdirection and giving a crucial sense of the unfamiliarity science fiction requires (and thus it has been a consistent showcase for musical and sound design technology). Science fiction dramas are often about human possibilities and potential, and consequently their sound and music can be about humanity's sonic present and future, and sonic capabilities. It thus has a particular sociocultural function. The "British/traditional" imagination evident in *Space 1999*'s first year is "futuristic" (electronic), as well as being "quality," which aids believability (orchestral). The "US/modern" imagination more evident in the second year screams that it is "now" – not the future! It reflects the acceleration of consumerism, shunting aside the protestant work ethic for an endless present of retail development through changing fashion.

Notes

1 Sylvia Anderson was known as the voice of "Lady Penelope" from *Thunderbirds*.
2 "While *Space: 1999* was a British series, the UK market was not as large or as important to its financial success (or failure) as the US market was" (Wood 2010: 40).
3 Wood notes that UK scheduling was intermittent, while the show's debut was on London Weekend Television on 6 September 1975, while the US debut was a day earlier on KRON San Francisco (2010: 40, 51).
4 Although neither of these were traditional "science fiction music" scores, and Gray's electronic input was a featured "otherworldly" element.
5 Wood states: "Whether poignant or powerful, light-hearted or terrifying, the soundtrack stands as one of the grandest in terms of scope and execution ever composed [and compiled] for a science fiction television series, and never ceases to impress" (Wood 2010: 32).
6 Interestingly, in 1975 an Italian film *Spazio 1999* was released on video. It comprised "Breakaway," "Ring Around the Moon," and "Another Time, Another Place" edited into an 88-minute feature but with music by Ennio Morricone.
7 For *Star Trek*, as one of its composers, Fred Steiner, pointed out union rules allowed the reuse of recorded music for that year only, and none from other sources. This had changed by the 1980s to require a score for each episode (Steiner, in Bond, 1999: 34–35).
8 For both years of *Space 1999*, a case might be made that music editor Alan Willis was an important "author" of the programme's music (and to a lesser degree the same for sound editors Peter Pennell and Alan Killick [for year 2]), who assembled from recorded sources and worked in a similar manner).
9 These are not quite the same as conventional "cues" or musical "motifs." So I am told, editors sometimes referred to these blocks of recording as "passages."
10 Indeed, Brian Hodgson's sound for the Tardis was later reclassified as music, for the purposes of copyright and royalties.
11 At times it is reminiscent of Weather Report or Return to Forever, and has occasional similarities to Alain Goraguer's music for French animated science fiction film *Fantastic Planet* (1973).
12 Musicians included Ronnie Verrell (drums), Martin Drew (drums, of Ronnie Scott's band), Barry Morgan (drums), Pete King (alto saxaphone, of CCS), Paul Keogh (guitar, played with Lou Reed, Kate Bush, and Roger Daltrey), Martin Kershaw (guitar, played with Chris Rea), Dave Lawson (synthesizer), David Snell (harp), Geoff Castle (organ), and the Jack Parnell Orchestra, who were the usual staff band for ATV.
13 The 2005 Network DVD release of Thriller includes these "American" programme frames. British examples series changing title music include *Z Cars* (1962–78), *Crossroads* (1964–87) and *Grange Hill* (1978–2008).
14 Originally, Gerry Anderson had commissioned music for the series from Elmes, who supplied some pop-inspired music, including the energetic disco-style part of the main titles. He was married to Sylvia Anderson's daughter,

had been in the group Christie (who had a big hit with *Yellow River*) and played guitar on the title theme.

15 The piece's structure is founded upon an eight-bar melody, which as a characteristic has one single guitar notes of the tune lasting for a whole bar each. This aspect apart, it is a fairly conventional structure, with a chromatic run downwards from the tonic.

16 Elmes recorded the guitar, bass guitar and drums of the title theme with John McCoy and Liam Genockey (who later formed the group Gillan with the ex-Deep Purple singer Ian Gillan) (Elmes no date).

17 It differs from Gray's in that the antecedent melody follows a major scale but reaches a dramatically held minor third at the top of its run. Such a mixing of major and minor scales is often taken as characteristic of blues-based rock and jazz.

18 Britain also had recourse to composers who were less specialised and had less experience of writing for the screen, which had fostered something of a tradition of less craft in matching action than in the USA.

19 The synthesizer is used less as a "sound source" (for its sound qualities) than as a solo instrument, or a textural "pad." Thus it is less like other music of the time, and other music in science fiction film and television, and has more in common with pop music of the following decade.

20 For Immodium Plus, where he was shown conducting Mozart (Wadsworth 1998).

Bibliography

Byrne, Johnny (interview, no date). http://www.space1999.net/catacombs/main/crguide/vcpff.html [accessed 12/02/2011].

Clark, Mike, and Bill Cotter, "An Interview with Fred Freiberger" in *Starlog*, no. 40, November 1980. www.space1999.net/marco/Fred%20(ENG).html [accessed 02/02/2011].

Donnelly, K.J., "Between Sublime Experimentation and Prosaic Functionalism: Music and Sound in *Doctor Who*" in David Butler, ed., *Time and Relative Dissertations in Space: Critical Perspectives on Doctor Who* (Manchester: Manchester University Press, 2007).

Donnelly, K.J., *The Spectre of Sound: Music in Film and Television* (London: BFI, 2006).

Elmes, Vic, "The Vic Elmes Interview" www.geocities.com/Area51/Jupiter/1630/vhelms.html, [accessed 20/4/2003].

Gray, Barry, "TV Greats: Barry Gray" (interview) www.televisionheaven.co.uk/ungray.htm [accessed 12/12/2010].

Hills, Matt, *Triumph of A Time Lord: Regenerating Doctor Who in the Twenty First Century* (London: I.B.Tauris, 2010).

Hirsch, David, "CD Microbreweries Part 1: Fanderson Records" in *Soundtrack*, vol. 10, no. 76, Winter 2000.

Hirsch, David, "Martin Landau – Space Age Hero" in *Starlog*, no. 108, July 1986.

http://www.space1999.net/catacombs/main/crguide/vcpff.htmlaccessed [accessed 02/02/2011].

Steiner, Fred, "Music for Star Trek: Scoring a Television Show in the Sixties" in Iris Newsom, ed., *Wonderful Inventions: Motion Pictures, Broadcasting and Recorded Sound at the Museum of Congress* (Washington, DC: Museum of

Congress, 1985), [no page number supplied], quoted in Jeff Bond, *The Music of Star Trek* (Los Angeles, CA: Lone Eagle, 1999).

Wadsworth, Derek, (interview, no date). www.space1999.net/catacombs/main/crguide/vczdw.html [accessed 02/02/2011].

Wadsworth, Derek, "Derek Wadsworth, Derek Wadsworth's Electronic Interview!" (no date). http://www.geocities.com/Area51/Jupiter/1630/index.html [accessed 20/01/2011].

Wadsworth, Derek, "Derek Wadsworth Interview 1998," Catacombs Reference Library www.space1999.net/catacombs/main/pguide/wrefidw1.html [accessed 20/12/2010].

Wood, Robert E., *Destination Moonbase Alpha: The Unofficial and Unauthorized Guide to Space: 1999* (Prestatyn: Telos, 2010).

13

LAWN OF THE DEAD

The Indifference of Musical Destiny in *Plants vs. Zombies*

Atavistic arcade game music has persisted into current video game culture, particularly in handheld games. Arcade-derived music engages distinctive aesthetics and psychology and is evident in PopCap's tower defence game *Plants vs. Zombies*. In this game, the player must defend a house (screen left) from slowly-moving zombies who from screen right traverse a lawn (sometimes with a swimming pool) and later a roof. Gameplay involves planting various vegetables, fungi, and flowers that counter the zombies by blocking, exploding, or showering them with projectiles. Rather than looking like many other horror games, it has a parodic quality, with comic zombies, a deranged neighbour (called Crazy Dave) with a saucepan on his head, and bizarre anthropomorphic varieties of plants. The game is part of a torrent of zombie products (films, games, television, books, comics, and other consumer goods) that have materialized since the Millennium, making the shambling undead one of the dominant metaphors of the times. *Plants vs. Zombies* has horizontal lanes of movement and 25 different types of zombies, beginning each level slowly with isolated attacking zombies but concluding with a massive torrent of them. It is a so-called tower defence game: a siege with the enemy's relentless forward movement towards the player's battlelines.[1] Although Atari's *Ramparts* in 1990 is considered the first game of this type, arcade Ur-text *Space Invaders* (1978) has an underlying structure that is precisely the same. Originally to be called *Lawn of the Dead* (Donski no date), *Plants vs. Zombies* was developed by PopCap Games and published in 2009 initially for PC and Mac, but has since been ported to Xbox, PlayStation, Nintendo DS, and mobile phones (iOS, Android, and BlackBerry).

DOI: 10.4324/9781003299653-13

The music is prerendered, recorded as a selection of pieces of distinct music rather than being interactive and dynamic, and although it is not tied securely to gameplay perhaps it is related to the game through a different logic, engaging with a primitive essence rather than functioning as the more modern procedure of interactive and dynamic video game music.[2] *Plants vs. Zombies* utilizes a cartoon graphic style and follows a similar strategy in its music. The music is cartoonish in that it appears exaggerated and burlesque, employing broad brush strokes, simple structures, and working through metonymy, with symbolic characteristics dominating any mimetic value. It has something of film music composer Danny Elfman's cartoonish gothic style to it (Jeriaska 2009). There are a number of dark comic pieces of music and a continuum of (musically derived) sound effects for shooting, impacts, and zombie biting. The music was composed and realized by Californian Laura Shigihara, a classically trained pianist who attended the University of California, Berkeley but to study International Relations rather than music. According to her website, she apparently already had secured a contract as a singer-songwriter in Japan but then went on to write game music (Shigihara, no date). *Plants vs. Zombies* won the VGChartz Game of the Year Awards 2009; it also won Best Music Score (and was released as an MP3 album) (Schnackenberg 2009). More generally, *Plants vs. Zombies* proved highly

successful, involving many tied-in products and the game's cultural status even being recognized through providing the theme to state lottery tickets in the US state of Virginia.[3] With the success of this game and its music, perhaps one would have expected *Plants vs. Zombies* to have music that was intimately interwoven with the gameplay, forming a dynamic and developing relationship. Instead, the music simply progresses, almost in parallel to the unfolding of the game, as a homology to the relentless shambling movement of the zombies.

Arcades and Beyond

In *Reading the Popular*, John Fiske called video arcades "the semiotic brothels of the machine age" (Fiske 1989: 93). In the early years of video gaming they certainly were exciting and unpredictable places (Ellis: 1984: 47–65). Arcades began with pinball and one-armed bandits. In 1978, the release of Taito's *Space Invaders* began the halcyon era of game arcades. The most successful games included *Space Invaders*, *Pac-Man*, *Ms.Pac-Man*, and *Galaxian* (all Namco); *Asteroids* (Atari); *Donkey Kong* and *Donkey Kong Jnr* (both Nintendo); *Defender* (Williams); and *Mr Do* (Taito). However, according to Steven Kent, 1983 was the beginning of the coin-op arcade decline (2001: 116) although Karen Collins dates the decline as starting later, in 1988 (2008: 63). Yet in the US in 1991, $8 billion was still being spent on coin-op games whereas only $1 billion was spent on home gaming (Kinder 1991: 88). The disappearance of video gaming arcades was caused directly by the rise of home gaming consoles. It was not however an overnight supplanting, and there was an early 1990s minor resurgence in arcades (especially in the UK) with kicking and driving games.[4] The move to home consoles initially made gaming less public and allowed more control of the sonic environment by the producers.

The music for arcade games appears not very interactive by more recent standards. It was just a presence, rather than being defined by gameplay. Indeed, arcade music functioned as Ballyhoo – the tradition of loud and raucous music that beckoned, aiming to call in punters to bars or fairground tents.[5] Thus it aimed at exciting sounds and music, as a promise of the game's qualities. Significantly, arcade games produced music when not being played (together creating a wonderful but random Ivesian arcade soundscape) and making for general excitement.[6] Music regularly has a high degree of autonomy from the game, relating to indifference to events and gameplay. It can prevail independently, almost as "absolute music," standing on its own two feet rather than making sense only when accompanying its video game.

Such music has been described in recent years as chip music, chiptune music, or 8-bit music. It was defined by technological parameters and limitations. 8-bit CPU and architecture (of the late 1970s and early 1980s) used 8-bit integers and code that was 8-bits wide. The technological capabilities led to the dominance of thin textures and particular timbres (generated rather than sampled), few available channels of noise generator, and synthesized waveforms. Indeed, arcade games commenced a certain novel tradition of music in association with images. This music was characterized by its decidedly restricted parameters, in early years often merely comprising unaccompanied single-voice melodies. The limitations on music were provided not only by the small speakers but also by a lack of software space for an extensive musical program, as well as dynamic and timbre limitations and restricted number of sound voices available.[7] The consequent genre of music is characterized by bright and simple musical melodies basic and unelaborated accompaniment, utilizing harsh tones with basic waveforms and thin textures.[8] It would often include the use of rapid arpeggios that could give the aural impression of more dense-sounding chords but cost less in software space. This particular style was evident in most video games until developments in the early 1990s, and sometimes still is.[9] This musical mode, originating in arcade games, sustained into early home console games. The arrival of more complex processing allied to 16-bit sample capabilities (and the availability of more sound voice channels) opened computer games to the same sonic options as film, television, and the music world more generally. Although available in 1987, it was the Super Famicom in 1990 and, more significantly, the Sony Play Station in 1994 that revolutionized sound for video games. The latter's reliance upon a CD-ROM drive allowed for 24 channels of CD-quality sound (using a sample rate of up to 44.1 kHz). According to Rod Munday, this technological development marked an end to "video game music" as a distinctive genre of music (2007: 51). While this is certainly arguable, it opened up radical new opportunities for video game music. The difference in the amount of dedicated memory-program space, as well as processor capability and working memory, meant game music could be more clearly interactive, and music could be more integrated with screen action. It could also be more complex and embrace a wider range of timbres and dynamics.

Published scholarship on video game music has rather neglected arcade games and even to a degree 8-bit games, too (Perron and Wolf 2003: 8–9). Karen Collins's systematic *Game Sound* contains relatively little about arcade or 8-bit music and is happier concentrating on more recent games. Similarly, Roberto Dillon in *The Golden Age of Video Games* concentrates on home consoles to the detriment of arcade games (2011). Writing about video game music has tended to privilege music written for high production values console games, where music has a particular form. This form is dictated by the gameplay and involves the use of software programs (known as engines) that marshal fragmentary cues into a continuous fabric through a dynamic relationship with the game events controlled by the player.[10] Yet a relatively common form of game music derives directly from video games' arcade origins: that of non-dynamic and non-interactive music. Its connection to the rest of the game is more complex and less composed or directed.

Video game studies should be careful not to overplay the ideal of interactive dynamic music as the centre of game music, particularly as disconnected non-dynamic music exemplifies a strong tradition in game music, tracing back to the arcade. The aesthetic remains. Indeed, it is more common than we might give credit: many real-time games use little more than fairly simple trigger and loop mechanisms for music accompanying active gameplay. According to Karen Collins there are eight in-game functions of video game music: "kinetic functions," "anticipating action," "drawing attention," "structural functions," "reinforcement," "illusionary and spatial functions," "environmental functions," and "communication of emotional meaning" (Collins 2007: 263–298). *Plants vs. Zombies'* music engages only two of these functions clearly: structural functions and environmental functions. So, is the music unimportant for the game? The fact that the game can be played without music augurs that it is not an essential part of playing the game (which seemingly differentiates it from dynamic, interactive music). Significantly, certain types of games have the capability to retain sound effects but remove music. We should never forget that there are many games where the musical soundtrack is not essential, such as EA's best–selling sports franchises like *FIFA* (annually since 1993)and the *FIFA Manager* series (annually since 1997 and different ranges). In games such as these, the player can change the music library for their own selection of MP3 files of music. Similarly, most mobile games do not require musical input for gameplay or immersion.[11] If the music is not integrated on an essential or functional level, then it is not missed. With games that are played on mobile phones, sound regularly is muted by the player. With *Plants vs. Zombies* not only music but also sound effects are lost when the sound is switched off, although this does not inhibit gameplay as much as it might in many games, as only a minimum of relevant information is communicated through the soundtrack.

"Lawn, Day": Non-Interactive, Non-Dynamic Music

So what connection is there between music and the rest of the game? The first levels, which take place during the day on the front lawn of the player's unseen house, are accompanied by a piece of music that lasts 2.20 (timed from the game rather than the MP3) and simply begins again once finished. The gameplay does not take a single standard time and thus the music does not correspond with activities on the screen. It mechanically restarts at the point where it finishes, irrespective of the events in the game.[12] Thus it is able to have a strong rhythmic impetus that is not going to be interrupted, and is in fact predominantly a tango or habanera with a regular pulse all the way through, superseded by a more conventional section with a regular 4/4 beat. The use of such a distinct dance rhythm as the basis of the music is remarkable. Dances, with their regular pulses, tend not to be an effective accompaniment to moving images unless there is a desire to unite disparate images in a montage sequence with strong rhythmic music holding them together.[13] The very regularity of dances means that as an accompaniment to audiovisual culture, they tend to marshal the proceedings, to make the action feel like it is moving to the beat of the dance rather than following any diegetic or narrative logic.

This piece of music ("Grasswalk" as the MP3 file is titled) is based on distinct tonal harmonic movement: the opening chord progression relies upon an alternation of A minor and F 7th chords. Derived from Aeolian harmony, this alternation of a minor chord and a major chord four semitones below it is a common harmonic progression in horror film music and dark rock songs. It is evident in Wagner's funeral march for Siegfried from *Götterdämmerung*, although the addition of the 7th here adds an air of irony not evident in Wagner's piece. This note also provides an unexpected turn to the melody. Across the whole piece the structure is based strictly on four-bar units, with melody from particular instruments (oboe, an arch deep comic melody in the strings, pizzicato strings). Indeed, this is a heavily regulated structure, based on a sense of integrity for regular rhythmic structure, namely four-bar, eight-bar, and 16-bar units. It is never far from traditional song form and melodies develop along highly traditional lines (often following antecedent-consequent, and AA'BA formations, etc.). Uniform regularity is essential. The piece's structure is premised upon units of four bars, bearing a distinct resemblance to the AABA form of the standard 32-bar song. The opening tango part lasts for 16 bars, followed by eight bars of soaring oboe melody (the same four bars repeated), then an orphan four-bar drop-out section (where almost all instruments recede), then pizzicato strings for eight bars followed by the same with added sustained strings for eight bars, leading to piano arpeggios of 16 bars (the same four bars repeated), after which the piece

repeats all over again. Apart from one section, all are eight- or 16-bar but the four-bar strophe is the fundamental structural unit, with regularity giving something of a mechanical character to proceedings. Just after the first eight bars, when the music begins repeating, an eerie sound accompanied by a voice intoning "the zombies are coming" gives warning that a zombie is about to appear on the right of the screen. The harmony never strays too far from the key of A minor (despite the F 7th chord), and the slow tango rhythm is held in the bass line, which plays chord tones with a short chromatic run. Some of the music on later night levels adopts a tango rhythm, too. Perhaps the regularity of the musical structure is slightly hidden by the syncopated melody in the opening section of the tango, which then leads to a section dominated by an oboe melody with a more uniform downbeat rhythm. Successful negotiation of the level triggers a burst of jazz guitar to crudely blot out the existing music. There is a sense of irony instilled by the playful tango section, which at least partially is due to its occasional chromatic runs (downwards in the melody and upwards in the bass, tending towards the predictable) and slightly out-of-kilter seventh chord on the m6 of the scale. Later the four-bar drop-out is of exaggerated tonic-chord-dominant-chord piano accompaniment, and an arch and overdone section of melody performed by pizzicato strings. There is a strong sense of notes being overstressed, given an inflated and incongruous rendering,[14] which moves the piece away from being normal and towards being parodic. In fact, the music has nothing to do with zombies and plenty to do with comedic notions of music, particularly in the form that they have been standardized by mass media such as radio and television. The sense of irony comes from overstatement, where the listener feels aware of the music being overly obvious for the purposes of effect.

Each level of the game has a different piece of accompanying music. The general sonic palette is overwhelmingly electronic although aping traditional instruments. It includes marimba-like tuned percussion sounds, as well as more traditional orchestral-style sounds. The synthetic strings and brass have an inactive and lazy character, wholly unlike the tradition of loud strident brass in horror films, but nevertheless deep and resonant.

The relation of music to action is almost negligible, with the regularity of the music furnishing something of a mechanical character to gameplay. However, on the later level set at night, there is a minor sense of action being matched by the music. The piece here is a long marimba melody, which consists of five similar melodies, each of which has slight variations. These make up a succession that is then looped *ad infinitum*. As the player waits for the zombies' appearance on screen left, an eerie wavy synth sound enters with a voice over whisper saying "the zombies are coming." At 0.17 a string melody enters and a lone zombie appears shortly afterwards. At 0.48 brass enters and another zombie appears. At 1.29

both strings and brass as two zombies appear simultaneously. Overall, the music is a loop of about 1.53 minutes, that fails to develop and simply halts abruptly when the level is finished with a crudely intruding burst of unconnected jazz guitar.[15] However, beyond this, there appears to be no notable connection. Apart from the concluding segment of the level, where a drumbeat enters as an accompaniment to the existing music, appearing kinetically to choreograph movement through grabbing proceedings by the scruff of the neck as what is billed on screen as a "massive wave of zombies" approaches at the conclusion of each card. The assumption is that the beat matches the excitement of action (and chaotic simultaneity on screen). However, again, if we turn the sound off, it does not have a significant impact on the experience of the game and arguably none at all on the gameplay. So perhaps I should reformulate my earlier question as: is the *game* unimportant for the music? Shigihara's music was made available as CD/download and indeed is not functional music (*Gebrauchsmusik*) that derives its nature from its cultural partner (in this case the game) but has its own integrity as music in its own right. The conclusion of each level breaks the music's regularity. Apart from the crude succession of jazz guitar that materializes if the player vanquishes the zombies, there is another possible conclusion precipitated again by a vulgar interruption. Four notes of ponderous sinister cartoon music materialize if the zombies break through and win (eating the player's brains). Overall, *Plants vs. Zombies* music expresses a burlesque of horror, warding off the possibility of any actual terror. However, it conceivably could fit another game with a profoundly different character. Having noted this, it might be connected most directly with the game but on a deeper level, where the music's regularity relates to the unceasing regularity of the gameplay.

Isomorphism and Psychology

So, how is the music connected to the images of the game? Is it connected to representations of zombies and plants? There appears to be nothing objective to connect the music with such traditions of representation. It also is not functional dramatic music in that it has little synchronous connection with the images. Yet while the music is not doing the same thing as the images in terms of dynamics and kinesis, perhaps there is a deeper level of unity. The principle of isomorphism suggests that objects, including cultural objects, might have a shared essential structure and matching character on a deep (below surface) level (Arnheim 1961: 308). Perhaps we can illustrate this process with reference to the fast food chain McDonalds. There is an expectation that in each restaurant, the architecture, décor, food, service, and even music all complement one another. Perhaps these elements are of the same essence. Rather than being radically different, these aspects are manifestations of the same cultural impetus, perhaps even the same cultural archetype, although concretized in different forms. We never hear any avant garde music in McDonalds. The character of the music is carefully chosen to fit the corporate character and match with everything else on some deeper level of unity. Nothing should stick out like a sore thumb. According to Rudolf Arnheim, such "homology" and "structural kinship" in cultural objects work on a psychological level as an essential part of its unity across forms. This likeness is central to the "psychophysical parallelism" of mental state and object perceived (Arnheim 1961: 308).

The game's aesthetics contain some clear homologies or parallels. The relentless forward movement of zombies in *Plants vs. Zombies* homologises the looped music. Such game music is in effect simply a countdown – and on one level potentially a more general metaphor for being overtaken by age and death. Furthermore, the music can often appear indifferent to developments in games such as *Plants vs. Zombies* (for instance, when the player is nearing death, it just carries on relentlessly). Such indifferent music is not anempathetic music but something even more emotionally disengaged. Rather than redoubling the emotional effect, the effect can often be a mental dislocation. Anempathetic implies that it is *important* to miss the appropriate emotion. The emotional effect can be redoubled, seeing as we expect emotional congruence but instead receive no emotional engagement, and realize the extreme poignancy of the overall situation.[16] On the other hand, the indifference of the unemotional music is a fundamentally different situation, where music does not provide any emotional tone for its accompaniment. Perhaps it is a film music-based idea that music should be emotional. After all, we are increasingly used to music with little or no emotional tone in public spaces, such as environmental ambient muzak (Kassabian 2013). From the point of view of emotional music that is functional in an audio-visual scenario, this unemotional music embodies an unacceptable indifference. While Chion claimed that anempathetic music was at the essence of cinema as a medium (Chion 1994: 8), such indifference in game music might tell us something about the nature of modern culture, and the desire to hide the lack of emotional engagement and empathy beneath the shiny surface of commercial culture.[17] Adverts aim to integrate us as consumers but we remain only an ace away from the clear indifference of such culture.

Perhaps we should not expect explicit interaction or involvement between sound and image. Indeed, a lack of focus on functionality or emotion might change much in the way of dominant audio-visual analysis.[18] Claudia Gorbman points out that music in film always signifies emotion (1987: 73), if not evoking and directing emotion. However, while anempathetic music redirects emotional vectors, redoubling effect through incongruent emotional tone (Chion 1994: 8), under discussion here is music that fails to have an emotional impact. This lack of such effect is due to primary dislocation between sound (music) and image (game on screen), meaning that the effect of emotional congruence between the two is minimal and the lack of momentary dynamic matching retains a sense of uninvolved parallel, where the player's emotional reaction to gameplay is not directed or enhanced by the music. It seems that the only way music can be unemotional is through eschewing any direct involvement with other aspects of audio-visual culture.

There is a telling contrast between the hot emotional aspects of shooting things in many video games and the cold indifference of planting destructive flowers, like mines or IEDs, which are destructive later rather than sooner in *Plants vs. Zombies*. The game portrays a relentless attack by mindless but deadly drones, while the music embodies a similar process. Musical destiny is already known and expected, through the music's repetitive structure (Fink 2005: 5). So, the game relies upon the indifference of musical destiny to match its steady, violent threat of action. However, while these two channels (of sound and image) may involve similar logic they are not strictly speaking matching. They are two separate and parallel paths of inevitability, and their lack of integration suggests a strange, aberrant psychology in play. Disconnection aesthetically dramatizes, embodies, or perhaps even causes disconnection emotionally. This appears to be a very current cultural malaise, one of the (the constant) repositioning of human psychology through technology. This aesthetic set-up has distinct ramifications for perception. Sometimes understanding may be forced into a déjà vu, splitting the signal in the brain with a delay in reception and processing, particularly as a discrepancy exists between the speeds of aural and visual perception and processing.[19] The lapse could be compounded by the physical makeup of the brain as a parallel processing device, which channels impulses to different regions and works upon them simultaneously. Indeed, on occasions brains appear able to go out of synch, dividing and confusing broad cerebral functions. Perhaps on one level, it is like the brain-dead zombies, who appear only to have lower brain functions. Such basic brain activity is dominated by the cerebellum, which governs motor activity and rhythm-oriented activity. On the other hand, the game forces the player into an a-rhythmic upper brain activity of thinking ahead in an advanced manner to halt the zombie attack rather than simply react to their immediate threat. If the game arguably embodies physically something of a split in the brain, this is compounded by the music's relationship to the gameplay. For the purposes of analysis, it proved extremely difficult to listen to and analyze the music while playing the game. Indeed, trying to do so underlined the schizoid processing needed to deal with both, while it was far easier to achieve one or the other alone. This seeming split-brain aspect of the game is also homologized by the game's central depiction of social division. The game's scenario adumbrates a clear metaphor: the zombies appear to be the social underclass invading the lawns of respectable suburbia. Here, garden plants – which are a seemingly useless sign of the cultivated middle class – prove effective against the great unwashed. Thus, cultivation destroys barbarism (and in terms of human development agricultural planters succeeded the more primitive hunter-gatherers). The player embodies the civilized and must play through prediction and forethought, while the zombies represent the mindless masses, who live (after a fashion) from hand to mouth. While it is not explicit, it is tempting to impute the use of a tango/habanera as the basis for the first assault on the house as in some small way ascribing a

Latin or Hispanic character to this underclass invasion of civilized suburbia. Perhaps reactionary sociocultural ideas are close to the surface, but further, perhaps the game embodies a social indifference, too. This, at least partly, is an effect of the indifference of both the gameplay and its musical mechanisms. Despite the seeming remoteness of the game's representations, connections between the cartoon zombies and the real world are tangible. One zombie character was clearly based on Michael Jackson, referencing his famous *Thriller* music video, while wearing one glove and moonwalking on the spot. The estate of the recently deceased Jackson's objected and the producers replaced him with a generic disco-dancing zombie (Anon, Bitgamer 2007). One might wonder if Jackson's video was tempting fate.

Conclusion

While much culture has such social resonances once the analyst scratches its surface, the processes of music that do not work explicitly to enhance and dovetail with the game's narrative and gameplay are less apparent. Such simple production (messy rather than heavily directed interactive music and image) potentially creates a much more complex psychology of sound-image relations. In isomorphic terms, the game and the music are both predicated upon relentless progress, irrespective of the gamer's actions, but this inevitability is more evident in the music, which loops and is unresponsive to the events of the game. Its lack of sympathy means that it persists with the indifference of musical destiny as a reminder of the cold logic of the game's progress.

To a degree, arcade origins have been retained as aesthetic tradition by some video games. The format has been determined by arcade games' loud, brash, music with its own integrity, and the technological tradition of 8-bit, with the dominance of clear, minimal, textures, simple tunes, and short pieces with regular structures looped. Such music appears more mechanical, deficient of the seeming empathy of music that transforms with gameplay and new situations. In games such as *Plants vs. Zombies*, in psychological terms, such indifferent music is not anempathetic but perhaps something even more emotionally disengaged.[20] Indifference seems particularly fitting to the relentless forward movement of zombies in *Plants vs. Zombies*. This is not the sort of immersive experience that so much expensive and meticulously composed game music aims toward, but a more complex cross-rhythm of temporal activities. This music is not crafted to make a seamless unified experience but instead at the heart of the game is a clash of musical integrity and often repetitive gameplay. Deep inside many contemporary games, the arcade heritage remains.

Notes

1 Carl Therrien lists variety of horror games ("sidescrolling action games," shooting galleries, first-person shooters, fighting games, text-adventures, point-and-click adventure games, role-playing games, racing/vehicular combat games, and strategy games) but does not include tower defence games (Therrien 2009: 32).

2 However, from a different perspective, the "prerendered" music forms a backing track over which the player can "solo" through causing different sound effects through interactive gameplay.

3 Shigihara made the soundtrack album available as a download, including the song *Zombies on Your Lawn*, which also had a music video using images from the game. Later, a song recording called *Wabby Wabbo*, credited to "Crazy Dave," the neighbour in the game, was released for Christmas 2011 as a charity record for Concern Worldwide. The music video included game icons of plants, zombies and Dave, while the press release noted that it was "the first hip-hop single ever released to feature a yodeling solo by a yeti zombie" (Anon, *The Guardian*, 2019).

4 Such as *Sega Rally* (1994, Sega) and *Mortal Kombat* (1992, Midway).

5 See the highly informative discussion of the antecedents of video game music in Lerner (2014). *Plants vs. Zombies*' death music derives almost directly from the silent film music clichés discussed by Lerner.

6 There is a memorable arcade sequence in the John Hughes' film *Ferris Bueller's Day Off* (1986), while arcade game sounds abound in the Clash's song *Ivan Meets GI Joe* (from the album *Sandinista!* [CBS-Epic, 1980]).

7 Although technological determinism is unfashionable in this case it is hard not to see the role of software and hardware limitations as defining.
8 The character of some of this early game music was reminiscent of cartoon music. Zach Whalen notes that "early cartoon and horror film music established certain tropes that videogames rely on today" (2004). Similarly, some children's games of this time included similar alliances of sound and image, such as "Major Morgan – The Electric Organ" in the 1980s.
9 Identifiable 1980s 8-bit video game-style music appears in the video game and the film *Scott Pigrim vs. the World* (game Ubisoft 2012, film 2010) and popular songs such as Kesha's *Tik Tok* (2010) and Nelly Furtado and Timbaland's *Do It* (2006), which controversially appeared remarkably similar to an existing chiptune recording.
10 Such as the Lucas Arts iMuse engine.
11 Mobile games "should be playable without sound" according to the Nokia guide (Collins 2008: 78).
12 Although, the player's actions trigger musically derived sounds, forming something of a random "solo" performed over the top of Shigihara's musical bed. It is not easy to conceive this as a coherent piece of music, however.
13 Isolated instances of dance forms in cinema include Bernard Herrmann's music for *North by Northwest* (1959), where the repetitive incidental music is based on another Latin dance, the fandango, and Stanley Kubrick's use of Strauss's *Beautiful Blue Danube* waltz in *2001: A Space Odyssey* (1968).
14 Leonard Bernstein (no date) points to incongruity as one of the key aspects of humorous music (2013).
15 These timings are derived from a recording I made of my own playing of the PC version of the game.
16 Michel Chion notes that the seeming indifference can intensify emotion (1994: 8).
17 This is utterly unlike conventional mainstream film incidental music. Indeed, it is more like avant garde film music – or should I say, music in avant garde film.
18 Although, of course, there is the phenomenon of pareidolia, the human propensity to find patterns where none was constructed or intended.
19 While individual responses vary, auditory information is processed faster. The brain commonly activates 30–50 msecs earlier for sound than for image (van Eijk, Kohlrausch, Joula and van de Par 2008: 955).
20 Gillian Skirrow suggested that video games constitute a "paranoiac environment" (1986: 130).

Bibliography

Anon, "Games Blog" *The Guardian*, www.guardian.co.uk/technology/gamesblog/2011/dec/19/plants-vs-zombies-charity [accessed 22/02/2012].
Anon, "Michael Jackson Removed from Plants vs. Zombies" in *Bitgamer*, 2010. www.bit-tech.net/news/gaming/2010/07/28/michael-jackson-removed-from-plants-vs-zomb/1 [accessed 20/02/2012].
Arnheim, Rudolf, "The Gestalt Theory of Expression" in Mary Henle, ed., *Documents of Gestalt Psychology* (Los Angeles, CA: University of California Press, 1961).
Bernstein, Leonard, "Young People's Concert: Humor in Music" (no date) www.leonardbernstein.com/ypc_script_humor_in_music.htm [accessed 05/06/2013].

Chion, Michel, *Audio-Vision: Sound on Screen* (New York: Columbia University Press, 1994).
Collins, Karen, "An Introduction to the Participatory and Non-Linear Aspects of Video Game Audio" in Stan Hawkins and John Richardson, eds., *Essays on Sound and Vision* (Helsinki: Helsinki University Press, 2007).
Collins, Karen, *Game Sound: An Introduction to the History, Theory and Practice of Video Game Music and Sound Design* (Cambridge, MA: MIT Press, 2008).
Dillon, Roberto, *The Golden Age of Video Games: The Birth of a Multibillion Dollar Industry* (London: Routledge, 2011).
Donski, "Plants vs. Zombies was Almost Named 'Lawn of the Dead'" *N4G* (no date). http://n4g.com/news/1052212/plants-vs-zombies-was-almost-named-lawn-of-the-dead [accessed 12/10/2012].
Ellis, Desmond Ellis, "Video Arcades, Youth and Trouble" in *Youth and Society*, vol. 16, no. 1, 1984.
Fink, Robert, *Repeating Ourselves: American Minimal Music as Cultural Practice* (Berkeley, CA: University of California Press, 2005).
Fiske, John, *Reading the Popular* (London: Unwin Hyman, 1989).
Gorbman, Claudia, *Unheard Melodies: Narrative Film Music* (London: BFI, 1987).
Jeriaska, "Interview: The Terrifying True Story of the Plants vs. Zombies Soundtrack" *Gamasutra* (2009). http://www.gamasutra.com/news/originals/?story=23666 [accessed 14/01/2012].
Kassabian, Anahid, *Ubiquitous Listening: Affect, Attention and Disturbed Subjectivity* (Berkeley, CA: University of California Press, 2013).
Kent, Steven L., *The Ultimate History of Video Games: From Pong to Pokemon* (New York: Three Rivers Press, 2001).
Kinder, Marsha, *Playing with Power: From Muppet Babies to Teenage Mutant Ninja Turtles* (Berkeley, CA: University of California Press, 1991).
Lerner, Neil, "The Origins of Musical Style in Video Games, 1977–1983" in David Neumeyer, ed., *The Oxford Handbook of Film Music Studies* (Oxford: Oxford University Press, 2014).
Munday, Rod, "Music in Video Games" in Jamie Sexton, ed., *Music, Sound and Multimedia: From the Live to the Virtual* (Edinburgh: Edinburgh University Press, 2007).
Perron, Bernard, and Mark Wolf, "Introduction" in Mark Wolf, and Bernard Perron, eds., *The Video Game Theory Reader* (London: Routledge, 2003).
Schnackenberg, Matt, "PC VGChartz Game of the Year Awards 2009" http://gamrfeed.vgchartz.com/story/6350/Pc-vgchartz-game-of-the-year-awards-2009/ [accessed 20/2/12].
Shigihara, Laura, "Composer's Blog" (no date). http://shigi.wordpress.com/profile/ [accessed 16/1/2012].
Skirrow, Gillian, "Hellivision: An Analysis of Video Games" in Colin MacCabe, ed., *High Theory/Low Culture: Analyzing Popular Television and Film* (New York: St.Martin's Press, 1986).
Therrien, Carl, "Games of Fear: A Multi-Faceted Historical Account of the Horror Genre in Video Games" in Bernard Perron, ed., *Horror Video Games: Essays on the Fusion of Fear and Play* (Jefferson, NC: McFarland, 2009).

van Eijk, Rob L.J., Armin Kohlrausch, James F. Joula, and Steven van de Par, "Audiovisual Synchrony and Temporal Order Judgments: Effects of Experimental Method and Stimulus Type" in *Perception and Psychophysics*, vol. 70, no. 6, 2008.

Whalen, Zach, "Play Along – An Approach to Videogame Music" in *Game Studies*, vol. 4, no. 1, November 2004. www.gamestudies.org/0401/whalen [accessed 12/12/2012].

INDEX

Page numbers in **bold** indicate tables, while page numbers in *italics* mark photos or illustrations.